The Evolution of Conservative Party Social Policy

The Evolution Of Conservative Party Social Policy

Ben Williams
Tutor in Politics, University of Salford, UK

First published 2015 by
PALGRAVE MACMILLAN

Palgrave Macmillan in the UK is an imprint of Macmillan Publishers Limited, registered in England, company number 785998, of Houndmills, Basingstoke, Hampshire RG21 6XS.

Palgrave Macmillan in the US is a division of St Martin's Press LLC, 175 Fifth Avenue, New York, NY 10010.

Palgrave Macmillan is the global academic imprint of the above companies and has companies and representatives throughout the world.

Palgrave® and Macmillan® are registered trademarks in the United States, the United Kingdom, Europe and other countries.

ISBN 978–1–137–44580–3

This book is printed on paper suitable for recycling and made from fully managed and sustained forest sources. Logging, pulping and manufacturing processes are expected to conform to the environmental regulations of the country of origin.

A catalogue record for this book is available from the British Library.

Library of Congress Cataloging-in-Publication Data
Williams, Ben, 1973–
The evolution of conservative party social policy / Ben Williams.
    pages   cm
ISBN 978–1–137–44580–3 (hardback)
1. Conservative Party (Great Britain)—History—21st century.   2. Great Britain—Social policy—21st century.   3. Great Britain—Politics and government—21st century.   I. Title.
JN1129.C7W546 2015
361.6'10941—dc23   2014049918

Typeset by MPS Limited, Chennai, India.

Contents

List of Tables and Figures

Tables

Figures

Acknowledgements

Thanks are due to my close family, friends and colleagues, who have been a great support during the five years it has taken to write this book. In particular I would like to thank Dr Kevin Hickson and Professor Jonathan Tonge for the conscientious and supportive way in which they have assisted me and guided me in terms of researching, putting together and writing this work.

I thank my colleagues at the universities of Liverpool and Salford for the advice and camaraderie that I have experienced while working on the project, as well as the various groups of undergraduate students whose seminars and lectures I have led. These teaching experiences have been stimulating and helpful in the development of my work.

Special thanks must go to my parents, who have offered me tremendous support and encouragement in pursuing my chosen career. Katie, my daughter, provided welcome distraction and has tolerated my preoccupation during the course of the writing. It is to her that the book is dedicated.

Introduction and background

The Conservative Party's defeat at the 1997 General Election represented a political rejection on a historically unprecedented scale,[1] and in subsequent years the party has faced a significant period of introspection regarding its future direction, its policy-making agenda, and on a broader dimension, its overall political identity. The confident aura of the Thatcher era of the 1980s, fuelled by a successful election-winning formula of free-market populism alongside the ideological certainty instilled by the thrusting capitalist agenda of the 'New Right', was shattered by a shifting public mood and a gradual erosion of popular support as the 1990s progressed. These socio-political changes culminated in the electoral outcome of 1997 when the 20th century's 'natural party of government', which had generally acknowledged that 'periods of opposition (were) the exception, and office the norm',[2] found its once-dominant position in a state of utter political disarray, 'being reduced to a rump' and experiencing its heaviest electoral defeat 'since the birth of mass democratic politics in 1918'.[3] This watershed election result was variously described by sections of the media as a New Labour 'Triumph' (*The Guardian*), a 'Landslide' (*Daily Telegraph*) and a 'Massacre' (*Daily Mail*), with the general consensus being that 'it was all of these'.[4]

A long spell in national political opposition appeared inevitable given the scale of this ejection from office, and such an electoral annihilation at the hands of a revitalised and modernised 'New Labour' juggernaut represented the nadir of Conservative 20th-century political fortunes in terms of both parliamentary seats and wider public support. Fundamental reasons for such plummeting levels of popular appeal were rooted in the party's faltering and uncertain ideological vision, a diminishing public reputation aligned with the unappealing nature of the party's policy menu, with the image of contemporary Conservatism

1

damaged in the eyes of significant sections of the electorate. This appeared to reflect a broader public disenchantment regarding its long-term political agenda: ultimately, the 1997 Conservative Party appeared too concerned with its own internal policy divisions and had grown out of touch with the views and interests of a rapidly changing and increasingly diverse British society. This dynamic social change evolved while the Conservatives were preoccupied with the political strains of governance, with a primary focus on the fundamental economic restructuring of the country. Consequently, the Conservative Party faced a scenario whereby:

> After nearly two decades of Conservative rule, the needs, anxieties, priorities and aspirations of the electorate had become harder for the party to decipher and comprehend. Many simply failed to acknowledge how British society had changed in the 1990s'.[5]

Therefore, despite the constant hum of such ceaseless background social developments, the Conservative Party of the mid-1990s appeared to be instilled with a sense of socio-political myopia and detachment that struck at the heart of its identity as the decade progressed. Consequently, policy-making relating to key social and economic spheres appeared increasingly disjointed and lacking in terms of a coherent connected vision prior to 1997, with the party's main focus from 1992 onwards appearing to be the short-term political survival of John Major's fragile administration, with its slender parliamentary majority of just 21 (1992–97), which had disappeared by December 1996 due to a series of parliamentary deaths and subsequent by-election defeats. In this atavistic context of focusing on its own sheer political survival, the Conservative Party in office seemed to be detached from the basic concerns and priorities of contemporary external society. From late 1990 onwards, the Conservative political machine experienced a prolonged crisis triggered by the demise of Margaret Thatcher and her legacy of explicit ideological emphasis. The shattering electoral defeat of 1997 ultimately marked the culmination of almost seven years of a post-Thatcher hangover that blurred the party's focus, confused its direction and blighted its fortunes. This limited its ability to navigate coherently any progression from its period of electoral and political hegemony. The electoral watershed ultimately brought such matters of identity and future policy direction to the forefront of the party's political priorities, as it faced such challenges while firmly located in national political opposition on a long-term basis.

In this book I seek to analyse and interpret the nature of the response of British Conservatism to this somewhat bleak electoral and political scenario, observing the subsequent evolution of its key social policies and broader social attitudes in the process. I aim to address how and to what extent the Conservative Party has sought to adapt its position and attitudes in relation to various key social policy issues, and to what extent its comprehensive policy review has subsequently imparted elements of uncertainty and insecurity about the party's long-term political prospects that complement existing socio-political vulnerabilities. My approach is based on the premise that the party's established attitudes and alignment relating to broader contemporary social policy issues had created an associated negative image by the mid-1990s, and this was a clear contributing factor to the party's recent relative political decline. This in turn provides additional context to the party's image pertaining to social policy, as well as offering general enlightenment regarding the broader identity and image problems facing modern Conservatism, which has in turn created political and electoral difficulties that have been prolonged during the post-Thatcher era in particular.

A long-standing and dominant political role has been a hallmark of the Conservative Party's image, an image derived from its longevity, durability, electoral success and political pragmatism: it held national office either alone or in coalition for approximately two-thirds of the 20th century. However despite this legacy of political dominance, its electoral record in the final years of the 20th century and the first years of the 21st has been far from impressive, with no outright general election victory achieved since 1992. This scenario has generated a perception that modern Conservatism appears to have plateaued in terms of generating wider electoral popularity, become primarily 'economic' as opposed to 'social' in its policy focus, and accordingly become somewhat dealigned with the prevailing social moods, aspirations and attitudes of contemporary Britain. This provides an important context for the book's academic approach: a central element of its analysis is to assess the recent political assumption that the Conservative Party is inclined towards a primarily economic policy agenda, and to discover whether the assumption remains a valid and accurate one in the early years of the 21st century.

An inclination towards a predominantly economic agenda implies that by contrast, social policy has often been neglected, and the party's past record in this sphere between 1979 and 1997 is therefore an important element to consider when assessing its electoral performance in the present era. In analysing the various elements that have shaped and influenced the Conservative Party's political agenda from approximately 1997 onwards, the focus is therefore placed on a social policy agenda that has been the bedrock of the party's 'modernising' socio-political strategy, aimed at refreshing its electoral brand and widening its overall political appeal. In reviving and reinvigorating an otherwise neglected policy dimension, social policy reformulation has been a challenge made more difficult by the pressing economic problems and austerity agenda that the post-2010 government has had to deal with. This book's analytical framework ultimately seeks to compare the significance of social policy with that of economic policy-making, and specifically how the two dimensions interact and overlap in terms of both electoral potency and political relevance.

In adopting such an approach, key influences that have shaped the nature and rate of change within this sphere of social policy-making are addressed, with those which have been of most significance and connected to the party's recent electoral misfortune particularly highlighted, notably issues such as health, education and the wider welfare state. In seeking to emphasise how the contemporary Conservative Party has revised and reformulated its focus on social policy the choice of 1997 as a starting point is crucial. It marked the beginning of 13 years in national political opposition following a remarkable 18-year period in office; such a significant exile from government represented an unprecedented length of national political opposition for the self-styled 'natural party of government', and this provides a distinct and original angle from which to examine and appraise policy development. In embarking on a process of significant introspective policy revision during its time outside government, the party sought to revise and reinvent both its image and core principles for the 21st century, with its modernising elements seeking to elaborate an innovative understanding of the key socially fused concepts of community, society and social justice. This formed part of a broader project to 'detoxify' the public image of Conservatism that had become polluted among parts of the electorate due to political events and policy developments between 1979 and 1997. It is, therefore, an important aspect of this book to consider whether such developments have resulted in the construction of a distinct and credible socio-political agenda for the British Conservative Party in the early years of the 21st century, or alternatively whether it has led to a reversion to more traditional forms of Conservatism and associated policy-making. In summary, the broad themes and influences that are identified as significant factors in this process of social policy evolution and reformulation are ideology, pragmatism, statecraft and (since 2010) the practical implications of an austerity agenda and coalition politics.

The period from 1997 onwards therefore represents a unique and significant phase in British politics (particularly from a Conservative perspective), due to the party's unusually long exile from national office. The Conservative Party has enjoyed unprecedented electoral success as a party of government in the modern political era, although this record has been clouded somewhat by its relatively poor electoral performances from the mid-1990s. Such recent electoral difficulties are a development somewhat inconsistent with the party's political hegemony for much of the 20th century. As a political movement, the Conservative Party has assumed a pivotal, integral position in the British political system over the course of the last century, and its prominent role in the UK's broader political structure has been summarised by one academic as representing 'one of the great certainties of British politics',[6] such has been its near-constant presence in the higher political echelons in the modern era.

There have been no other periods during the age of mass democracy where the Conservative Party have been out of national government for such a long period of time. This prolonged absence from national office as a consequence of successive general election defeats between 1997 and 2005 means that the historical period being focused on represents the Conservative Party's most sustained period of opposition since 1832, a distinct period of modern history, an unprecedented era on which to focus.

This absence from government circles has appeared to some to have taken the Conservative Party to the brink of self-destruction, and indeed, following the party's second successive landslide electoral defeat in 2001, one commentator has described the Conservative Party as being 'shocked, frightened and hollowed out',[7] such was the extent of its identity crisis and sense of disarray and disorientation as a coherent political organisation. It is a reflection of the party's powers of durability and recovery that it was in a competitive electoral position again by 2009–10,[8] although this period of long-term opposition had motivated a root and branch review of Conservative ideology and policy in a number of key areas, on a scale not witnessed since the advent of Thatcherism from the mid-1970s onwards. In contemplating this concerted revision of post-Thatcher Conservative policy evolution, there has been contemporary good deal of conjecture in both media and academic circles as to just how extensive it has been in both a practical and theoretical sense.[9] This monograph offers a thorough analysis of the theoretical basis and the practical implementation of Conservative social policy both before and after 2010, examining a policy sphere perceived to have been given less priority by the party during the post-1979 political era in particular.

This book addresses some core questions in relation to the Conservative Party's deep internal policy review, and in particular offers a post-2010 perspective in assessing whether it has resulted in a fundamental revision of traditional Conservative ideology in order to embrace a more dynamic policy position in line with 21st century values and attitudes. An alternative view is that the Conservative leadership under David Cameron (from 2005 onwards) has, rather, gone no further than the implementation of a 're-packaged', cosmetic and cautious image change, instead being more inclined to embrace 'statecraft'[10] and a heightened focus on delivering practical governance and competence in office; a mere modification rather than a radical overhaul of traditional policy positions, shrinking away from fundamental changes.

In apparently diluting (rhetorically at least) some of the overt and explicit ideological emphasis of the past (for example during the Thatcherite hegemony of the 1980s), Cameron's Conservatism could be argued to have embraced a more pragmatic approach to its broader strategy for governance, merely moderating traditional values and attitudes with the aim of ultimately securing national office. However, once in power, some commentators such as Phillip Blond have argued that it has reverted to 'Thatcherite' type;[11] and this dynamic debate about the true nature and approach of modern Conservatism to social policy matters and the extent they have changed since the mid-1990s lies at the heart of this study.

In exploring and analysing the extent of the apparent 'change' in contemporary Conservative social policy, David Cameron's specific type of Conservatism has been the subject of much political conjecture and has been found to be difficult to specify, fuelled as it may be by his sustained rhetorical focus on changing the party's social policy. His notable involvement in formulating the Conservative Party's more right-wing 2005 general election manifesto[12] has generated debate among commentators in relation to how great his influence over it actually was, with some observations that he was more 'midwife' than 'creator' of such a 'core-vote' policy agenda.[13] Given how the party's 2010 manifesto was comparatively modified and 'modernised' in both tone and substance,[14] this has raised legitimate questions about how sincere Cameron's later endorsement of more socially orientated 'compassionate conservatism' has been, and whether such a changed emphasis on policy and a new style of governance is due to pure pragmatism and political opportunism on his part, or is rather due to a healthily evolving ideological compass and a genuine desire to rebrand and 'modernise' the Conservative Party.

A further pertinent context for this book is evident in the fact that the 2010 electoral outcome resulted in the formation of Britain's first post-war coalition government, a consequence of the first hung parliament since 1974,[15] and the first peacetime coalition since the 1930s. The subsequent dynamics and tensions of coalition government are therefore also an important dimension to be taken into account when assessing how the coalition with the Liberal Democrats has influenced the evolution of Conservative Party social policy on returning to national office. Such unusual circumstances and original elements have been further sharpened by atmosphere climate of unprecedented economic austerity since 2010, and this has created a further distinct element to frame the development of the Conservative Party's post-1997 social policies in practical terms. In this post-Thatcherite framework, and regardless of all of the warming words and changed rhetoric, the pivotal debate is whether the Conservative Party under David Cameron's leadership has represented and reflected a genuinely new and reformed social policy agenda in practical terms, distinct and different from past policy experiments, and it is this that the book seeks to rigorously explore. In assessing to what extent the Conservative Party's approach to social policy-making since 1997 has represented real change or has been merely a rhetorical emphasis on carefully-chosen words, some long-established and historical Conservative attitudes and beliefs regarding the role of government, social justice, the state and civil society have been rigorously reviewed, with the primary aim of determining to what extent they have either shifted or remained aligned to the party's traditional, instinctive approaches.

1
Ideological influences on Conservative Party social policy

In understanding how ideology has shaped the formulation of the Conservative Party's social and welfare policies over the course of the 20th century, particular attention must be paid to the contemporary political era, namely from the mid-1970s and the emergence of 'Thatcherism'. This chapter, therefore, seeks to assess and analyse the major influences on Conservative Party policy development, and determine to what extent both ideological and pragmatic factors have driven and shaped the party's policy-making agenda since 1997, particularly in the sphere of social and welfare policy.

Which aspect is the most influential over a government's policy-making processes is clearly a key factor to consider in this debate, and will probably vary over time. The 1980s era of Conservative rule has been perceived as being more ideological in nature than the previous post-war era, leading to a phase of policy prioritisation within the governing Conservative Party that saw the economic domain generally given greater emphasis and precedence over the development of social policy. The primacy of economics, many observers have claimed, was primarily due to Thatcherite ideological factors, although practical considerations were not entirely absent. As a consequence of this ideologically driven, economy-centric focus to policy-making, a wider public perception developed of a party that neglected social issues and was inclined to be socially illiberal. The 'Conservatives were disinterested in, and unable to offer solutions to, problems beyond the economic sphere'[1] and, Hayton suggests, they (the Conservatives) 'had become identified with the free market and individual freedom, but were perceived as being indifferent to social problems'.[2] This perception has been identified by various scholars and commentators as a key factor in the Conservatives' prolonged absence from national office.[3]

This apparent social 'neglect' provides the context for Conservative policy formulation with regard to the maintenance of key public services in the early 21st century, and which in turn has been rooted in the broader contemporary political debate about the ideological direction of the Conservative Party, the future development of the British welfare state and the evolution of social policy in general. This socio-political context ultimately goes to the heart of illustrating what factors fundamentally drive the Conservative Party's pursuit of political office, namely whether it is motivated by an inherent ideological policy-making agenda, or, instead, a pragmatic reaction to the economic realities and social attitudes of the day, or maybe even a mere atavistic desire for power at all costs ('the politics of power'[4]) aligned with the party's traditional image as being 'the natural party of government'.

It is usually the case that political groups or organisations in any society are broadly influenced by some sort of ideology or set of fundamental beliefs and principles, and it is these shared beliefs that tend to unite those within the same party who seek political office. Such unerring constant underlying ideology distinguished one party from its rivals for government in terms of the evolution and implementation of specific policies while in power. However, an ideology is not a simple concept in terms of definition and practical implementation; it can be viewed as 'a collection of aims, arguments and assumptions'[5] that are not always clear in their meaning. What makes the concept of an ideology even more difficult to define comprehensively and explain wholly is that even within specific ideological viewpoints there are often significant variations and differences. Ideologies can, therefore, appear to be fluid and dynamic concepts, and have been described as 'a complex phenomenon in itself manifesting a notable variety or internal differences'.[6] Particularly since the advent of mass democracy in the early 20th century, there has been a considerable amount of academic and political debate about the significance of ideology in influencing how governments of various political persuasions have performed while in office, and there has been particular focus on the ideological influences behind the specific policy-making agendas within contemporary party politics.

Within this robust debate over the relevance of ideology in motivating and guiding the actions and behaviour of recent politicians, the conservative historian Maurice Cowling sought to reject any uncertainty: he completely downgraded the significance of ideology in wider British politics for much of the past century,[7] dismissing the 'romanticism of "causes"'[8] and instead arguing that 'high politics' is broadly dominated by a small elite driven not by ideology but by 'self-interest... ambition and rivalry'.[9] By promoting such an argument during a century that appeared to feature some significant ideological debate, Cowling suggests that in the modern political era (20th century onwards), the senior hierarchy of the main political parties have broadly emerged from similar backgrounds and have traditionally had much in common in socio-economic terms, with fundamental political and ideological differences limited as a result. Cowling's viewpoint can be seen as contentious and open to dispute, particularly from the perspective of partisan and tribal politicians who would claim that there are clear ideological dividing lines between the various political parties. However it could be viewed as a valid analysis within the era of 'consensus politics' between 1945 and the mid-1970s, and even in the post-Thatcher 'consensus' from approximately 1990 onwards. In the context of the debate that assesses how significant ideology is considered to be in the process of governance, it provides a distinct angle of argument that suggests that perhaps all administrations of all political persuasions are ultimately driven by the desire for power and the fulfilment of both personal and collective group political ambition, with ideological motives having a limited role.

Changing British society and its impact on Conservative ideology and policy-making

The fluid and evolving social structure that became evident in Britain during the 1990s (much of which was ostensibly shaped by Conservative policies and governance), appeared to disorientate British Conservatism, and this dazed and disconnected response culminated in the 1997 electoral massacre. In formulating a concerted response to this shattering election result and its aftermath, distinct party divisions reflecting rival party traditions and factions came to the fore in seeking to shape and determine the party's position in the new political landscape being carved out by New Labour. This was initially evident in the guise of high-profile 'social authoritarian' and moralistic party figures such as Ann Widdecombe and, to a lesser extent, William Hague, demanding a return to traditional social values, even 'Victorian' ones as a means of reviving the party's fortunes by an attempted reversion to a more undiluted version of morally-infused social Conservatism. This clashed with the more socially liberal Conservatives of the post-1997 era, people like Michael Portillo and Francis Maude, often viewed as 'modernisers', who felt that political recovery was reliant on the party acclimatising to the changing social and political landscape and adopting 'a much more liberal line on "lifestyle" issues such as gay marriage and multiculturalism',[10] effectively embracing much of the 'modern' Blairite social policy agenda. Contemporary academics and commentators have seen an analogy for this division over social and moral issues in the 1960s societal divisions between 'Mods' and 'Rockers'.[11] Such divisions went to the heart of the typologies of Conservatism analysed by Heppell (2002),[12] who highlighted a three-dimensional model, which identified the party modernisers as embracing a broadly liberal line on 'social, sexual and moral policy', with the traditionalists taking a more conservative position on such matters. Such a contemporary liberal variant of Conservatism has been typified by recent comments of George Osborne (Chancellor of the Exchequer, 2010 onwards), who in publicly supporting moves to legislate in favour of gay marriage, warned the Conservative Party in late 2012 that 'ditching the policy would be toxic electorally'.[13]

This sense of friction between traditionalists and modernisers reflected the common perception that the party lacked a core, consistent ideological identity in the post-Thatcher era, and was also somewhat detached from changing public attitudes. This precarious political position was aligned with a basic need for political survival during the insecure Major years. The subsequent brutal removal from national office, exacerbated by two further general election defeats in 2001 and 2005, ultimately instigated a period of sustained self analysis within the Conservative Party. Such a process is arguably a natural response by any political movement to such a series of significant electoral setbacks, and various academics and commentators such as Seldon and Snowdon have viewed the Conservatives in this period of the late 1990s as 'suffering from a crisis, battered by years of uncertainty about the party's identity'.[14] This post-Thatcher state of turmoil and ideological haze was an unfamiliar experience for the Conservative Party, accustomed as it was to the general sense of political certainty that prevailed during its long periods of government for much of the 20th century. Thatcher's insertion of ideology and conviction into a party that had previously embraced pragmatism and consensus created a significant identity crisis following her departure from the political frontline in 1990, and this disruption to the party's equilibrium culminated in a sense of almost bewildered detachment from contemporary society for much of the remainder of the 1990s. Such a dislocation from the general public mood (on social issues in particular) resulted in thirteen years in the relative wilderness of national political opposition, which provided the party with the necessary time to adequately reflect and focus on what it essentially stood for in terms of its core beliefs, its overall identity, its ideological direction and to decide what should shape its policy agenda.

This sense of confusion over its identity had been a key legacy for the Conservative Party when the Thatcher era ended in 1990, with the ideological and political dominance of the 1980s now vanquished. In pure political terms 'Thatcherism posed as much of a challenge for the Conservatives as it had done for Labour'.[15]

> In a broader historical context, the cataclysm of three successive electoral setbacks is a significant and original backdrop to the period under scrutiny; policy development and renewal subsequently evolved in an unprecedented manner and focused on a whole range of socio-political issues, with the Conservative Party in opposition having to pragmatically acknowledge and embrace a plethora of 'popular' economic and social policies implemented by the Labour governments of Blair and Brown up until 2010. It has been in the area of social policy in particular that some of the most fundamental Conservative ideological soul-searching since 1997 appears to have taken place within the policy sphere that broadly incorporates issues such as welfare, education, the NHS as well as to some extent more 'modern' environmental policy –dimensions of public policy where the Conservatives have been eclipsed by the Labour Party with its more active and interventionist 'social' agenda. Subsequently there has been a general perception of a left-of-centre hegemonic influence over the evolution of social policy and a more 'socially just' policy direction within modern British politics, and a view that non-Conservative administrations have led the way in terms of initiatives and setting the agenda in this sphere. This can be said to have originated from both the 'years of consensus' after 1945 when the post-war Labour government set the social policy agenda, and the New Labour approach to public service reform since 1997. Both periods saw the development and implementation of various social policy initiatives that traditionally demanded a more interventionist, statist focus more aligned with the Labour Party's approach to statecraft and governance.

Accordingly, during the 1980s in particular these were not policy areas that the Conservative Party appeared to give as much priority or emphasis to in comparison to the fundamental problem of sorting out the country's unsatisfactory economic status as they saw it, although attempts to streamline the size and scope of the welfare state in particular were a long-term focus of mainstream Conservatism during this period. The party in office instead sought to mould a long-term neoliberal economic settlement that fundamentally shifted the economy's balance from the public to the private sector, and which has been broadly sustained to the present day. However a recurring criticism attached to the legacy of this period of Conservative government is that social policy (particularly in terms of addressing long-term poverty and welfare reliance) was neglected in comparison to economic matters, ultimately being denied the appropriate attention and policy-making effort that it required. This was within the political context of the Prime Minister Margaret Thatcher pursuing a revised 'free market' approach to both economic and social policy-making, in 'seeking to roll back the scope of the welfare state and therefore revers(ing) some of the more compassionate achievements of the post-1945 consensus'.[16]

This perception of a Conservative neglect of social and welfare policy in terms of both intellectual influence and practical policy-making thrust has led to a broad acknowledgment within political circles that many aspects of contemporary social policy in the UK have been associated with and shaped by the left-of-centre values of various post-war Labour governments, particularly given the Labour Party's more traditional 'social' core agenda, which has contrasted with the Conservatives' more 'economic' focus (since 1979 in particular). In analysing the extent of both change and continuity in the formation of Conservative social policies since the late 1990s onwards, one is struck by its coincidence with increasingly fluid and dynamic social attitudes in the UK, as public opinion generally appears to have taken on a more socially liberal outlook, though endorsing some significant, paradoxical cutbacks in welfare expenditure even while simultaneously desiring wider public spending on specific services. Within such a context, it is a challenge to address and identify the main driving forces behind the evolution of specific social policy approaches. A comparative approach seems to be required to assess whether the decisive influence has been the persistent presence of traditional ideology, the emergence of genuinely innovative socio-political ideas aligned with a genuinely 'New Conservatism', or a reversion to pragmatic statecraft.

Statecraft as a model of governance

The Conservative Party has been viewed as the least ideological of the mainstream British political parties. Unlike its principal Labour opponent with its deep-rooted links to socialism, Conservatism has traditionally not been burdened by an emotional attachment to an abstract ideology with a utopian vision of the future. It has been seen by academic observers as essentially 'a pragmatic rather than an ideological party',[17] and the Conservative politician David Willetts has observed that that party's inherent political pragmatism 'has never settled on a conclusion'.[18] Such an interpretation of the British Conservative Party focuses on its beliefs in an organic and gradually changing political and socio-economic structure, aligned with the image 'of a slowly evolving society'.[19] Given the broad perception that for most of the 20th century Conservative administrations have traditionally rejected ideology and been more inclined to embrace a more pragmatic approach to governance compared to Labour variants, there has been considerable academic analysis of the motivations of Conservative governments and their associated policy-making agendas, particularly in the post-war period. Motive for governance has come under further scrutiny since the more ideological Thatcher era from 1979 onwards, and one contemporary Conservative commentator has highlighted the fundamental importance of achieving political office in order to fully explain the true nature of the Conservative viewpoint, remarking that 'Conservatism, unlike socialism, is not merely a bundle of ideas, or a disposition, or a way of viewing the world. Rather, it must be realised in government to have substance'.[20] Two notable contributions to this academic analysis of the Conservative Party's fundamental attitudes and motivations to political office include the notion of 'statecraft' as developed by Jim Bulpitt[21] in the early 1980s, and also an analysis of the alleged key factors that contributed to the party's political hegemony for much of the 20th century, as outlined by Andrew Gamble[22] in the mid-1990s. Each researcher covered a different end of the Conservative Party's 18-year monopoly of national power (1979–97), and in analysing the early period of the Thatcher years, Bulpitt argued that ideology played a marginal and secondary role in the Conservative Party's political performance over most of the modern political era. He instead suggested that its main focus for governance has traditionally been 'statecraft', essentially 'the art of winning elections and achieving some necessary degree of governing competence in office'.[23]

Bulpitt's key argument is that the Conservative Party's historical tendency has been to adopt a pragmatic approach and react to circumstances rather than follow a clear ideological plan or blueprint while in political office, preferring to deal with the 'high politics' of public office rather than focusing on more ideology-driven grassroots political influences. In similar yet distinct vein to Cowling's notion of ideology-free party political motivations while in power, Bulpitt relegates ideology below pragmatism and managerial competence in explaining the various motives and influences behind Conservative political behaviour for the majority of the modern political period, particularly from the mid-19th century onwards. In one sense this analysis acknowledges an elitist model of politics like Cowling's, rejecting the significance of ideology as a determinant of political action and instead seeing Conservative administrations as essentially representing 'a philosophy of government or a ruling-class ideology'.[24] This argument suggests that flagship Conservative policies of the 1980s, such as privatisation, were not part of a grandiose ideological vision but were in fact low-key priorities at the start of the party's tenure in office and only gained momentum due to circumstantial developments as the decade progressed. This represented a rejection of the viewpoint that Thatcher was an ideological crusader, although it must be noted that Bulpitt's analysis is based on the early part of the 1980s when much of Margaret Thatcher's ideological vigour and most of her practical policies had yet to appear.

Bulpitt's analysis concluded that statecraft was the key driver of government policy-making and formulation of core actions in office; essentially the need for a political party to prove its competence in office in the shorter term so as to ensure a credible and competent reputation and subsequently a long-term maintenance of political power. Bulpitt's view is partially acknowledged by Philip Norton in a further analysis of Thatcher's period in office carried out in the latter phase of the 1980s, with Norton's study equally rejecting the perceived ideological predominance of Thatcherism, instead arguing that the Conservative Party of the 1980s vintage again adhered to 'something central to Conservative thought: circumstance'[25] (as opposed to a focused ideology). In this context, Norton claimed that most MPs during the Thatcher era were essentially party loyalists who would support the leadership as opposed to adhering to any clear ideological position, and this argument again emphasised that the Conservative Party in office has had a tendency to focus on a pragmatic approach alongside short-term events and developments, rather than following a clear pre-ordained blueprint of designated political actions within a long-term ideological focus.

Many political commentators have subsequently offered competing analysis and assessments as to the extent of ideological influences on the Conservative Party throughout the 20th century, with one more modern political viewpoint arguing that the party has tended to explicitly reject ideology for a more pragmatic and instinctive political approach (at least until the Thatcher era of 1975–90), as it has been 'wary of grand statements of principles and beliefs' and as a consequence 'many attribute the political success of British conservatism to its pragmatism- its concern with political practice not political theory'.[26]

Such an analysis adheres to the inherently pragmatic and flexible nature of Conservative policy-making, notably its desire for power and government tending to outweigh aloof and detached philosophies associated with the theorising of more abstract ideologies such as socialism. On this basis academics have argued that Conservatives traditionally reject and 'have nothing to do with theory, ideology and abstractions',[27] and, as an established political movement, over the course of modern politics it has therefore generally adopted a pragmatic approach to governance that is inclined to over-ride and transcend ideological considerations. Conservative academics and theorists such as Michael Oakeshott have referred to this pragmatic vision as representing a practical approach to politics that rejects incomprehensible theories and complex, rationalist ideologies that are beyond the comprehension of everyday life, and indeed often detached from the natural mood and instinctive feelings of the average citizen.[28] In this sense, such an interpretation of conservatism is that of a political outlook not guided by some overarching ideological blueprint, but which instead seeks to proceed 'without a pre-conceived plan or dogma, taking advantage of circumstances and building on successes',[29] and indeed seeks to pragmatically adapt to the various tides of change within society. Some conservative schools of thought view any ideological attachment as a negative phenomenon: the 19th-century Conservative leader Benjamin Disraeli dismissed contemporary ideological alternatives such as socialism as being 'mechanistic' and also 'bleak and materialistic' in their essentially rational analysis of society. In seeking to modernise the Conservative Party's image as a political force in the late 19th century, Disraeli established a tendency within British conservatism that embraced various social and democratic changes taking place, and favoured 'pragmatic empiricism';[30] in short, deliberately keeping ideology as a low-profile and often an anonymous feature of the Conservative Party image and appearance. For much of the 20th century, this pragmatic streak within the Conservative Party remained dominant, and certainly until the Thatcher era the party succeeded in ensuring that any tendencies towards 'Conservative (ideological) exhibitionism (were veiled) in a decent obscurity'.[31] This attitude was possibly influenced by the regular public outbursts of internal division evident within the more ideological Labour Party since its emergence in the early 1900s.

The Legacy of One Nation Conservatism

In seeking to mould an explicitly alternative approach to an ideological emphasis on policy-making, Disraeli adopted a vague 'One Nation' brand of Conservatism that was more in tune with a pragmatic governing instinct and general 'paternalistic' social responsibility as opposed to any specific blueprint for governance or policy-making. Indeed in his novel *Sybil (The Two Nations)*, Disraeli coined the phrase when alluding to:

> Two nations between whom there is no intercourse and no sympathy; who are as ignorant of each other's habits, thoughts, and feelings, as if they were dwellers in different zones, or inhabitants of different planets.... The rich and the poor.[32]

However, some of those more sceptical of Disraeli's ostensibly noble and moralistic motives have claimed that the great Conservative statesman was fully aware of the significance of protecting his own 'class' and the maintenance of the traditional social order, and this in itself was a form of underlying and implicit ideological influence that ultimately moulded his overall style and approach to governance.[33] Nevertheless, the social basis of Disraeli's analysis of a divided and class-ridden Britain resulted in a political remedy that required paternalistic state intervention and progressive, enlightened social policies in the name of maintaining legitimate social order. This remedial reaction appeared to be influenced by a fusion of humanitarian concern for the broader social welfare with a degree of party political calculation, and such a non-ideological emphasis established a political seam that would run deep in the Conservative Party for years to come. For much of the 20th century, therefore, this meant that there were clear distinctions in the differing attitudes towards ideology between the Conservative Party and its main political rival, as summarised below:

> Since its formation in 1900, Labour has been the ideological and sectional party in British politics..... (and) it was comparatively easy for the Conservatives to appeal to all sections of the nation, (with) their "dogma-light" approach.[34]

In short, such an analysis of the Conservative Party's approach to governance reflects a tendency for its adherents to be scornful of Labour's traditional inclinations towards a more ideological agenda, and instead seems to prefer the approach that 'doctrine and theory were subordinate to political calculation'[35] and indeed, circumstance.

In this context of facing an ideology-driven principal political opponent, some 50 years after Disraeli was in office there emerged the figure of Stanley Baldwin, Conservative Prime Minister on three separate occasions in the 1920s and 30s, the period's dominant political figure.

He further embraced this tradition and firmly rejected the ideological approach to governance amidst a period of inter-war class tensions and the steady growth of socialism. Baldwin, whose own son became a Labour MP, was ostensibly non-ideological to the extent that he 'even thought socialism and capitalism did not really exist',[36] and he is therefore associated with the 'One Nation' conservative tradition by virtue of such a political approach. In pursuing this political style, Baldwin developed a paternalistic image that emphasised national interest over divisive class divisions and ideological differences that were prevalent in this era, although despite cultivating this approach he did preside over the 1926 General Strike, one of the bitterest class-based disputes of the 20th century. This 'One Nation' tradition appeared to reach a zenith of influence within the party with the publication of *The Middle Way*[37] in 1938. This was Harold Macmillan's rejection of the 'laissez-faire' attitudes espoused by some Conservatives during the 'hungry thirties', and an affirmation of the party's moderate 'centrist' image, which sought 'to save capitalism from itself' by rejecting unregulated free market ideology as a 'combination of misery and inefficiency'.[38]

However, despite this non-ideological and paternalistic tradition being broadly associated with the liberal, moderate and left wing of the party, it has always attracted an eclectic mix of supporters to its cause, including free-market Conservatives such as Enoch Powell, who became a key Thatcherite influence and acolyte in his later years. What ultimately bound the 'One Nation' Conservatives together was a primary focus on the significance of society and social policy, with a paternalistic approach to maintaining strong communities alongside adequate and benevolent welfare policies in particular. In this context, in the post-war years after 1945, 'One Nation' politics remained at the forefront of Conservative governance and political behaviour while in office, embracing 'an active state approach' that 'saw the state as the key player in ameliorating social problems'.[39] As a consequence of this non-ideological tradition and heritage it was said that for much of its modern existence, and up to the emergence of Thatcher's 'New Right' in the mid-1970s in particular, that there was a notable limitation of ideological focus within the Conservative Party with its politicians generally being 'non-doctrinaire, pragmatic and capable of adjusting to the exigencies of the moment'.[40]

This tendency within the Conservative Party had manifestly been well-established over many decades, and it had been broadly associated with a pragmatic and moderate approach to governance, with the development of fluent and innovative social policies emanating from the centralised state being a key aspect of this 'paternalistic' political outlook. Established figures in the post-war Conservative Party between the early 1950s and mid-1970s such as Macmillan, Butler and Heath appeared to be generally imbued with the over-riding post-war consensual mentality,[41] and this moderate political viewpoint appeared to reject the extremities of left and right-wing ideological conflict and embraced the 'years of consensus' after 1945, regardless of the period's prevailing social-democratic slant that was a source of grievance for the Conservative 'New Right' in later years. Indeed, this right-of-centre party faction resented such a policy settlement in an ideological sense, ultimately rejecting its values and ethos as being part of a 'social democratic' political settlement. In this context, the overt ideological tendencies of 'Thatcherism' that erupted in the 1980s were viewed by many of the party's established 'grandees' as a political aberration, a dynamic break with the steady evolution, conventional methods and 'organic' approach of Conservative governments of the past, something whose legacy was perceived as destructively disrupting the Conservative Party's natural equilibrium for the next 20 years.

The emergence of ideological Conservatism

We see, then, that some academics and commentators (Norton and Bulpitt to varying extents) argue that, contrary to the perception of some parts of the media and the wider public, the perceived Thatcherite dominance of the 1980s Conservative Party was something of an illusion in terms of its long-term impact, and that the majority of Conservative politicians continued to adhere to a less ideological approach. In this context, while the Thatcherites may have seized the party leadership in 1975 and sought to inject a more ideological direction to governance, the reality was that they were actually 'in a minority within the party' and that there was 'no Thatcherite hegemony within government'.[42] This argument would claim that the Conservative Party from the mid-1970s onwards was in fact a balanced and diverse body that reflected the varying political traditions of the party, and that the explicit ideological emphasis towards governance associated with Thatcherism was in fact a deviation from an inherent and historic non-ideological Conservative pragmatism. However, the political reality was that Thatcher and her close allies held the reins of the party leadership between 1975 and 1990, and in policy terms their ideological focus arguably created a less balanced and conciliatory style of government after 1979, regarding the post-war settlement of social policy issues and related aspects of public welfare as less of a priority than the need to address economic matters, and this exacerbated the potential for further social divisions in the process. An interesting 'fused' interpretation of Thatcher's motives has been offered by Andrew Gamble, who acknowledges that there was no intricate blueprint for power, but perhaps instead a more strategic vision:

> Thatcherism is sometimes presented as though in 1979 there existed a set of policy blueprints ready for immediate implementation. No actual policy process could ever work in that way. What distinguished the Thatcher government from its predecessors was not detailed policy plans but its strategic sense of its long-term, objectives and its pragmatism concerning the means to achieve them.[43]

However, there have been politicians and commentators who challenge this politically 'pragmatic' interpretation and emphasis, and instead declare that core ideological beliefs have been at the root of the party's political direction over the course of modern history and have been the ultimate driving forces behind how the party has functioned while in office. A further analysis by Gamble examined the Conservative Party's fortunes during a nadir of the party's modern history in the mid-1990s. He argued that far from lacking an ideological bedrock of inherent beliefs, the Conservative Party was in fact traditionally aligned with some fundamental political principles ('The Pillars of Conservative Hegemony'[44]), which, according to Gamble, were the Constitution, the Union, Property and Empire (nationalism). Such pillars will certainly have driven the Thatcher 'New Right' project in a broad direction, without offering precise policy formulation. However Gamble's argument was that by the mid-1990s the Conservative Party had seen its association with such principles and 'pillars' weakened by their apparent lack of relevance to changing public attitudes, which could provide a key explanation for the party's significant electoral malaise of this period. However while Gamble's position did accept the importance of core ideological foundations in driving the party's policy formulation and behaviour in office, he did not accept that such changing social and political developments should detract from the fundamental priority of winning elections and governing competently in the process (the basic principles of the 'statecraft' theory).

This interpretation of Conservative motivations for governance, with its greater emphasis on the significance of ideological thought and a set of beliefs, was therefore most explicitly exposed and highlighted by the ideologically-driven years of Thatcherism during the 1980s. This counter-argument to the pragmatic approach to holding office has been partially acknowledged by some cerebral Conservative politicians, such as David Willetts, who has suggested that 'Conservatives do indeed have political principles- but they have emerged from political practice. Conservatives like their ideas made flesh in particular historical figures and circumstances'.[45] Such an analysis appears to suggest that a specific variant of ideological principles derive from empirical experience of political office, and this interpretation has also been reaffirmed from a more politically neutral perspective as reflecting a scenario that 'while formally eschewing abstract doctrine and the policy blueprint, Conservatives have usually been prepared to (adopt an) instinctive approach to politics, (based on) a rather vaguely formed disposition or "mode of feeling"'.[46] This would suggest that Conservatives do have inherent principles that derive from deep-rooted experiences, instincts and lessons from the past, and this in turn informs and directs contemporary policy-making in an appropriate 'ideological' direction deriving from an essentially empirical basis. This approach is said to have ideological implications in that the practical outcome has been a tendency to defend the existing status quo, and within this interpretation of British Conservatism (even before the Thatcher period), there has been an acknowledgement that as a political organisation it has tended to embrace a specific 'political mood' as opposed to just stubbornly resisting change. It can therefore alternatively be perceived as being a political movement that over the course of the 20th century has developed policies that have been moulded and fuelled by specific values and experiences, and these elements have created an 'ideological' undercurrent that has been utilised to broadly justify the existing political order, social hierarchy and levels of inequality, alongside various established traditions.

This perspective fuses a hazy degree of 'empirical' ideology with a defence of the status quo that is skewed in favour of Conservative interests, and which in turn is said to inspire the political actions of Conservative politicians and their formulation of policy, despite the absence of a clear blueprint for action in dealing with various circumstances and occasions that an ideological creed or explicit doctrine would perhaps provide. Any sense of ideology, therefore, derives from the actual activities and pragmatic experiences of previous spells of governance, and it is argued by academics like Leach that any existence of a 'conservative ideology has to be substantially inferred from the actions of Conservative governments'.[47] Consequently, an ideological guidance and tradition can be said to emerge from the practical and empirical realities of governance in the past, not from a detached and abstract philosophy that may never have been practically applied to everyday situations. This criticism could be applied to the explicitly ideological concepts of socialism or social democratic theory as broadly associated with British Conservatism's main political rival, the Labour Party, although this analysis could perhaps be open to debate after the political pragmatism of the New Labour era (1997–2010). This emphasis on practical experience ultimately influencing future administrations is not dissimilar to Bulpitt's basic analysis of the significance of 'statecraft', although unlike Bulpitt it does promote the value of ideas and principles over mere pragmatism and managerial competence. This more ideological emphasis would ultimately argue that the Thatcherite policy programme of the 1980s was 'not some kind of aberration..... (but) the adoption of an agenda consistent with tradition'.[48]

However, given the broader context of a perceived absence of clear ideological direction during the post-war years (particularly in relation to Heath's government from 1970 to 1974), a direct and recurring internal party criticism of the Conservative governments of this period has been that in attempting to run the machinery of government with such a pragmatic 'managerial' ethos, such an approach to governance can be viewed as an affront to the party's intrinsic ideological traditions, as it has been claimed that a 'Conservative cannot simply approach politics in such a managerial spirit (due to the) bedrock of principle on which a Conservative government has to rest'.[49] In this context of enshrined and deep-rooted principles, it has been argued, (and cited as both a strength and weakness) that there are some notable examples of Conservative administrations that have been vehemently ideological, most prominently the Thatcher administration between 1979 and 1990. This specific historical period witnessed explicit ideological influences rising to the surface on an unprecedented scale, evident in the clear influence of the academic F.A Hayek and his seminal anti-collectivist work *The Road to Serfdom*[50] along with the developing views of the economist Milton Friedman and the Chicago School of Economics in shaping policy-making during this sustained period of Conservative government. Indeed, in sharp conflict with Bulpitt's alternative theory that pragmatic 'statecraft' (and not ideology) was the main driving force behind much of the Thatcher period of government,[51] there do exist strong suggestions to the contrary, not least deriving from the direct sentiments of the dominant political figure of this period herself (as recalled by a contemporary Cabinet Minister):

JA [Jonathan Aitken] remembers one or two specifics about MT [Margaret Thatcher] at these meetings..... she did say at an early one, 'We must have an ideology. The other side have got an ideology, by which they can test things, we should have one as well.'[52]

While such comments could perhaps be interpreted as reflecting a somewhat simplistic and adversarial approach to politics from one perspective, at another level it indicates that Thatcher recognised the significance of ideology in presenting a clear, focused and coherent message to the electorate within the political climate in which she operated, as well as acknowledging its significant function of establishing a cogent political identity in the process. Subsequently, the Thatcherite ideological focus on core economic issues and key political priorities such as monetarism and the control of inflation led to a situation whereby the Thatcher government progressively '...inserted into Conservative policy ... a dogmatic tone that had previously been lacking'.[53] 'One Nation' critics from the left of the Conservative Party, derided by the Thatcherites as 'Wets', fully acknowledged the more explicit ideological direction of the post-1979 Conservative government from the outset, despite being sceptical of the approach that Thatcher was taking, as observed by one such critic below:

the 1979 government had an ideology (or something very like one) ... and (took the view that) attempts to reach consensus or compromise would merely ... reproduce the deficiencies of previous governments.[54]

This ideological approach to governance appeared to stem from the inferred failures of previous Conservative governments (in both economic and social policy terms), and it certainly antagonised some factions of the contemporary party. In particular, 'One Nation' Conservatives were collectively concerned with the specific implications for social policy and related welfare issues in particular, primarily due to the apparent downgrading of such issues as political priorities from 1979 onwards in comparison to other areas such as taxation, industrial relations and law and order. Such was the impact of this ideological shift and the wider repercussions for society of the Thatcherite economic focus on retrenchment in the early 1980s, and in this context therefore the post-1979 approach represented a marked contrast to previous post-war Conservative governments as it focused on 'reversing the collectivism of the post-war years'.[55] This was specifically the case in its rejection of the (social-democratic) consensus politics of the previous three decades, 'consensus' being the anathema to ideology and conviction, a term dismissed by Margaret Thatcher as being associated with those who had abandoned 'all beliefs, principles and values'.[56] Thatcher's disdain of consensual, relatively high-spending previous administrations (of all parties), was coupled by a rejection of her belief in their limited and timid ideological direction. This Thatcherite analysis was rooted in the perceived financial profligacy of successive post-war governments, which had subsequently fuelled an over-generous welfare state that encouraged dependency, and this would have significant implications for the formulation of both economic and social policy-making during the watershed political decade of the 1980s.

Over the course of the 20th century the Labour Party's more explicit adherence to socialist principles has meant that it has often had a stronger association with ideology and theory, with the Conservative links to this aspect of political behaviour downgraded and being generally inclined to a more pragmatic and adaptable approach to such matters. However, various political and media commentators have argued that such a situation has been reversed in recent years, particularly with the Thatcherite agenda of the 1980s, with its imposition of 'an ideological dogma upon the traditionally non-ideological Conservative Party'.[57] This notably contrasted with the New Labour stance from the mid-1990s onwards, which was broadly and deliberately 'ideology-light' in its political approach, particularly under Tony Blair from 1994 who preferred moulding and formulating policy on a more flexible and pragmatic basis. However, despite the determined desire of some acolytes to instil an unerring element of ideology and theory into the doctrine of Thatcherism, commentators such as Letwin have firmly rejected its claim to have theoretical aspects, primarily due its pragmatic yet simultaneously 'vigorous virtues', as its 'concern has been with action ... (for) Thatcherism has not got what it takes to be a theory'.[58]

Modern Conservatism and future approaches to governance

In the context of analysing the varying influences of pragmatism, ideology and theory on the various post-war Conservative governments, the key question is 'How much weight have ideological and theoretical influences had on driving Conservative ideas and practical policies (notably of the social and welfare type) since the late 1990s, as opposed to the alternative approach of more flexible pragmatic influences?' The subsequent analysis has therefore focused on which has been the primary factor in shaping the party's social policy agenda in the modern political environment, or alternatively whether a fusion of several factors has been the practical reality. This question is particularly pertinent given the revolutionary economic upheaval that Britain experienced during the 1980s, a decade in which management of the economy appeared to take precedence in terms of government priorities. Questions were subsequently asked about whether appropriate attention and innovation was given by the governing Conservative Party to social policy and the promotion of 'civic society' by comparison, and political critics have subsequently suggested some definite neglect of the social policy agenda as a consequence. This debate has therefore been specifically prominent in the wake of the Thatcherite socio-economic 'revolution' of the 1980s and then in the aftermath of the 1997 electoral disaster, the latter date being the starting point for Conservatives striving to reinvent a core policy agenda and a political identity.

In the post-Thatcher era, the ongoing debate about the relative prominence of ideology has continued to generate many internal party tensions and divergent views as to whether more or less ideological emphasis and focus is desirable in future Conservative administrations, with an uncertain overall picture as to whether the prominence of ideology will strengthen or weaken the party's identity and practical electoral appeal in the long-term. Some academic analysis has subsequently asserted that following a decade of apparent certainty in the art of governance and statecraft that was arguably the source of the party's political success in the 1980s, in stark contrast the party has struggled to administer power in a similarly competent way from 1990 onwards; it is claimed that the 'electoral decline and fall of the Conservative party in the immediate post-Thatcherite era demonstrates that contemporary British conservatism has been characterised by a failure of party statecraft'.[59] This viewpoint (with added hindsight) appears to draw a contrast between the key argument put forward by Bulpitt in the early 1980s that Thatcher's key political focus was the achievement and maintenance of 'statecraft' and stable, competent rule (rather than an ideological crusade) and Norton's analysis of the late 1980s as a time when pragmatic party loyalists prevailed over the Thatcherite ideologues within the Conservative parliamentary ranks and maintained a responsible and moderating influence over the direction of governance in the process. However Thatcher's apparent over-emphasis on ideology and its associated rhetoric the longer she was in office ultimately eroded the potential for successful and sustained 'statecraft' and damaged the party's delicate internal equilibrium, and as a consequence its traditional unity was severely weakened. This in turn adversely affected the political fortunes of British Conservatism in the long term, culminating in the intra-party policy divisions of the 1990s and the electoral carnage of 1997 that led to 13 long years in political opposition. This Thatcherite legacy has gone to the heart of the party's definitive ideological identity and emphasis, therefore, although the argument put forward by Andrew Gamble suggests that ideology could indeed complement competence in office and not necessarily be a substitute for it, due to the belief that Thatcherism represented a revised version of party statecraft that merely promoted more explicit conservative ideological principles already lurking beneath the surface. However Gamble did acknowledge in the late 1980s that 'the short-term success of Thatcherite conservatism as an instrument of party statecraft would not be sustainable over the longer term',[60] an argument ostensibly vindicated in his 1995 analysis[61] which painted a more pessimistic picture of Conservative political fortunes.

This debate over the importance and emphasis of ideology within British Conservatism has significantly influenced the context of David Cameron's leadership since 2005, specifically how his brand of post-Thatcherite 'modern' Conservatism ultimately comes to be defined in both social and economic policy terms as well as electoral performance. Cameron has sought to pursue a delicate balancing act of utilising occasional Thatcherite rhetoric while simultaneously embracing a pragmatic position on various socio-economic issues and emphasising greater emphasis on a distinct model of community-based 'compassionate conservatism' (evident in 'The Big Society' policy agenda); an approach aligned with more explicit public concern for the poorer members of society where it is considered politically expedient and appropriate. This quixotic fusion of contrasting Conservative traditions has therefore often made Cameron's agenda elusive and difficult to attach a specific label to, and in embracing both social and economic elements, has found itself being somewhat distinct from both the traditional left and right of the party's 'ideological' spectrum. This fundamental question of the relative significance of ideology in relation to the formation of party policy is a dynamic area of contemporary socio-political debate, and in assessing the evolution of specific Conservative Party welfare and social policies over the period of coalition government (from 2010 onwards) and in future years, political observers will continue to analyse to what extent such policy has been shaped by explicit ideology, pragmatic 'statecraft', or a fusion of both.

2
The 'New Right' and its impact on Conservative social policy

This chapter focuses on the development and evolution of the specific 'New Right' ideology in its guise as a contemporary and modern variant of Conservative political thought. As a viewpoint with a global context and influence, it aspired to revive the individualistic values of the liberal 'free-market' economic environment that prevailed in the mid to late 19th century, while seeking to dismantle the post-1945 welfare settlement. This 'neo-liberal' economic outlook subsequently established itself as a distinct influence within the British Conservative Party during its period of political dominance in the 1980s, rejecting much of the party's paternalistic social policy of the post-war period in the process. In exploring precisely what the beliefs and key principles of this brand of Conservatism are, it is necessary to analyse its origins and assess how it has developed as a political concept within the modern political framework, as well as how it became firmly attached to the policy-making agenda of Margaret Thatcher from 1975 onwards. We will see how the New Right's ideological thrust influenced the welfare and social policies of the Thatcher government between 1979 and 1990, and how it potentially continues to influence party policy to the present day.

The Origins and evolution of the New Right

Having gained influence over the direction of the Conservative Party in the mid-1970s with the accession of Margaret Thatcher to the party leadership, the challenge for the advocates of the 'New Right' was to craft specific policies that could be implemented while in power. This would be a significant challenge as the 'New Right' vanguard were a minority within the wider parliamentary Conservative Party,[1] and far from politically secure in the early years of Thatcher's leadership.

Nevertheless, the Thatcherite or 'New Right' viewpoint heavily influenced the party's sustained spell in political office from 1979, pushing the Conservative administration of the 1980s in a more explicitly ideological direction than had been associated with the party's approach to governance for much of the 20th century (see Chapter 1). This political perspective owed much to a philosophical strand of British and international (notably American) conservative thought that rejected the structure of the post-war consensus regarding state intervention and regulation of the mixed economy, along with high levels of taxation and corporatist trade union power, and which argued instead for a smaller state and reduced taxation within a neo-liberal 'free-market' economic framework.[2] It was argued by advocates of the 'New Right' perspective that only in such a neo-liberal framework could wealth be both created and shared efficiently across society, free from the constraints of an interfering and repressive state, creating a scenario where 'the less well-off are indirectly aided by the rich through the "trickle-down effect", whereby the expenditure and investment of the wealthy percolates downwards and outwards to the rest of society, and thereby generates employment and finances welfare provision'.[3] The historical period from 1979 onwards witnessed the ideological edge of the 'New Right' wielding increasing power and influence within British politics, absorbing popular support in the process and being clearly in the ascendancy in terms of public opinion and electoral support. The 'New Right' ultimately became established as a transatlantic political presence and was increasingly influential on a global level from the mid-1970s onwards, reacting to both international and specifically domestic political and economic events with its own policy remedies for the socio-economic problems of the time.

This ideology promoted a meritocratic and entrepreneurial model of society, though, despite its 'free-market' emphasis, it still acknowledged the need for some variant of a welfare state to exist, albeit a less vast and bureaucratic one. Under this 'New Right' political vision therefore, welfare provision would be funded and moulded by the dynamism of the 'neo-liberal state' and its economy. However, while it offered the prospect of greater organisational efficiency and less bureaucracy, as a consequence it would also be potentially less comprehensive, a bad outcome for the more vulnerable members of society who generally use such services most. The political left has consistently questioned the effectiveness, fairness and 'socially just' implications of such a free market focus and 'trickle-down' approach in spreading wealth and providing an effective welfare service in practical terms, and argues that the neo-liberal economic and social model is in fundamental conflict with an egalitarian socio-political model as promoted and idealised by socialists and social democrats. Neo-liberals would certainly acknowledge that a more egalitarian model of society is not a likely outcome from their ideal economic structure (a position developed further in Chapter 3), but they view this as a natural and desirable outcome. The 'New Right' variant of conservatism views inequality as a natural state of affairs, as the economic liberal distinguishes 'sharply between equality of rights and equality of opportunity, on the one hand, and material equality of equality of outcome on the other'.[4]

The growing intellectual and theoretical influence of the 'New Right' culminated in a sustained period of political popularity and hegemony due to the perceived failures of the post-war 'social-democratic' model of a mixed economy. Politicians aligned with its vision, such as Ronald Reagan and Margaret Thatcher, gained a political foothold from the mid-1970s onwards; and held political power in the USA and Britain for most of the 1980s.

The Thatcher government in Britain was heavily influenced and intellectually bolstered by the neo-liberal agenda of economists such as Milton Friedman and F.A Hayek.[5] Friedman was associated with the 'Chicago School' (University of Chicago),[6] while Hayek was attached in academic terms to the 'Austrian School'.[7] Both economists agreed on a fundamental rejection of the Keynesian post-war economic settlement[8] that had been consolidated across much of the Western world since the mid-1940s. Both argued that this 'social-democratic' model of the state represented a 'source of coercion'[9] in relation to the autonomy of the individual citizen; they instead advocated economic deregulation, greater promotion of 'free-market' capitalism and its associated culture of enhanced individual economic liberalism and personal freedoms. The works of Friedman and Hayek influenced Thatcher's own British sources of ideological and political inspiration and prophecy, notably Enoch Powell, described by one commentator as 'the heretical voice of the fifties and sixties'[10] in terms of questioning the post-war consensus. As a primary British source of Thatcher's political agenda, Powell expressed a devout, idealised faith in a society influenced by the principles of economic liberalism, genuinely believing that due to the 'statist' nature of the post-war settlement, there was a growing real threat as 'to whether a free society was to survive in Britain or be destroyed by socialism'.[11] Powell's vocal and sustained critique of the post-war consensus was bolstered by the Institute of Economic Affairs (IEA, founded 1955 under the considerable influence of Hayek), which challenged the Keynesian post-war settlement. This body was in turn supported by the emergence the Centre for Policy Studies (CPS) in 1974, co-founded by Sir Keith Joseph, Alfred Sherman and Margaret Thatcher, who established it as 'an institutional base for the dissemination of (their) revisionist agenda'[12] seeking to challenge the post-war political consensus and advocate a free-market alternative. Such bodies promoting economic liberalism were to challenge the cost and scope of the British welfare state and its various policies with increased vigour, with such financial aspects an increasingly relevant issue in an era of growing economic difficulties. Powell's rhetoric, alongside the pamphlets, seminars and publications of the IEA from the 1960s onwards, and Joseph's CPS from the mid-1970s, set the scene for 'Thatcherism' to emerge as a credible political force within British politics:

> Arguably, Keith Joseph did as much as any other single person around the world to reshape the debate about government and marketplace, to take a variety of ideas and bind them together into a powerful critique of the mixed economy and... help shape them into a political programme (that) was articulated and put into effect by his most important student, Margaret Thatcher. She made the ideas "happen".[13]

Thatcher's administration sought to develop this socio-economic blueprint practically, aiming to steer Britain in a new and distinct 'neo-liberal' political direction, offering a stark contrast to the period since 1945, which was essentially an era anchored in the apparent certainties of the Keynesian analysis of post-war economics and society and the necessity of a 'mixed economy'. However, by the late 1970s such certainties had become distorted and undermined by major global and domestic economic failings, and Thatcher sought to challenge them with her own brand of 'conviction' and ideology-driven politics. However her own ideological certainties were not manifest from the outset of her period in office; they were to develop further as her confidence and political power grew during the 1980s. She was, however, guided from the outset by some principles that shaped her political actions and colour her legacy to the present day. She set off on her time as Prime Minister believing 'that modern Conservatism was barely distinguishable from the social-democratic path forged by successive post-war Labour governments (and that) Britain had lost its economic dynamism and, as a consequence, a culture of decline and dependency had been allowed to take hold'.[14]

In pursuing the approach to governance that it did, the post-1979 administration had to formulate, develop and implement some crucial and distinctly original policy decisions as Britain reached a socioeconomic crossroads in terms of the sustainability of its long-term levels of taxation, public spending and overall public service and welfare provision. In seeking to transcend and move on from a period viewed by the 'New Right' as being stagnant and regressive in its entrenched left-of-centre socio-economic agenda, Thatcher desired to lead a crusading and more ideological administration that would revolutionise the direction and emphasis of policy-making in the UK, dragging the centre of gravity of British politics back to the right in the process. By enthusiastically embracing this 'New Right' approach to governance, and providing a much more economic-centric edge to the government's policy agenda, Thatcher would subsequently be described as 'the most controversial prime minister in post-war British history'.[15]

Within the British political context, the 'New Right' movement ultimately evolved as a potent political force in a pragmatic and circumstantial manner, as its emergence and prominence as a key influence within the British political sphere was 'not originally an ideological conversion but more a response to events'.[16] The 'events' that the British New Right variant sought to respond to were the tumultuous climax of the sustained 'years of consensus' from 1945, which were reaching crisis point in the mid-1970s. There was mood emerging in the 1970s that post-war British governments of all political persuasions taxed and spent too much, had failed to address Britain's post-war economic relative decline and industrial inefficiencies, and that the 'corporatist' nature of trade union power was out of control. This led some to label the country as 'the sick man of Europe'[17] and such a mood reached a shattering crescendo in the winter of 1978/79, when militant trade unionism heralded the 'Winter of Discontent' and the apparent crippling of the British system of government, with even prominent Labour figures such as Harold Wilson acknowledging the alienation of public opinion from the government due to the existence of 'Garbage piled up and rotted in the streets... picketing and closure of schools, and... action preventing the burial of the dead'.[18]

This socially chaotic scenario appeared to vindicate the alternative political and economic agenda espoused by the 'New Right' thinkers of the period. As a consequence of such sustained industrial and economic disruption, a significant public backlash was evident in the 1979 General Election when the Conservatives were elected on a higher than average swing,[19] with Labour punished for its trade union links and its association with high 'tax and spend' policies. The specific policy-making agenda and political priorities of the incoming government after 1979 were therefore focused on the development of innovative policies to instigate a long-term restructuring of the British model of government from its traditional post-war collectivist appearance, seeking to instil a more individualist structure. This political and socio-economic vision was shaped by ideology but also influenced by the vagaries of circumstance, 'Thatcherite policies did not spring out of nothing. The way was prepared for them by a confluence of ideas, activities and circumstances'.[20]

In particular, circumstances derived from the perceived expense and inefficiencies in the size and scope of the post-war state that had been identified from the vantage point of the New Right's position as an acute observer of government and society during the Conservatives' time in political opposition from 1974 onwards. Now with its recently-acquired and notable influence over the party leadership, from the mid-1970s the radical 'New Right', inspired by the work of Joseph, the IEA and CPS, identified the ever-growing and increasingly expensive welfare state as an area that needed significant reform and retrenchment in the context of the industrial unrest and negative economic growth of the 1970s. This political approach marked 'a major departure from the political consensus on welfare... (and) also a fundamental change of direction for the Conservatives',[21] who had previously supported its somewhat bloated and bureaucratic existence for the majority of the post-war 'consensus' period. Many within the 'New Right' were sceptical and even contemptuous of the scale of British welfare provision, identifying it with Britain's sustained post-war economic difficulties. Such an attitude had significant implications for the traditionally bipartisan approach to maintaining the generous British welfare state, and, in adopting such an approach, Thatcher's administration sought to drive Britain away from consensus politics. The premier made 'no secret of her dislike of political consensus between the parties'[22] that had existed for much of the post-war period.[23] This attitude was applied to the welfare state along with many other aspects of post-1945 British politics. Hence, the 'New Right' Thatcherite crusade should be understood as 'a libertarian project bent on destroying the "liberal consensus"'[24] within British politics and society. This notably different agenda simultaneously sought to break away from a dormant period of history by applying a new, contrasting ethos for governance that aligned 'the notion of conviction with the metaphor of movement and direction'.[25] This move was intended to instil dynamism and broader electoral appeal into the

Conservative Party's political programme from 1979 onwards, as is argued by Letwin's notion of the 'vigorous virtues' as being an essential component of the Thatcherite policy agenda. Such a conviction-based 'libertarian' angle emphasised that greater economic freedoms and a reduced role for the state would be the practical repercussions.

The Economic Implications of the New Right policy agenda

The overall thrust of Conservative policy-making after 1979 consequently appeared to take on a greater economic focus as opposed to a social one, although there were explicit social and welfare policy implications for an economic approach tinged with a distinctly 'New Right', neo-liberal flavour. Although by the mid-1970s there were concerns across the political spectrum over the long-term rising costs of the welfare state, the development and innovation of social and welfare policy was often downgraded and was initially overlooked as a policy priority by the incoming government in 1979.

During the period from 1945 to the mid-1970s, there had been broad bipartisan agreement on the levels of public spending and investment in social policies and public services, resulting in the state taking on a gradually increased degree of social responsibility for British citizens, reflected in progressively enhanced levels of welfare provision. This in turn led to increased government spending and economic activity to support social policies, and as a consequence of such trends UK government expenditure as a percentage of GDP steadily grew until it reached a peak of 48.9% in 1975.[26] This zenith of government expenditure prompted the Labour government of James Callaghan, even before the advent of Thatcherism, to acknowledge that Keynesian economics linked to an ever-growing state and its associated generous and costly social policies was no longer economically sustainable.[27]

Margaret Thatcher's administration had an ideology-tinted political strategy, despite the party's traditional aversion to such an approach to governance. It was shaped by a coherent set of ideas, primarily focused on the perceived need to tackle deep-rooted structural economic problems which were a side-effect of generous welfare provision. Yet, according to one commentator, this economic emphasis did not mean that Thatcherism was only about economics, but was rather 'not so much an economic policy as a way of doing economic policy – or, more precisely, a way of not doing economic policy'.[28] The Thatcher government placed emphasis on developing and radically restructuring the country's fundamental economic framework (a distinct approach from the mainstream post-war era), in order to address and tackle the high-spending social policies of successive governments of previous decades. The 'New Right' emphasis on economics could be clearly seen in one of its first forays into British social policy, when the Thatcher government abolished the link between the state old-age pension and earnings in 1980, a move that appeared to be primarily motivated by economic factors rather than social ones – a means of saving money. Such an emphasis on financial retrenchment appeared to downplay the potential for social policy innovation, although social policy and economics certainly fuse in many areas of contemporary politics, particularly in welfare provision whereby the scale, cost and overall scope of welfare services are linked to the health of the host economy. It has been a recurring challenge of modern British political administrations to achieve a satisfactory balance between these different nuances in the policy-making process, and socio-economic priorities often change as governments change, as governments in the post-Thatcher era have demonstrated.

Thatcherite critics of the Keynesian settlement, deploying the terms and concepts of monetarism, claimed that it had served its immediate purpose in promoting a short-term stimulus to encourage post-war recovery, but in the long-term it had simply increased levels of taxation, inflation, and public spending as a percentage of GDP, all of which factors had restricted long-term economic growth. As a consequence, by the 1980s Britain's post-war economic performance had been sluggish compared to other Western nations, and this had restricted the scope, efficiency and effectiveness of social and welfare policies. In general political terms therefore, social policy programmes and priorities could be broadly moulded and influenced by prevailing economic forces and conditions. Such economic pressure was certainly evident in the social policy expenditure of the Labour government (1974–9), particularly in its twilight phase following the significant cutbacks imposed following the IMF's dramatic intervention in 1976.[29] This period marked the end of the so-called 'Golden Age' of economic growth,[30] initially brought to a halt by the 1973 global oil crisis and culminating in rising unemployment, surging inflation and significant cuts in public spending and areas of social and welfare policy in the late 1970s, which in turn prompted the 'Winter of Discontent' and the consequent injection of 'New Right' theories into the realities of political power.

As a reaction to the global socio-economic developments and trends that were increasingly evident as the 1970s progressed, the New Right's advocates enthusiastically promoted monetarist theory (as espoused by its founding father Milton Friedman,[31]) and in doing so opposed government 'interference', as evident in excessive 'welfarism', high levels of public expenditure, rising levels of inflation and significant economic regulation. As an economic theory, it therefore espoused a less 'statist' approach, pursuing a greater emphasis on 'marketisation', generating greater fiscal and monetary flexibility in the process for those governments that adhered to its principles. In adopting this approach the Thatcher government endorsed a 'neo-liberal ideological assault on the post-war settlement'.[32] It argued that instead of targeting zero unemployment (as the prevailing post-war social-democratic model of governance had done), the market should determine a natural rate of unemployment. Inflation would instead be prioritised, ultimately reducing the government's traditional role in post-war economic management, with consequences for social and welfare policy provision in the process. In this context, the New Right's influence sought to 'nurture the values and attitudes needed to maintain capitalism in the new circumstances',[33] with such circumstances being the acknowledged eventual failure of post-war Keynesian economics, exacerbated by the impact of the globalised slump on the British economy. Friedman's monetarist doctrine claimed that by rejecting interventionist and 'futile attempts to push unemployment to zero [it would] no longer trigger inflationary spirals'.[34] The fact that such sentiments appeared to be shared by both an incumbent British Labour Prime Minister and a neo-liberal economist seemed to affirm that there were severe implications for the long-term sustainability of the post-war model of social policy.

The New Right's political narrative argued that the core of Britain's economy needed to be drastically revised and its welfare scope reduced in order to ensure a more effective and efficient management in the future. Inflation peaked at 26% during the mid-1970s; the Thatcherite analysis proclaimed that this was primarily due to decades of post-war economic intervention, with the government sustaining and subsidising inefficient industries and surplus jobs in the name of maintaining social harmony, often in defiance of the demands of the 'laws' of the free-market. This interpretation appeared to have been accepted by various members and supporters of Margaret Thatcher's administration from an early stage of its existence, as there was a 'growing number of Conservative neo-liberals, emboldened intellectually by the ideas and critiques adumbrated by the New Right, (who saw) many of the economic problems being experienced by Britain during the 1970s... (as) a consequence of successive post-war governments, Conservative and Labour alike, not allowing "the market" to function freely'.[35]

This suggested that a radically different 'free-market' approach to government policy-making would be pursued from 1979 onwards. The Thatcherite reaction to the spiralling socio-economic trend of inflation that peaked in the mid-1970s was to explicitly reject the interventionist, statist nature of the Keynesian legacy, and instead preach a return to the liberal economics of the 'Victorian era', in line with Thatcher's adherence to Victorian social and economic values of thrift and self-help. 'Thatcherism' represented a firm viewpoint that the economic policies and principles that had driven the dominant social democratic model of government during much of the post-war Britain had to be rejected 'in order to relaunch Britain as a successful capitalist economy',[36] and in doing so the Thatcher administration represented a fermenting ideological backlash against the socio-economic conditions of the time. From this political perspective it was 'a necessary response to the perilous state Britain was in prior to Thatcher's electoral victory in 1979',[37] and this required a 'free economy and a strong state', as described within Andrew Gamble's notable analysis of the New Right agenda,[38] that highlighted its fusion of economic liberalism and social conservatism. Such a marked change of government direction, with a distinct and contrasting political outlook from what had gone before, triggered a clear shift towards fiscal retrenchment, marketisation, the streamlining of public services and a significant review of overall government spending levels.

This approach has been summarised by scholars such as Gamble as requiring a 'strong state' to instil the necessary structural framework that allows a government to impose its moral values and political tendencies, but at the same time allow capitalism to flourish by seeking to actively 'unwind the coils of social democracy and welfarism that had fastened around the free economy'.[39] Indeed, a key principle of the New Right is that a strong state is an essential factor for capitalism to work at its most beneficial and effective, being 'dynamic and productive' yet still reliant 'upon institutions that the market itself cannot generate spontaneously... (leaving) a major role for government'.[40] The post-war model of social democratic government was condemned as fundamentally flawed, being a system that was 'alien to the Thatcherites... To them, Keynesianism was anathema'.[41] This would have drastic implications for social and welfare policies: from the 'New Right' perspective the creaking socio-economic structure of Britain required radical alteration; indeed, in the most radical Thatcherite analysis it perhaps even needed to be dismantled and rebuilt in a completely new guise. It was in such a context that the 1980s witnessed 'concerted attempts... to refashion the welfare state'.[42] The new Prime Minister clearly sought to rebalance the political consensus that had been firmly established in the years following 1945. In doing so, the state was nevertheless required to play a distinct role in fashioning the appropriate socio-economic conditions, social order and political structures.

The New Right's Influence on Thatcherism and its social policies

This socio-economic environment allowed Margaret Thatcher to initiate a range of drastic economic cutbacks in public spending as part of her 'monetarist experiment' from 1979 onwards. This was a prominent feature of her political agenda during her early years in power. By the start of the 1980s, the immediate short-term social consequences of such an austere approach to reducing the cost and scope of public service provision were fairly severe in terms of social unrest. It appears, therefore, that the clearest evidence of a correlation between economic and social policy can be seen when extreme economic pressures or a sustained period of recession put strains on the maintenance and funding of social policies within the overall structure of the welfare state. When such severe economic factors lead to a 'rolling back' of the state and cutbacks in the funding of welfare and social policies, there are often potentially serious social repercussions. In the aftermath of Chancellor of the Exchequer Geoffrey Howe's controversial 1981 'retrenchment' Budget in particular, the extent of such discord was such that 'throughout 1981, Britain was a country nowhere near to being at peace with itself,[43] with many inner-cities such as Liverpool, Bristol and London erupting and providing the backdrop to extreme and destructive rioting and social unrest, reflecting a mood of dissent among poorer social groups towards the sharp reductions in government public spending levels. The more moderate 'One Nation' faction of the Conservative Party was alarmed at such direct and brutal social implications of Thatcherism, claiming that on two fronts, 'economically and socially, the government was steering for the rocks – and hit them'.[44] Their fears appeared to materialise: 'Riots in Brixton a month after the budget and in Toxteth in July showed they had good reason to be worried'.[45] Such fears of widening social unrest contrasted sharply with the views of the Thatcherite 'New Right' ministers within government, most prominently Norman Tebbit, who, in the midst of such escalating unemployment and social disharmony, infamously referred to growing up "in the

'30s with an unemployed father", adding that "he didn't riot. He got on his bike and looked for work, and he kept looking 'til he found it".[46]

The Thatcherite reaction to such social unrest contrasted sharply with the 'One Nation' Conservative viewpoint, and such differences marked a key fracture within the Conservative Party in relation to economic policy and its wider social consequences. There has been much political debate as to whether the early phase of Conservative government of 1979 achieved more failure than success (on various levels), and political commentators and academics ranging from David Willetts to Shirley Letwin have identified this initial period of Thatcher's Conservative administration as pursuing a 'New Right' inspired policy agenda that was 'above all, economic' in its core emphasis.[47] As a consequence, social policy, social issues and broader welfare reform were seen to be relatively neglected and even expendable in some cases, being subordinate to the fundamental aim of 'balancing the books' and achieving greater long-term economic efficiency. As Letwin argues when she refers to the 'vigorous virtues', such an emphasis on economic liberalism and dynamism grew in its boldness and ideological vigour the longer Thatcher was in power, and it was during her second term (1983–87) that her policy agenda developed its more definitive economic edge, as her overall political focus became 'increasingly committed to the privatisation of public services and the reduction of public expenditure ... on the welfare state'.[48]

Margaret Thatcher's primary economic emphasis is often epitomised by the statement she made in an interview with *Woman's Own* magazine in the wake of her third election victory in 1987 that "There is no such thing as society",[49] a phrase often used out of its full context but which nevertheless appears to emphasise her focus on economic individualism as opposed to a social agenda. However, those who worked closely with her during this period do not accept that social policy was neglected or even abandoned to the extent that critics have claimed, as explained below:

> In her early days... (she was) preoccupied with the economy and industrial relations and she turned to social policy in the mid-80s when welfare reform and then education became a priority. So it is true that it wasn't a priority early on, but it became more of a priority later ... there was a caricature of Thatcher that came from the notorious 'Woman's Own' quote – she was not really saying that she rejected society, she really attempted to correct a misapprehension about her views on society.[50]

Despite such a determined defence of her attitudes and outlook regarding social policy matters, there continue to be critical academic interpretations of the Conservative Party's record in this broad policy area during the 1980s, reinforcing the perception that Conservatives of the New Right variant were 'not interested in society, and were merely concerned with economics',[51] culminating in the socio-economic outcome that 'under-funding on public services was one of the key legacies of Conservative social policy in the 1980s and 1990s'.[52] There were clear social consequences to the revolutionary economic policies pursued by the Thatcher government, often perceived as being negative; this again emphasises the strong link between economic and social and welfare policies in most political models. According to one contemporary Conservative activist looking back at this period, the British economy's need for radical medicine meant that 'the inevitable consequence of this was that social policy took rather more of a back seat than perhaps it should. The generalised perception of Conservative welfare and social policy throughout this period is thus probably negative'.[53] Having acknowledged such negative perceptions however, there were nevertheless tensions within the broader New Right family between the Conservative neo-liberals who wanted more radically deregulated public services and those of a more authoritarian and socially conservative nature who favoured maintaining the 'strong state' as alluded to by Andrew Gamble. Some distinct flagship social policies emerged from these ideological tensions, an example being the acceleration of council house sales with its associated reduction in state responsibility that proved to be popular with many voters.[54] However, with welfare and social policies directly affected by the government's desire to shrink the size and scope of its economic footprint, this would arguably set a precedent for future Conservative administrations in the pursuit of restructuring and reforming welfare and social policy while cutting public spending, with potential parallels evident in the Conservative–Liberal Democrat coalition administration that took office with an explicit 'retrenchment' agenda in May 2010.

Some Conservative figures of the moderate 'One Nation' wing, a faction of the party that was steadily overlooked and sidelined during the Thatcher period, have indeed acknowledged the apparent downgrading of social policy during this era, regretfully commenting on how it was unfairly sidelined and neglected: 'We do not make enough of our social record... Why not develop our ideas about choice and better provision as a genuine social policy we are proud of?'[55]

It transpired that the need to secure a restructured economic model that would deliver long-term stability was awarded greater political emphasis during the 1980s, but the focus on providing greater choice within social policy would nevertheless develop as the decade progressed, and would significantly shape post-Thatcher Conservative thinking (and indeed wider politics). During the 1980s such a focused emphasis on economic restructuring as the primary medicine for addressing society's deep-rooted problems remained more at the forefront of government policy direction, although, despite this, it has been argued by academics such as Howard Glennerster that the Thatcher decade 'was a decisive one for social policy', although it was only after she had departed from office in 1990 that 'distinctive legislative changes were placed on the statute book'.[56] However, despite this inference that social policy and related welfare issues were revitalised under John Major's administration from 1990 to 1997, it has been acknowledged in the midst of this post-Thatcher period that it remained a low priority in policy terms and that future party leaders would have to grapple with it much more earnestly, with accurate predictions that the 'new theme of more fundamental change in Britain's welfare state... will fall to the younger generation of Conservatives to elaborate'.[57] This line of analysis will certainly have struck a chord with the Conservative politicians and 'modernisers' of David Cameron's ilk, who, having surveyed the wreckage of the 1997 general election defeat, gradually sought to steer the Party back on the road to electability and a wider public appeal. This focus on the need for a refreshed and more attractive electoral message has led to a revised interpretation of the New Right's legacy in terms of shaping a practical and long-term social policy focus for the Conservative Party, and this has particularly resonated with David Cameron's leadership agenda from late 2005 onwards.

Social and political consequences of the 'New Right' policy agenda

The historical example of how the New Right tradition explicitly influenced the last sustained period of Conservative government and how it in turn created divisions between different sections of the Conservative Party has had contemporary repercussions in terms of how the party has functioned in office from 2010 onwards. Given such an unconvincing and uncertain legacy in the sphere of social and welfare policy from the 1980s onwards, the Conservative Party's more explicit economy-focused approach employed during this period ultimately had some harsh consequences in terms of broader social harmony; evident in notable social unrest such as the inner-city riots of 1981, the Miners' Strike of 1984–5 and the poll tax protests of 1989–90. In this context and as a modern-day comparison, parallels can be made between the policy priorities of the early phase of Conservative government from 1979 onwards and the proposed economic cutbacks of the Conservative–Liberal Democrat coalition as outlined from May 2010 onwards. Such an approach has the potential to generate similarly negative implications for long-term levels of welfare provision and the broader social fabric, and there was some evidence of this in autumn 2010 with the protests against the increase in university tuition fees, alongside the serious social unrest across much of urban Britain in the summer of 2011.

As a consequence of such episodes of social turmoil in the 1980s, David Cameron's generation of 21st century Conservatives have been sensitive to criticisms that have aligned them with previous Tory administrations regarding the perceived neglect of poorer, urban areas and their inhabitants who are reliant on greater levels of state provision and welfare support, and who were adversely affected by funding cutbacks for various welfare policies during the 1980s.[58] However, it remains unclear as to whether the approach to retrenchment from 2010 onwards has been specifically influenced by the legacy of the 'New Right' socio-political agenda or whether it has anything different to offer from the 1980s in terms of enhanced 'compassion', namely in ensuring that adequate levels of social policy and welfare provision will remain in place for the most vulnerable, while delivering adequate social order in the process. Fears of repeated scenes of social unrest have been expressed in the context of the proposed economic cutbacks that commenced in 2010–11 to deal with Britain's large economic deficit, with similarly negative implications predicted for the implementation and delivery of social policy across the country. However, such internal party divisions and tensions have perhaps been initially less apparent amidst the scenes of public unrest in response to the economic retrenchment imposed to tackle the national deficit from 2010 onwards, for example in relation to the protests at student tuition fees increases in late 2010. However, the rioting of summer 2011 (arguably linked to significant reductions in government expenditure), may have had more significant implications for the social policy agenda for the long-term duration of the Conservative–Liberal Democrat coalition's time in office, with some moderate Conservatives and Liberal Democrats expressing more vocal fears of the ongoing social unrest that could be caused by sustained draconian cuts to key public services. The broader social consequences of the summer riots of 2011 may be merely symptomatic of a negative public reaction to government austerity measures, and the damage to government may be ultimately measured by the numbers of people affected, the extent to which they represent a significant fraction of the electorate, and whether the changes have a long-term electoral impact.

There is some potential for a coherent connection to be made between the socio-economic approach of the New Right and the style and model of governance adopted by the Cameron administration. While gloomy contemporary parallels between the 1981 Budget and the post-2010 austerity agenda have been drawn by many on the left, the 'New Right' interpretation of events offers the alternative viewpoint that on a purely economic and fiscally responsible level, 'The budget of 1981 is considered the epitome of soundness, an exercise in rigour that laid the foundations for the strong economic recovery'.[59] This budget can therefore be viewed as of one of this historical period's most significant socio-economic developments and is an episode used as a benchmark by the New Right-influenced 'fiscal' Conservatives of the present day, offering a blueprint for Conservative administrations in how to deal with tough economic conditions and the implementation of necessary measures of retrenchment while maintaining stable overall governance. Indeed, many Conservative politicians in the coalition government of 2010 ultimately aspired to similar concerted and high-profile efforts to balance the books over the course of the 2010–15 administration, hoping to create a similarly restructured economy and accompanying socio-economic change.[60] It has, however, been noted by various political commentators that David Cameron appears to be the first Conservative Party Leader since 1997 who has sought to place spoken explicitly on the need to acknowledge and address the social implications of the neo-liberal economic model in a way that the Thatcherites did not. With his 'emphasis on social issues… intended to demonstrate that, notwithstanding his continued support for the neo-liberal economic agenda… he accepted that the party had ignored the adverse social consequences that accompanied such radical social change'.[61]

David Cameron's focus on the social implications of neo-liberal economics and a smaller state sit uncomfortably next to the social unrest that engulfed parts of urban Britain in the middle of 2011, and his attitude on this subject has appeared to blur the extent of his Conservative identity, given that he has consistently expressed a 'One Nation' style paternalistic concern for the poorer members of society, but has also expressed little sympathy for those involved in such unrest, and has acknowledged the need for significant economic cutbacks aligned with the New Right's general analysis and neo-liberal economic model. There appears to be some inconsistency and a paradox within the Cameron socio-economic prescription, namely how the circle can be squared between reduced government expenditure, fewer public services and the subsequent personal hardships that ensue. This may be clarified during the course of his premiership in the face of changing circumstances.

In contrast to its perceived neglect and indifference to social policy, during the 1980s the Conservative Party appeared to have established a positive reputation for economic competence as a key component of the radical New Right agenda. Economic credibility, therefore, appeared to be the cornerstone of its political dominance, and this reputation was a key factor in the party's impressive achievement of four election victories in a row between 1979 and 1992, with economic competence perhaps the crucial factor in its success in the closely fought general election of 1992.[62] This positive economic reputation had been carefully cultivated by the New Right's policy actions that had featured privatisation, tax cuts and concerted anti-inflationary measures pursued throughout the 1980s. However, this reputation was shattered following the debacle of 'Black Wednesday' on 16 September 1992, 'the day the pound toppled out of the ERM... a political and economic calamity'.[63] In the wake of this event John Major's Conservative government found that its former superiority on economic policy matters (as definitively established during the 1980s), was eradicated by a collapse of public trust. New Labour subsequently eclipsed the Conservatives in terms of economic reputation as the 1990s progressed, and the outcome of the 1997 general election was arguably sealed some years beforehand on the basis of such fundamental economic factors affecting electoral fortunes,[64] although issues such as sleaze and party divisions would also later have an effect. The disruptive legacy of 'Black Wednesday' could therefore be viewed as a major deviation from the New Right's economic blueprint, and it certainly played a part in the Conservatives seeking to widen their overall policy appeal and extend their emphasis on social issues after 1997, as they could no longer rely on a formidable economic record.

Given the electoral annihilation of 1997 and further heavy defeats in 2001 and 2005, it became apparent that not only had the Conservative Party lost its previously unrivalled mantle of economic probity and competence, but perhaps more significantly, it was also perceived as being out of touch with significant swathes of contemporary British society, particularly in relation to aspects of the modern lifestyle and the associated social policies that had become important determinants in many people's voting habits. This perhaps indicated that just as 'Keynesianism' had appeared to have had its day as a socio-economic model by the mid-1970s, so, therefore, had the principles and policies associated with Thatcherism and the 'New Right' by the mid-1990s. Some Conservative politicians were resistant to such suggestions, including the 'modernisers' within the party leadership after 2005, (in government from 2010),[65] along with key groups of backbenchers such as the traditionalist 'Cornerstone'[66] group of socially conservative MPs. This went to the root of the Conservative Party's troubled and uncertain identity in the post-Thatcher period from 1990 onwards, with rival influences grappling for the party's soul and its future political direction. In some respects it can be argued that while society appeared to have evolved and developed during the party's eighteen years in power (1979–97), the Conservative hierarchy, its broad attitudes and the wider party structure had seemingly failed to adapt and mould its own social policy agenda and social outlook accordingly. This was despite there being evidence of some notable demographic shifts across society in terms of gender politics, greater sexual diversity, more non-conventional family models and higher levels of multi-ethnicity within a more diverse and tolerant British social structure. This became evident in ongoing electoral difficulties and lack of broad appeal, as outlined by a Conservative MP at the start of the 21st century:

> My children... are all bright and ... in their mid or late twenties, and probably natural Tories. But none of them would ever vote Tory. They think the party is totally out of touch. All the stuff about gays is totally incredible to them... We have not selected a woman or an ethnic minority candidate for a single winnable seat. That's the sort of party we have become.[67]

Once the Conservative Party was firmly consigned to opposition after 1997, this definitive electoral development provided party reformers and modernisers with a significant impetus to reform and explicitly re-align the party's 'post-Thatcher' position in relation to some specific key issues and areas of social policy in particular, without abandoning Thatcherism and the 'New Right' legacy entirely. Therefore although the Thatcherite focus on neo-liberal economics, free-markets and Euroscepticism seemed to have been broadly maintained as important undercurrents of conventional Conservative identity, social policy had emerged as a key competing factor in determining the nation's broader political agenda and electoral behaviour. This renewed focus on devising distinct social policies and liberalising the party's collective social attitude was further influenced by the fact that by the early 21st century, despite economic setbacks like 'Black Wednesday', there was broad cross-party agreement in support of the Thatcherite 'neo-liberal' economic agenda that appeared to have been irreversibly established following the sustained period of Conservative government in the 1980s. By default, therefore, social and welfare policy issues now required enhanced political attention, alongside associated hostility to the perceived dependency culture engendered by the post-war social and welfare policies. The New Right's economic agenda of the 1980s had ultimately shifted the broader political debate and wider public mood in favour of the perspective of New Right Conservatism, but the diverse social trends and developments of this period were less aligned with such neo-conservative social values and therefore somewhat undermined the Conservative Party's long-term electoral position. It is within this context that David Cameron's leadership of the Conservative Party since late 2005 has from the very outset accepted and embraced the evolution of contemporary British society as an integral aspect of his determined vision to reverse the tide of repeated electoral defeat, aspiring to rebalance its focus as he felt that 'towards the end of the 1980s we did become too much the economics party', stemming from his belief that 'his party has won the battle of ideas in political economy, and that New Labour's success was very proof of that'.[68]

This viewpoint acknowledging the need to address and give greater emphasis to welfare and social policy fitted with the views of party heavyweights who had preceded Cameron in holding prominent positions in the party following the loss of office in 1997. In 1998 Michael Portillo, the former cabinet minister and Shadow Chancellor (2000–2001) had claimed (as part of his transformation from a 'New Right' disciple of Thatcherism to a socially liberal Conservative), that the Tories needed to address welfare reform, particularly 'getting away from the sense of entitlement'[69] evident in some welfare recipients, as well as tackling the negative image of some aspects of the party's approach to welfare policy. Even William Hague (party leader 1997–2001), and viewed as being less socially liberal than the post-1997 Portillo, accepted that the 'Tories cannot any longer be just an "economic party"... [and] implied a desire to open up on the welfare and other social issues'.[70] Therefore, despite such ostensible success in shaping the country's long-term economic values and infrastructure during the watershed decade of the 1980s, there was a growing feeling by the early 21st century that there was a need for a more explicit focus on the social issues that had been neglected during the period of Thatcherite political hegemony, and that the Conservative Party had been responsible for 'shirking responsibility for industrial and social issues where it ought to act'.[71] Such apparent neglect, lack of priority and limited interest in social issues ultimately appeared to result in the Conservatives developing a sense of disconnection with the mainstream electorate's general social values and expectations that had been shaped in conjunction with the dramatic economic changes of the 1980s. This culminated in uninspiring and disjointed social policies that were unappealing to significant swathes of society, and which provides one explanation for the major loss of electoral support the party experienced from the mid-1990s onwards.

This post-Thatcher legacy generated the phenomenon of the Conservatives being increasingly perceived as being 'out of touch' with broader society during the final years of the 20th century, a 100-year period that the party had dominated the UK in political terms. This was observed by major Conservative donor Michael Ashcroft after the party's third successive General Election defeat in 2005, when he warned that despite a modest electoral improvement (an increased in its vote of 0.7%), the level of popular support for the party was effectively 'flatlining' and had risen minimally in eight years (1.7%).[72] Ashcroft subsequently concluded that there needed to be urgent 'modernisation' and radical reform of Conservative Party values and identity if the party was to make any kind of significant electoral recovery[73] in a post-Thatcher British society. Such persistent limitations in wider public support was arguably influenced by both the negative economic performance of the last Conservative government, and the party's perceived unpalatable and unsympathetic approaches to socio-economic issues such as unemployment, the benefits system and welfare reform. A concerted attempt to rebalance this approach has been evident under Cameron's leadership since 2005, with a 'modernising' focus on supporting core services such as the NHS instead of cutting taxes, '(and being) at ease with modern Britain, with a multicultural society and with people who had different lifestyles and sexual preferences'.[74]

This introspective analysis and subsequent desire for a fresh strategic approach is aligned with existing external opinions about the Conservative Party's image, identity and wider public perception in the aftermath of the dominant 'New Right' era, and specifically the Thatcherite association with conservative Victorian social attitudes, a position that could often be identified with intolerance. At the

2002 Party Conference, Party Chairman Theresa May accepted that Conservatives needed to extend their popular appeal and effectively 'catch up' with the changing British social agenda that had evolved while the party had been in power up to 1997. In this context, May controversially acknowledged that many people had bad memories of the previous Conservative government and some of its social attitudes:

> There's a lot we need to do in this party of ours. Our base is too narrow and so, occasionally, are our sympathies. You know what some people call us – the nasty party.[75]

Such a brutal self-assessment is perhaps a reflection of the fact that in the three general elections between 1997 and 2005, the Conservative Party's New Right legacy of economic neo-liberalism appeared out of touch with the aspirations, social priorities and contemporary attitudes of modern, multicultural, heterogeneous Britain. It was also often abruptly and instinctively opposed to the Labour government's 'social liberalism'[76] and its associated bureaucratic measures, yet had little in terms of a constructive alternative agenda to offer. Thus, the New Right vocabulary and rhetoric that was politically appealing during the 1980s now appeared to hinder efforts to articulate a coherent and persuasive Conservative Party programme or image in terms of an innovative and coherent set of social policies for the early 21st century. For example, in a throwback to the Thatcherite 'Victorian' mentality on both social and economic issues, after 1997 the party opposed policies such as adoption rights for gay couples, repeal of the infamous section 28 about the teaching of homosexual lifestyles, initially opposed the minimum wage and 'targeted' tax credits aimed at poorer social groups; all of which in turn often created adverse headlines about the party's stance appearing out of touch with a more benevolent and tolerant public opinion. Conservative Party modernisers have therefore attempted to detach themselves from the intolerant and moralistic aspect of the New Right's legacy, fully conscious of the party's 'weak standing with the electorate, particularly on health and welfare issues',[77] and subsequently sought to progressively and pragmatically develop a more appealing image for moderate floating voters under David Cameron's leadership since 2005. The New Right's intense ideological emphasis ultimately appeared to have destabilised the party's internal equilibrium in the long-term, affecting the long-term balance of its policy focus. By the start of the 21st century this led to demands for re-alignment and the 'detoxifying' of the Conservative image[78] in relation to the more negative aspects of the New Right's agenda, and an opportunity to address its 'divided ideological legacy... (of) economic liberalism (and) social conservatism'.[79] Cameron has, therefore, purposely sought to eradicate negative perceptions by revising the party's position on social and welfare policy issues and made concerted efforts 'to distance the Conservatives from their image as the "nasty" or "uncaring" party... to "decontaminate" the brand'.[80] A high-profile example of this approach can be seen in the government's groundbreaking policy of legalising gay marriage in 2013.

Conservatism and the New Right legacy in the 21st century

In seeking to achieve the visible 'detoxification' and 'decontamination' of its own political brand, in the early years of the 21st century the Conservative Party sought to speak with a more 'compassionate' and liberal tone on matters relating to social and welfare policy-making in particular. In doing so it has aspired to adopt a modernised, pragmatic and 'reformist' policy approach, and in opposition between 2005 and 2010 it adapted to much of Labour's additional investment in public services and the associated increased taxation. This was a consequence of 'New Labour's politics of dominance in the area of public services'[81] and the associated electoral success in the form of three successive general election victories. Election results between 1997 and 2005 would therefore suggest that the electorate broadly supported this enhanced attention to public services as espoused by Blair and Brown, although the Conservatives consistently demanded greater efficiency and value for money in the use and expenditure of public finances as a qualification for supporting associated social and welfare policies. In responding to such political realities in a more pragmatic and flexible manner, the Conservatives therefore began to adapt their image and renewed their focus on refreshing their policy agenda within this specific sphere. This resulted in a departure from the more ideologically robust agenda of the 1980s, although in seeking to revitalise the Conservative Party brand, David Cameron has been careful not to completely detach himself from Thatcher's influence and legacy and alienate sections of his party in the process, in rhetorical terms at least.

Nevertheless, the more socially liberal and tolerant 'modernising' tendency within the Conservative Party has notably progressed under the leadership of Cameron since late 2005. This has arguably been at the expense of the economic neo-liberals, and possibly as a consequence of the difficult years of William Hague's leadership (1997–2001) and that of Iain Duncan Smith (2001–3).[82] During this phase of national opposition (1997–2003), the party appeared particularly confused about its political identity and reverted to speaking primarily to its core supporters and its media allies, with its popular vote remaining static accordingly: 'Between 1999 and the 2001 election campaign, Conservative policy changed direction to focus on bolstering the Party's "core" support... (while) the leadership appeared increasingly to shape policy in response to the latest headlines in the *Daily Telegraph* and *Daily Mail*'.[83] Yet despite an approach under Cameron that has been intent on widening the broad appeal and revised policy agenda of modern, post-Thatcher Conservatism, even in 2010 the party's level of popular support was disappointing in comparison to former levels, rising less than 6% between the electoral nadir of 1997 and the return to national office in 2010. David Cameron subsequently moved into Number 10 'with a smaller proportion of support from the electorate than any previous Conservative prime minister',[84] although marginally more than Tony Blair's level of support on his third election victory for Labour in 2005. This reflected the Conservative Party's image problems within some sections of society, suggesting an inability to eradicate the wider public's memories of various unpopular policies from its previous spells in office.

While such statistics of declining contemporary political support may provide succour to those Thatcherites from the New Right tradition who seek a return to the 1980s populist brand of Conservative policies, these bleak electoral statistics indicate a long-term decline in popular support for the Conservative Party, the 'natural party of government' for much of the 20th century. This illustrates the dilemma facing any incoming Conservative government and its efforts to remould distinct and radical social and welfare policies along with a greater degree of decentralisation and economic efficiency fuelled by its 'Big Society' vision. With such limited, falling and volatile levels of popular support, this fragile public mood is likely to further undermine the party's popularity after 2010 as it pursues the streamlining economic reforms it claims are necessary to tackle the national deficit amidst a lingering recession and global economic crisis, significantly hampering its room for manoeuvre in its social policy-making agenda. However, from the financial and banking crisis of 2008 onwards, the Conservative leadership's decision to adopt the language of retrenchment and abandon its initial support for the Labour administration's spending plans suggested an opportunistic move in the direction of the Thatcherite 'neo-liberal' approach of the 1980s. In pragmatically adapting to the economic fluctuations of the time, Conservative politicians subsequently argued with greater confidence for 'small government' and in the process inserted some clear divisions between the two main parties on economic and social policy.

This approach has been viewed by some as an opportunity for the Conservatives to reassert their case for the New Right's agenda of a smaller state and reduced expenditure on welfare and social policies, with a prolonged recession and global financial crisis creating the appropriate conditions for this. This strategy came to fruition when having returned to office at the head of a coalition with the Liberal Democrats in May 2010, £17.5 billion was initially trimmed from the welfare bill alone in the Emergency Budget that took effect from October 2010.[85] This appeared to reflect in economic terms that the party had retained some core Thatcherite New Right principles, particularly regarding the modern party's 'historic scepticism towards public spending'.[86] Therefore, in this revised analysis of the country's economic policy-making approach:

> Cameron ditched his previous pledge to match Labour spending levels... (and) rediscovered virtues in Margaret Thatcher, the woman hitherto largely airbrushed from history in his speeches. Cameron and Osborne made themselves champions of fiscal conservatism, opening up the biggest divide on economic policy between the parties for more than a decade.[87]

In this context of a re-evaluation of Conservative economic and social priorities and levels of public expenditure, there appears to have been an apparent reversion to the Thatcherite language of retrenchment amidst a major recession, and Cameron appears to have revised and redefined his approach to the promotion of 'compassionate conservatism' in practical policy terms, taking the opportunity to downgrade the dominant spendthrift tendencies of the centralised state in pursuit of reduced debt and deficit levels. Utilising the language and rhetoric of social responsibility and community action, Cameron has therefore initiated flagship policies such as 'The Big Society' which despite criticisms of its vagueness, has symbolised a willingness to take the ideological argument to Labour about how to operate both economic and social policy within a tighter financial strait-jacket, seeking to reclaim the Conservative Party's economic reputation while simultaneously infiltrating Labour's traditional hegemony in electoral terms on social and welfare policy matters.

The long-term challenge for the contemporary Conservative Party in the early 21st century remains to convince key socio-economic groups within the electorate that it seeks to pursue a credible agenda of public service reform, modernisation and innovation of social and welfare policies for this specific historical era, and that a simultaneous economic approach moulded by fiscal conservatism, retrenchment and a nod to the New Right's neo-liberal traditions, is in fact a genuine attempt to balance the nation's books and restore stability to the country's finances. Such an approach has had to be reviewed by changing economic circumstances, however, as 'The politics of the welfare state has been changed by the economic downturn. As a *Times* leader put it [2008], "Compassionate conservatism is a more difficult proposition in a recession".'[88]

In pursuing this challenging scenario therefore, the New Right's legacy of fiscal conservatism has reappeared on the political horizon, and the clarity of David Cameron's socio-economic outlook has been hampered by the challenges of a global economic recession, making it even more difficult to fulfil the primary aims of party modernisers to streamline the British welfare model in a compassionate way while simultaneously maintaining sustainable and genuine welfare and social policies.

In cultivating a more compassionate image, the Conservative Party's leadership of the early 21st century has been wary of the potential dangers and hazards in preserving this appearance while engaged in a political agenda focused on retrenchment; reflecting the prevailing socio-political mood since the party returned to national office in 2010. There are, therefore, both potentially negative perceptions and radical implications of pursuing welfare reform amidst a recession, as identified by some elements of the 'New Right' from the 1970s onwards:

> In many countries, a conservative resurgence accompanied the economic turmoil of the late 1970s. Conservative parties gained strength, and within these parties leadership shifted to those most critical of the post-war consensus on social and economic policy. These newly ascendant conservatives viewed the welfare state as a large part of the problem... (and) viewed retrenchment not as a necessary evil but as a necessary good.[89]

This suggestion of a sense of political opportunism amidst economic uncertainty among acolytes of the New Right has been observed by academics, including Andrew Gamble, who has stated that dissident figures on both the left and right of politics in the 1970s who were disillusioned by the apparent failings of the post-war consensus, subsequently 'welcomed the political space created by the recession and the possibilities for refashioning institutions and redesigning policies in radical ways'.[90] Gamble has referred to this development as being part of a 'crisis of social democracy'[91] which gave the more pro-capitalist 'New Right' agenda an opportunity to fill a socio-political vacuum with a model of government more aligned with the principles of free-market liberal democracy instead, namely a 'free economy and a strong state'. Within such a socio-political context, the New Right's attitude and legacy in terms of the possibility to radically restructure the welfare state has meant that contemporary groups of floating voters have remained more sceptical of the Conservative Party's position towards social policy and ensuring adequate welfare provision in recent years (evident in declining levels of popular support at recent general elections). This is based on perceptions that the Conservative Party did not sufficiently invest in or sufficiently focus on the core welfare state during the 1980s, and which explains its pursuit of a 'broader decontamination strategy' in this respect.[92]

In such a context, the new generation of Conservative politicians have to convince more sceptical audience of their genuine interest and benevolent concern in both the maintenance and innovation of credible social policies as part of the party's strategy to establish a sustainable model of welfare provision for the 21st century. This may be a significant challenge, given that there is evidence from within the Conservative Party's 2010 intake of MPs of an appetite 'for the Thatcherite agenda of tax cuts, continued marketisation and downward pressure on public spending'[93]. In this context it would appear, therefore, that some within the Conservative ranks have seen an opportunity or a 'necessary good' (as was ostensibly the case in the 1970s) for radical socio-economic restructuring and the resurgence of a Thatcherite 'rolling back' of the state and the instillation of some 'vigorous virtues' into the British welfare model as a consequence of economic difficulties faced. Public opinion towards this approach is open to conjecture, as there appears to be significant fluidity in voters' attitudes towards taxation and public spending, with some recent analysis indicating a shift towards increased support for retrenchment, particularly so as the New Labour years in office progressed, 'with 'strong evidence for a decline in support for tax-funded increases in state provision and hardening of public attitudes towards welfare recipients'[94] during the Blair/Brown era. However such increased scepticism of Labour's perceived financial profligacy from 1997 onwards has not appeared to translate automatically into an enthusiastic endorsement of alternative Conservative models of economic retrenchment, perhaps evidenced by the inconclusive outcome of the 2010 General Election[95]. Such apparent wider suspicion of Conservative public spending proposals on social and welfare policies has been heightened by the economic slump and associated employment insecurities of those who may come to rely on its provisions, and in such a context the Conservatives' ongoing focus in this policy sphere will be to convince the electorate that the maintenance of core services can be complemented by greater economic efficiency within a framework of fiscal conservatism.

The New Right restructured some key components of the established post-war welfare state in Britain during the 1980s, but a more radical restructuring of core public services and reduction of welfare expenditure remained an uncompleted aspiration of the Thatcherite project during its decade of political ascendancy. The failure to fulfil its idealised vision of welfare and social policy provision was fundamentally due to reasons that remain to this day: 'that the structural impediments involved are little short of immense'[96] and 'a crucial constraint on the Conservatives was the sheer popularity of welfare institutions'[97]. Public opinion and significant bureaucratic impediments were therefore key factors that ultimately prevented the New Right's imprint on British society and policy-making from being as deep as it could have been during its period of political hegemony throughout the 1980s. This raises the key question as to whether the same impediments are in place in the early years of the 21st century should any new version of such reforms be pursued.

3
Conservatism and social justice in theory

This chapter seeks to address and analyse the meaning of the concept of social justice and the ways its presence on the political scene has influenced the formulation of Conservative Party social and welfare policy. In focusing on the party's policy evolution since its comprehensive loss of power in 1997, we see that the concept of social justice has been a constant, ambiguous, dynamic factor in the modern political arena, with its contested interpretations forming the basis for debate among political parties and politicians, particularly from 1979 onwards. A concise yet fundamental definition of this key socio-political term might be the desire for a moral and 'fairer' justification for the distribution of material rewards within society, which implies a general requirement for a more equal social and economic outcome. (Who or what defines 'fairness' has been a major source of contention.) Such emphasis on equality implies an essentially 'egalitarian' flavour being attached to the term 'social justice', reflecting an acknowledgement of the need to foster and generate a more equal society on a range of levels, and this has developed into a prominent issue within British political debate over recent years. In this role the concept has shaped and influenced the formulation of social and economic policies of the mainstream political parties, who have paid attention to it primarily because it retains a significant resonance and appeal with key parts of the electorate.

The meaning of social justice

The conventional political interpretation of social justice implies the need for an active, interventionist role for the state as the mechanism that can deliver a morally-based and 'fairer' allocation of social and economic benefits. This is 'justice' achieved through social policy. The concept has been of particular significance to Conservative fortunes, as recent polling has indicated that there is 'greater scepticism about the Conservatives' broader policy agenda, which to some extent supports the data from the British Social Attitudes survey... (indicating) relatively high levels of support for state provision'.[1] Such public attitudes indicate scepticism about the Conservatives' broader social policy agenda, as well as firm support for a positive and active role for the state.[2] These attitudes have been displayed consistently since the 1990s, resulting in a persisting emphasis on the concept of social justice and its associated practical outcome of active state-instigated social policies. The term has been increasingly used as a rhetorical device by mainstream politicians of all parties, with the desirability of achieving a policy-making outcome aligned with the principles of social justice often being a prominent element of political debate. However, given that the concept of social justice is not always clearly explained, and its meaning disputed by adherents of all ideological traditions, the precise nature of the principles of social justice has been and still is keenly debated.

So, although vague in terms of its meaning, 'social justice' has been a pervading feature of the evolution and formulation of social and economic policy for all political parties and viewpoints. The conventional, widely held interpretation of social justice, fundamentally linked to the values of fairness and equality and with an active role for the state, has tended to be more generally used and emphasised by politicians of the left and centre-left. In such a 'conventional' interpretation, the state has been viewed as a fundamental tool for achieving social justice, either by government social or economic policy and/or via state intervention to achieve a more egalitarian or 'socially just' outcome by addressing long-term social inequality and poverty. The strength and persistence of this association affirmed the leftist hue of the concept, and as a result many Conservative figures (both politicians and commentators), came to be critical and at times even resentful of the left's monopoly and specific interpretation of the term. Many became sceptical of its 'egalitarian' meaning, and, indeed, of its actual effectiveness and practicality. In short, egalitarianism and fairness are concepts that have been regularly used as justifications for policies intended to improve social justice as part of an 'emotional appeal'[3] by mainly left-wing politicians over the course of the 20th century, and this has presented politicians who are dubious of its meaning and interpretation with a challenge: to develop an alternative analysis that negates such emotional appeal and offers a distinctive alternative with popular political support.

From a traditional Conservative political perspective therefore, 'social justice' that is nourished by state-generated egalitarianism creates potential difficulties when large numbers of voters embrace it as a desirable model of society. Indeed, many Conservative academics and politicians have condemned the left-of-centre interpretation of social justice that seeks to promote enhanced levels of social equality as 'one of the central prejudices of modern British politics' that emerges in practical form as a flawed 'belief that it is the proper function of the British state to influence the distribution of wealth for its own sake'.[4] The standard Conservative position fundamentally rejects the philosophical basis behind this view of social justice, opposes its emphasis on greater egalitarianism and a more 'statist' style of governance, and questions the need for such an approach to public policy. Joseph and Sumption argued that in practical terms an inflated role for the state is a natural consequence once this concept is established as a key guidance for government policy-making.[5] Conservative and free-market thinkers, academics and politicians have therefore preferred to endorse a position that favours a less interventionist approach by the state, instead focusing on the value of individual capabilities, an approach that involves 'privileging liberty, [compared to] socialists prioritising equality'.[6]

Conservatives' traditional scepticism of the concepts of egalitarianism and conventional social justice can therefore be attributed to the fact that both terms are associated with the left of politics, with the socialist or social democratic vision of society. Many Conservatives have a deep-seated 'wariness of egalitarianism',[7] in that they feel it is part of a left-wing myth that justifies a particular version of social justice that relies on significant and 'unnatural' state provision to achieve its aims, and cleaves to a social philosophy that argues that greater equality of outcome is both inherently desirable and practically achievable. This perception and interpretation of how society should ideally function is rejected as a 'myth' by the 'New Right' tradition that has come to prominence since the mid-1970s. New Right adherents have been notably strident in articulating a viewpoint, endorsed by many conservative politicians and thinkers all over the world, that inequality is 'natural and inevitable, a fact of life which cannot be altered, and which therefore should be readily accepted, rather than viewed as a problem to be eradicated'.[8] Indeed, stemming from this distaste for egalitarian vocabulary and sentiment, Conservatives with links to the Thatcherite tradition have referred to social justice as a 'slippery term',[9] suggesting that it is an ambiguous concept that reflects an inaccurate vision of how human nature operates in practice. The 'social-democratic' interpretation of social justice therefore stands in clear and fundamental distinction to core Conservative principles of the post-1979 era. An enhanced role for the state in social policy matters is fundamentally opposed to the individualist thrust that that modern Conservatism has sought to promote – more competition, greater private economic freedoms, extended choice and better opportunities for the individual. Conservative critics of the leftist usage of the term argue that the implications of this approach are an inevitable growth in 'statist' regulation, which in turn creates a state-instigated outcome that could also be viewed as unjust from a free-market perspective. The New Right argues that such 'unnatural' and impractical desires for greater equality of outcome directly led to the bureaucratic and interventionist tendencies of the state that were a prominent feature of the post-war years of consensus up to the mid-1970s, evident in both economic and social policy initiatives.

Conservative social policy priorities: liberty over equality

Most Conservatives view political and economic liberty as of far greater importance than the achievement of social and economic equality,[10] the latter being a concept which is generally viewed by those on the right of politics as being a goal that is 'undesirable and unattainable'[11] in practice. They instead emphasise the importance of securing and preserving core socio-economic freedoms and protecting them from the potentially dominant and repressive power of the state, which the left perceives to be the key mechanism that enables individuals to progress within society. Some Conservative thinkers and politicians would link this broad scepticism about the practicality of a society based on collectivism and equality with the more pessimistic characterisation of human nature that is often associated with right-wing politics. This viewpoint dates back to the 17th-century analysis of Thomas Hobbes and his advocacy of strong government to deal with "nasty, brutish" mankind, aligned with his negative perception of human nature[12] as inherently unable spontaneously to behave in harmony with other individuals. Conservative-minded thinkers and politicians over the centuries have developed a general position that views an aspiration towards greater socio-economic equality as an unrealistic notion that is contrary to the savage and competitive nature of human beings. They are, therefore, only willing to tolerate greater individual freedoms if there is a framework of a strong state to regulate society and to instil political authority and social order.[13]

In these times, this belief is fuelled and consolidated by the influences and pressures of a capitalist, competitive society. For many conservatives, of both past and present, 'inequality is ultimately rooted in
human nature itself',[14] and the 'idealistic' socialist emphasis on blaming
external social and material forces for inequality, e.g. the unregulated
and arbitrary forces of capitalism, is therefore a flawed analysis of contemporary society. The Conservative, and particularly the 'New Right',
perspective holds that such a socialist interpretation and promotion of
greater equality is in fact contrary to basic, fundamental tenets of both
human behaviour and the 'invisible hand'[15] of the free-market, and
while social mobility is a perfectly wholesome aspiration for a dynamic
'vigorous' society, this is not the same as greater equality of outcome,
which should not be aspired to. As a supplement to this Hobbesian
analysis, this 'New Right' conservative philosophical perspective argues
that within an environment of general individual freedom regulated by
the state's rule of law, it is a further inherent aspect of human nature
for there to be such natural inequality among individual citizens, due to
the fact that 'some people innately possess more ambition, intelligence
or talent than others... (and this) unequal distribution of such charac-
teristics inevitably results(s) in an inherently unequal society'.[16]

The mainstream Conservative political view of equality (both One
Nation and Thatcherite) is that both 'equality' and the standard left-
wing view of 'social justice' are vague, abstract and illusory concepts
that defy basic aspects of human nature relating to competition, material well-being, individual talent and self-interest, which, it can be
argued, are the key factors that 'individuals are motivated primarily
by'.[17] As a consequence of differing skills and talents, a natural social
hierarchy is said to emerge, further supporting the premise that neither
equality nor an egalitarian version of 'social justice' are achievable or
desirable goals. Indeed, there are some Conservatives who would argue
that when the state attempts to equalise social conditions or to restore
greater social justice by intervention, it distorts and disrupts the intentions of the 'free market' or the natural social order. The state, therefore,
is actually functioning in an unfair and unjust manner. Even moderate
conservatives such as Ian Gilmour[18] acknowledged such potential consequences of this explicitly interventionist approach to governance. A
state-led redistribution of resources in accordance with the principles of
'social justice' is unacceptable for the principal reason that 'in a morally
pluralistic society, any principle of distribution is subjective and contentious'[19] and the state's motives can often be seen as somewhat arbitrary,
random and questionable.

Despite this sceptical critique, particularly from the perspective of the New Right's position of political hegemony in the 1980s, the concept of social justice has stubbornly refused to be excluded from contemporary political debate and has continued as one of the important motives behind social policy formulation. It grew in momentum during the post-Thatcher political era in particular (from approximately 1990 onwards), when politicians across the spectrum sought to offer a distinct, refreshed and more inclusive political image in the aftermath of such a dominant and socially divisive phase of leadership. They increasingly appeared to compete in terms of being seen as 'fair' and 'just' in their development and expression of social and economic policies and their impact on society. From John Major onwards, post-Thatcher Conservative leaders have in implicit and explicit terms sought to gradually moderate the tone of their social policy agenda rather than adopt the more abrasive ideological emphasis as witnessed during the Thatcher era, perhaps an acknowledgment that the New Right's socio-political approach in 1980s Britain had created the perception, indeed the fact, that socio-economic inequalities were becoming wider and more evident.[20] In recent years, having condemned New Labour for presiding over the continued widening of the gap between rich and poor during its 13-year term of office,[21] modernising Conservatives from the Cameron inner-circle have openly spoken about the need to reduce the disparity.[22] In adopting a more emollient tone in relation to this policy area, there is certainly potential for 21st-century Conservatives to revise the language used in relation to the concept of 'justice' in order to positively connect with key groups of electors, although the Thatcherite diehards of 1980s vintage have generally appeared less willing to embrace such an approach. This is primarily due to their ongoing concerns with the left's use and interpretation of the term 'social justice', principally because it symbolises a political and philosophical retreat from the New Right's perspective of a socially 'just' society based on meritocratic and economic 'rights' and linked to personal endeavour. This society would always have 'naturally' unequal socio-economic outcomes, unlike the alternative 'leftist' ideological variant. '[T]he only clear and consistent meaning one can give to the (left's) rhetoric of social justice is the pursuit of ever-greater material equality. That is the issue'.[23]

The New Right's anti-egalitarian analysis therefore bolsters Thatcherite scepticism towards 'social justice'. It appears to imply, and even demand, an egalitarian distribution of material resources, an approach that many modern Conservatives find undesirable, 'unjust', unrealistic, and ultimately contrary to the fundamentally 'selfish' and competitive instincts of human nature and the 'natural' inequalities that exist within all societies. The post-1979 Thatcherite Conservative tradition rejected the left's conventional and more communitarian emphasis, and for much of the modern historical period the Conservative Party was broadly united on this issue, rejecting the left's interpretation of social justice as being essentially a form of 'reverse discrimination'. Such sentiments were a particularly evident feature of the party's 1987 general election manifesto, which many would identify as the most explicit expression of Thatcherite political strength at its electoral zenith, as it argued that 'Reverse discrimination is itself an injustice and can have no place in a tolerant and civilised society... it would undermine the achievement and example of those who had risen on their merits'.[24]

In this context, the Thatcherite 'meritocratic' vision of social justice is significantly different from the left's traditional interpretation, and as the dominant form of Conservatism from the mid-1970s it has therefore embraced a model of society and social behaviour from a notably different political perspective. This viewpoint has placed greater emphasis on individualist meritocracy being central to the achievement of greater social justice, and from this different political angle 'social justice is interpreted as a reward for individual success, rather than as welfare ideology has it, the equal treatment of all'.[25] As a result of such scepticism towards traditional notions of social justice and an enhanced focus on economics, individualism and variable personal abilities, it has been asserted that 'Thatcherism scarcely had a social policy'[26] throughout her sustained period of governance. However, despite her obvious focus on a radical restructuring of economic policy, this is an exaggerated and unfair analysis, given that there clearly were social policies developed between 1979 and 1990, with some significant attempts to reform and scale down the welfare state, notably from the mid-1980s onwards. The 'New Right' or 'Thatcherite' position would therefore argue that the principle of social justice has been 'hijacked' and manipulated by elements of the left due to their specific formulation of the concept. Consequently, left-of-centre politicians have depicted themselves as having enhanced and more enlightened social policies due to them being associated and influenced by their interpretation of 'socially just' principles, moulded by the ethos of a more active and interventionist welfare state.

Equality can be viewed as a key component of the social justice agenda. It is ultimately an ambiguous concept that is open to interpretation from various political positions, with the left more traditionally focused on generating a greater equality of outcome using state intervention. New Right Conservatism has consistently opposed such state-generated equality of outcome, principally due to its vehement belief that such an approach conflicts with the human realities of individual ability and competition, alongside its philosophical preference for a smaller-state model. The New Right tradition has emphasised the importance of equality of opportunity, individual freedom and associated 'meritocratic' principles, as identified on the British political scene by Michael Young in 1958.[27] This aggressive counter-reaction has been in contrast to paternalistic 'One Nation' Conservatives, dominant for much of the post-war period of 'consensus', who broadly accepted the relative definition of poverty and traditionally endorsed the role of the welfare state in raising the standard of living of the poorest members of society. This more traditional variant of Conservatism has been willing to embrace a generous and interventionist state in the name of maintaining social order, while resisting the meritocracy and social dynamism espoused by Thatcherites.

Within such a context, given their preference for a hierarchical, class-based and ordered society, with a benevolent upper social hierarchy seeking to provide a generous level of paternalistic government support for the lower classes, moderate One Nation Conservatives have broadly rejected the New Right's focus on fluid social mobility between classes. While the 19th-century Disraelian brand of British Conservatism focused on the duty of the state and the governing classes to assist the poor and to manage the more extreme examples of inequality,[28] this has created some friction within Conservatism between the One Nation tradition and the New Right variant 'about how far inequality should be permitted to develop'.[29] An important difference between the two groups has been whether poverty levels should be gauged by absolute values (the measurement of the most basic globalised standards of living) or relative values (more focused on comparative divisions between rich and poor within a specific society). Mainstream Conservative viewpoint across all traditions reached the conclusion during the course of the 20th century that inequality is an inevitable consequence of the different talents and resources of individual citizens within a competitive, capitalist-orientated society. Nevertheless, there is a strong Conservative paternalistic tradition that argues that it is possible to support distinctive social policies around a relatively active model of state welfare provision, yet reject the ultimate 'egalitarian' motives and aspirations of the left-of-centre vision of a contemporary welfare state and its associated version of social justice. This 'One Nation' tradition would appear to firmly reject the socialist-orientated notion that if 'one does not believe in equality, one must oppose the welfare state',[30] as this version of Conservatism generously supported the British welfare state for much of the second part of the 20th century.

The 'One Nation' paternalistic Conservative tendency, with its traditional emphasis on significant state intervention alongside a more explicit collective social conscience in the form of a generous welfare state, has never, however, embraced the sentiments of a left-wing interpretation of social justice and its focus on equality in terms of material rewards and/or outcome. Rather, it has focused on reducing inequality in order for an unequal social model to be deemed acceptable to the rest of society. Such a view 'did not mean any acceptance of equality, but it did entail an acknowledgement that socio-economic inequalities needed to be kept within boundaries or limits',[31] primarily to ensure the long-term prospects of the established governing class.[32] This justifies the 'One Nation' Conservative support for a generous welfare state and the expenditure involved. Therefore, despite many differences with the 'New Right' Thatcherites over social and economic issues, this moderate faction of Conservatism has never embraced equality, and has broadly adopted the view that 'inequality is an inevitable and immutable fact of life'[33] based on birth, individual qualities and socio-economic circumstance.

Therefore, due to this sense of ideological detachment from the evolution of the modern meaning of social justice (with its left-of-centre origins and abstract implications), many contemporary Conservatives of all 'factions' have had to struggle to express or articulate a coherent view about it. Most Conservatives have had concerns about the Rawlsian theory of 'justice' within society, a significant and innovative socio-political analysis that has flourished since the 1970s, and which advocates that equality and co-operation are natural inclinations of human activity at the beginning of most societies. According to this perspective, such behaviour is classified as the instinctive attitude of human nature. John Rawls'[34] hypothetical 'veil of ignorance' concludes that rational mankind prefers equality to inequality, and therefore seeks to justify a redistributive model of social justice with enhanced levels of fairness and equality within society, although through his 'difference principle' inequality can be justified as long as its existence benefits the least advantaged members of society; for example when within a growing economy a relatively wealthy employer continues to provide steady employment for a lower paid employee. Rawls' deductive perspective concludes that some degree of redistributive social justice can only be achieved via the intervention and mechanisms of a welfare state and appropriate legislation, and in practical terms such intervention takes the form of specific social policies to meet a needs-based model of social justice.

This analysis appeared to vindicate various long-established arguments of socialists and social democrats about the appropriate means and justification for delivering social justice, and to affirm the belief that man is by nature a creature inclined towards co-operation and equality within society in order to fulfil basic social needs, both on an individual and a communitarian basis. According to the Rawlsian perspective this vision of social justice is primarily achieved via the proactive influence of the state. Most conservatives do not accept this hypothetical 'social contract' within an imagined 'state of nature', arguing instead that in terms of equality being the alleged 'natural state of mankind ... there is scarcely any instance in recorded history in which mankind has actually experienced it'.[35] This viewpoint again emphasises the conservative-minded disdain for left-of-centre hypothetical theories and abstractions, instead preferring practical and empirical realities and acknowledging that inequality and a clear social hierarchy is an inherent part of the natural order of things that can be justified in behavioural, social and civic terms. This core conservative critique of the Rawlsian approach to equality and social justice automatically concludes that its emphasis on enhanced equality of outcome is a highly questionable prospect based on the practical experiences of most modern societies.

Conservatives of all variations and across different nationalities have therefore sought to revise and counteract this social democratic version of 'social justice', with one notable alternative being the development of the 'social market', a pro-capitalist concept that emphasises how communities can thrive and benefit in positive social terms from a fluid and accessible free-market environment that can deliver a fair, just and stable society without excessive government intervention. This contrasts with the more 'statist' and 'interventionist' conclusions reached by the left-of-centre variant of social justice, and the dynamic potential of the 'market' as a concept therefore creates an alternative 'capitalist' framework that can develop a more conservatively-inclined model for the achievement of a socially just society. Such a viewpoint represents a capitalist approach to challenging and demolishing the egalitarian arguments and implications of left-leaning social justice theorists and academics, instead emphasising 'the mutual dependence between the free market and the community'[36] in creating and sustaining a more just social order in the long term. Originating in 20th century, specifically post-war, western Germany, and with strong continental links, the concept of the social market has led to the emergence in recent years of significant think-tanks such as the 'Social Market Foundation' (founded 1989), seeking to influence the development of social and economic policy in Britain, and in the process aiming to steer policy-making in a less statist, more economically liberal, direction. Focus on the development of a choice-based quasi-market within the provision of public services has been influential in shaping the contemporary political debate in the modern Conservative Party, as well as its revised approach to the ways that the state delivers public policies with reduced levels of intervention and control. This has been particularly prevalent during the post-Thatcher era, with many of the party's modernisers recognising the importance of maintaining capitalist free-market values, while acknowledging the need to stabilise community structures in a way that was overlooked during the 1980s.

The New Right and neo-liberal view of social justice

As previously highlighted, social justice is a dynamic and contestable concept that is open to interpretation within political circles, and its ambiguity means that its meaning in practice has generated disagreements throughout the course of the modern political era. In basic terms those on the left envisage a direct and essential role for the state in creating enhanced social justice, while those on the right argue for a less 'statist' or interventionist approach, with less government regulation and more reliance on the laws of the free market as the determinant as to what is the 'just' basis of material rewards. Indeed, within the British Conservative Party, a fairly new tradition of conservatism sought to promote an aggressively revised version of the concept, namely the Thatcherites, who actively contributed to ending the 'years of consensus' by vigorously promoting a more marketised approach to public service delivery (and in turn creating a 'social market'), at the expense of a universal and generously state-funded welfare provision as the means of achieving social justice. This tendency argues that laissez-faire capitalism is incompatible with a traditional 'liberal–left' social justice agenda which views the state as the vital tool for achieving the desired outcome of greater equality. Many within the New Right tradition, such as Hayek, Friedman and Thatcher, have interpreted 'social justice as social welfare'[37] in the context of its practical application, and have consequently attached to it associated negative implications in its conventional application to contemporary society.

The most important ideological thrust in the drive to reduce the power and expenditure of the modern state and its attempts to shape social justice was provided by the work of the Austrian economist F.A Hayek, a key philosophical and ideological influence on the evolution of Conservative social and economic policy-making, particularly during Margaret Thatcher's administration in the 1980s. Hayek's influence was most important in the specific 'neo-liberal' economic tradition of modern Conservatism, forming an essential element of the broader New Right agenda that promoted a smaller role for the state in economic and social policy matters, and which obtained intellectual succour from Hayek's writings in developing this political outlook.[38] In promoting a socio-political agenda that was an 'amalgamation of economic liberty and social conventionalism',[39] Hayek helped to instigate a distinct response for both British and international Conservatism in the mid-20th century to the growth in 'statist' tendencies that had been established across various political systems before, during and particularly after World War Two. While not unexpected in communist regimes, the growth of the economic power of the state in traditional Western capitalist societies alarmed Hayek. The New Right has derived particular inspiration and guidance from his distinct, unorthodox revision of the concept of 'social justice', which condemned the 'statist' left-of-centre interpretation of it as representing a 'mirage' that was not as desirable or attainable as those on the socialist left claimed it to be. The Hayekian 'Austrian school' argues that the conventional view of social justice, with its emphasis on an active state, is an illusion constructed to suit a specific political agenda framed by interventionist social democrats, and that it can be rejected as a purely hypothetical concept that is fatally flawed on both an intellectual and practical basis, primarily due to its promotion of a socio-political model that does not deal in economic or social realities or indeed human nature (of the competitive and brutal Hobbesian variant).[40] This anti-collectivist perspective firmly proclaims that 'there could be no injustice perpetrated against those in poverty',[41] given that they had reached such a social status not because of a repressive and deliberate government policy, but rather due to arbitrary factors such as individual ability, personal circumstances and socio-economic influences beyond their control. From a modern perspective, Hayek's version of social justice can therefore be summarised as reflecting the belief that: 'Returns from the market were not moral returns and we shouldn't see them as moral returns, but if a pop star earns more than a nurse it's not that the pop star is morally superior to a nurse, it's just that the distribution of economic returns in a market economy does not align, and is not supposed to align, with a set of moral judgements'.[42]

This anti-redistributive position therefore rejects the rationalist morality that shapes the egalitarian nature of 'justice' as concluded by Rawls, and instead argues that the social-democrat interventionist approach to delivering social justice drives people towards dependency and 'serfdom'[43] due the extension of the state's powers. In formulating a critique of Rawls' modern justification for social justice and the broader social democratic approach to governance, an appropriate academic response along Hayekian lines was developed by Robert Nozick, whose analysis rejected Rawls' conclusions and argued from a more libertarian perspective for the 'inherent superiority of markets over all other forms of social organisation'.[44] Nozick sought to justify the inevitability and justification of inequality as derived from his specific version of the 'state of nature', instilling his own moral streak as to how 'just' such a scenario was, due to it being an ultimate consequence of free exchange and varying individual abilities within the free market environment.[45] According to this libertarian viewpoint, social justice is achieved and framed by an emphasis on the economic rights of each individual citizen, with their own endeavour and achievement the ultimate arbiter and measurement of what they receive in both social and economic terms; and which entails a limited and detached role for the state within this process. Although most advocates of the mainstream New Right approach have advocated a greater degree of state intervention than Nozick, the 'free economy' as depicted by Gamble in the late 1980s illustrated how the Thatcherite socio-economic model of society emerged and resulted in a significantly reduced role for government, less state regulation, and greater individual economic freedoms. This in turn provides the principled framework for an associated neo-liberal version of social justice that was 'achieved through the daily plebiscite in the market'[46] rather than intervention by politicians in pursuit of an 'artificial' and 'arbitrary' redistribution of resources.

Neo-liberals such as Hayek, in association with the libertarian outlook of Nozick, have developed a critique that perceives social justice as being paradoxical in its traditional liberal sense, claiming it to be an empty and meaningless doctrine due to its emphasis on rewarding individuals in accordance with an artificial and socially-imposed (statist) moral framework, rather than focusing on their talent and variable individual abilities which are allowed to flourish in the free-market. In turn, the neo-liberal New Right proposed its own morality-fused framework to generate an alternative version of social justice, one that was essentially market-driven and that 'was buttressed by the revival of moral arguments against equality'.[47] In adopting this distinct approach that sought to reverse the post-war trend towards greater equality and erode the liberal–left's moral monopoly regarding the usage of 'social justice', this New Right analysis fundamentally challenged the subjective liberal morality that has underpinned the traditional interpretation of the term. In arguing that 'the moral merit of each individual is hidden, and can be known by no one',[48] the neo-liberal argument therefore seeks to undermine Rawls' proposed 'veil of ignorance' as a coherent philosophical basis for social-democratic style social justice. On this premise, it is therefore a legitimate question to ask how the state can have sufficient knowledge to determine precisely how social justice should be formulated and goods redistributed in the wider social interest.

In adopting such an anti-statist position and opposing the egalitarian and redistributive principles of 'natural' justice imposed by Rawls several decades later, Hayek's core position, developed at the zenith of state power during World War Two, dismisses the artificial nature of the left's version of 'social justice' as the driving force behind its idealised model of welfare policy, concluding that such an approach inevitably results in a bloated and bureaucratic welfare state. The Hayekian model instead promotes an idealised 'neo-liberal' economic influence that creates the appropriate political structure for its associated society, with limited powers of regulatory intervention in pursuit of a revamped 'New Right' version of social justice. This approach asserts that the market is the ultimate determinant of wealth and status, with dynamics that are driven by individual spontaneity and economic liberalism, rather than the 'dead hand' of the monolithic state.[49] Such an interpretation of social justice therefore places ultimate faith in the forces of laissez-faire capitalism and a less regulated state as the most effective guarantors of a fair and 'socially just' outcome, on the premise that the very concept of social justice is 'a vague and contested idea'.[50]

The neo-liberal version of social justice, therefore, seeks to allow individuals to achieve their most appropriate socio-economic status primarily on the basis of merit, while aligned with a governmental model that promotes the dynamism of a 'free economy'[51] and a minimised amount of government intervention in economic matters, because 'using the welfare state to realize an ideal of social justice is, for neoliberals, an abuse of power'.[52] However, critical academics such as Raymond Plant have examined neo-liberalism from a left-of-centre perspective, and argue that such an approach will practically succumb to a more social democratic and 'statist' outcome, citing empirical evidence that the state's powers and capacity actually grew in many respects during the Thatcher period of government in the 1980s. This critical analysis views the practicality of a neo-liberal state with scepticism, seeking to highlight the New Right's paradoxical reliance on elements of the conventional post-war state, particularly to maintain social order and core elements of welfare provision during periods of economic difficulty. Given the essentially cyclical and unpredictable nature of free-market capitalism, these unstable elements aligned with the strategic pursuit of a smaller state, ultimately cast doubt as to how a neo-liberal political structure (in comparison to a social democratic model), could effectively maintain a coherent and stable form of governance in the long term.

The neo-liberal analysis and approach to social justice views any significant state regulation of economic activity as an unnecessary encroachment on individual freedom, while also rejecting what is viewed as an 'artificial' redistribution of wealth as advocated by the social democratic model of welfare provision. According to such a free-market perspective, therefore, the left's approach to delivering social justice is hindered by the state bureaucracy that its approach to governance tends to create, and as a consequence, New Right-influenced Conservatives claim, for much of the post-war period social justice and greater equality have not been achieved in the way the liberal left have desired. The Hayekian and 'New Right' analysis has subsequently identified fundamental problems in achieving the conventional (liberal) post-war version of social justice, namely due to its over-reliance on a bureaucratic model of government which embraces 'social-democratic' principles and associated political institutions as the key tools for achieving such a socially 'just' outcome. New Right thinkers and academics have dismissed the state's regulatory role as being at the heart of a deeply flawed analysis in terms of explaining the existence and tackling the causes of social inequality and injustice. Accordingly, when writing about the neo-liberal state from a left-of-centre political angle, Plant has observed that a core belief of this approach is that there is a more limited yet more efficient role for government in the delivery of enhanced social justice which requires the proposed neo-liberal political structure not to follow 'such a distributive agenda, [instead being] committed to a more objective and less expansive form of safety net welfare provision'.[53]

Such a neo-liberal model therefore rejects the rationalist and redistributive capacity of the state and its associated bureaucracy, and in turn ultimately questions whether the conventional interpretation of 'social justice' and its subjective formulation of the welfare state is a legitimate basis by which society can function or be driven. For, as Hayek himself argued, 'since only situations which have been created by humans can be called just or unjust... what is called 'social' or 'distributive' justice is indeed meaningless within a spontaneous order'.[54] Hayek ultimately devised this unconventional alternative analysis of the modern social-democratic variant of social justice and simultaneously defended individualism in the face of a 'statist' onslaught, defying the socio-political orthodoxy of post-war British politics in the process. Hayek could therefore be said to have 'placed social democrats on the defensive'[55] in seeking to justify their previously dominant and subjective interpretation and manipulation of social justice, ultimately questioning their ability to address the accepted social injustices of contemporary society and even challenging the practical meaning of the concept of social justice. This 'neo-liberal' critique of social justice was rediscovered and revitalised in the 1980s, coming to be highly influential in the dominant political administrations of Thatcher in Britain and Reagan in the USA. During this decade, when the Thatcher government and its distinct political agenda dominated the British political landscape, this theoretical framework offered a more individualistic and unorthodox interpretation of social justice, with the 'New Right' in government practically challenging its traditional definition by a confident counter-assertion that 'any form of distribution of social goods not based on individual attainment, which would introduce compensatory elements or appeal to a collective social responsibility, is excluded from the intention of social justice'.[56]

This approach sought to reassess the perceived reasons for the existence of poverty and inequality across British society, along with the established mechanisms and motives for dealing with it. As the 1980s progressed, such an approach to this aspect of government policy-making created a political landscape that featured a 'distinctively Thatcherite approach to poverty and social justice',[57] offering a more confident brand of social conservatism that contemptuously dismissed social democrats as being motivated by the 'politics of envy' in their advocacy of redistributive social justice as the remedy for ameliorating long-term poverty. At the same time, the sidelined 'One Nation' Conservatives were dismissed for their implicit justification for redistributive social policies, an attitude fuelled by heightened social consciences and a degree of paternalistic guilt at having levels of wealth that the majority of the population did not. Nevertheless, it was within the context of such a confident legacy that members of the Major administration of the 1990s, including ministers with politically moderate reputations,

such as William Waldegrave, appeared buoyed by the ideological conflict and eventual victory of the previous decade and therefore argued
for a fairly radical review of post-war social and welfare policies, primarily 'a move towards the insurance principle, together with an element
of compulsion – i.e. people being obliged to provide for themselves'.[58]

Modern Conservatism's revised social policy agenda sought to explore
the development of continental models of national insurance along
with inspiration from the American individualist welfare model, as
opposed to the post-war British focus on universalised welfare and
associated social policies. This approach represented a notable shift of
mood, indicating an apparent ideological victory for the 'New Right'
during the 1980s. It was an increasingly common position of radical
and open-minded thinkers within both the Conservative Party and
the fledgling New Labour movement in the mid-1990s to question the
hegemonic role of the state as the sole provider of welfare provision,
and such developments align with the view of some academics who
argue that the Conservative approach to dealing with 'poverty and
social justice actually became more radical after 1990'.[59] The escala-
tion of this school of thought as the 1990s progressed is evident in
the relatively low-profile viewpoint (which contradicts the critical and
pessimistic perception of Thatcherites), that John Major was in fact a
more effective and practical advocate than his predecessor in pursuing a
neo-liberal approach to 'marketised' and diversified public service provision, more wholeheartedly embracing the New Right's version of social
justice.[60] Privatisation and deregulation continued and even accelerated
under Major's rule, supporting the argument that 'a process of ideological realignment... occurred during the Conservative leadership of John
Major'.[61] This suggested that the party became ever more confident in
its free-market rhetoric and focus during the 1990s, although it undermined its ideological purity by resorting to some notable public spending increases as a means of staving off political unpopularity.

The essential Hayekian influence that sought to shape such political
developments was the notion that 'government activity (be) limited primarily to establishing the framework within which individuals are free
to pursue their objectives',[62] and this automatically implied a limited
role for the state, along with a reduced financial and bureaucratic presence. The government would secure and provide a minimalist outline
framework of state activity, which in turn would allow a more explicit
degree of personal freedom and relative individual autonomy. While
the Thatcher era sought to earnestly embrace and pursue such principles of socio-economic conservatism, the 20 years that followed from

1990 were perhaps less consistently loyal to this Hayekian vision of the world, beginning with the increased curve of public spending that developed under Major, and then more significantly the longer that Labour was in power after 1997. Following the 2010 General Election result, while not necessarily endorsing Hayek's vision of a shrunken state with the same avowed enthusiasm of the Thatcherites in the early 1980s, Cameron and his coalition partners were provided with the opportunity and appropriate context to transform their vocal criticisms of Labour's legacy of 'statism' and ongoing welfare dependency into the concrete implementation of their own distinct political remedies for the country's various social ills.

The revival of civic Conservatism

This burgeoning alternative debate in relation to the traditional inter-pretation of social justice and conventional post-war British welfare provision developed throughout the 1990s in particular, and it has con-tinues to generate significant levels of political discussion to the present day. However, despite this attempt to construct alternative variants of welfare provision and a radically different interpretation of social justice during their 18 years of dominant political rule (1979–1997), contem-porary political opponents of the Conservative Party were sceptical as to how wider society and civic community interests were positively served by the Conservatives' neo-liberal, less 'statist' approach to government delivery of social policies. The clear suggestion from political oppo-nents was that as a consequence of such an economics-driven political agenda, social and welfare policy was broadly overlooked, as evident in comments from rival political figures from this particular era: 'He (Ashdown) thinks the Tories are utterly bereft of any ideas about society/ community. Willetts and his Civic Conservatism[63] is the exception – but they don't want to know'.[64]

Such high-profile observations indicate how attempts to rebrand and re-ignite the Conservative Party's distinct interpretation of 'society', social justice and innovative social policy-making both during and after the Thatcher era have been questioned by opposing politicians as being generally devoid of coherence and direction. However, the 'Civic Conservatism' referred to did emerge as something with sufficient dis-tinction to engage the attention of the political classes, primarily as a post-Thatcher theory devised in the 1990s by the Conservative politi-cian David Willetts, a cerebral figure with a background as a political advisor and with a reputation as an intellectual. This 'intellectual' aura provided some credibility to this emerging variant of social policy, with Willetts' model of 'civic conservatism' seeking to articulate an alternative model of a 'civil society' that focused on the relationship between the individual and a number of interconnected yet separate political institutions (as opposed to just the monolithic, centralised state). This 'civic' focus sought to free individual citizens from the tentacles of excessive state regulation and control; while also not being wholly reliant on the neo-liberal laissez-faire ethos of free-market economics, but valuing the importance of individual civil action, community-based localism and more diverse public service provision as opposed to the dominance of the all-encompassing state. In many ways it was legitimate attempt to respond and interact with Labour's advocacy of the 'Third Way', an ideology-light, flexible political philosophy originating from Anthony Giddens in 1994, which rejected both traditional positions of left and right, while embracing communitarianism and conventional social justice on one hand, and general principles of free market 'efficiency' and economic liberalism on the other.

The emergence of 'Civic Conservatism' ultimately sought to restore some broader public credibility to the Conservative Party's approach to managing key public services, while acknowledging the important social elements and implications of government policy-making. This stemmed from the fact that in the dying days of the Major government in the mid-1990s, 'the Conservative Party was perceived by the voters as indifferent or even hostile to public services'[65] and in espousing this reformist position, Willetts appeared to signal a departure from the Thatcher mantra of the late 1980s that 'there was no such thing as society', despite having a reputation as a figure from the New Right wing of the party. During the New Labour era from 1997, despite evidence of overlap between the 'Third way' and Civic Conservatism, Willetts developed a critique of New Labour's approach to governance and offered specific criticisms of its 'reliance on the state and public spending', and instead sought to emphasise the important role of 'the voluntary efforts of citizens themselves'.[66] Within this context, there emerged a revised and adapted shape to this specific vision of Conservative social policy, rejecting the hegemonic state yet embracing the value of 'society' and the need for viable, good-quality public services to be delivered more diversely, specifically by fusing individualism and community-driven actions in an appropriate balance. This sought to create a distinct message when formulating Conservative social and welfare policies, namely 'the need to show that such a thing as Civic Conservatism exists and is vital... (representing) a real difference between the parties'.[67]

Willetts' role in this evolution of 'civic conservatism' and a new variant of social policy was significant, given that he appeared to be modifying his earlier Thatcherite scepticism about the traditional social-democrat interpretation of social justice. However, this approach did not represent a point-blank acceptance of the conventional version of this concept, but was instead a pragmatic right-of-centre attempt to devise a new and distinctive approach to the role of the community, 'society' and localism in delivering a new variant of social justice and a subsequent formulation of appropriate social policies to reflect the changing socio-political landscape. As the 1990s progressed, there was a growing perception among non-Thatcherites that Margaret Thatcher's administration had manifested a degree of neglect and indifference to social justice during its years in office, and as a consequence the Conservative Party's attitude to this concept lacked clarity and focus in comparison to the New Labour agenda that promoted 'social justice' more explicitly and vigorously from the mid-1990s onwards. This lingering negative attitude towards such an increasingly prominent political concept attached itself to the Conservative Party throughout the 1990s and beyond, generating electoral unpopularity in the process, as 'the Conservative Party... seemed for some time unable to learn the lessons of defeat in 1997 and to move away from its Thatcherite position and its influences on the development of social policy within the Conservative Party'.[68] 'Civic Conservatism' was the initial and formative catalyst that aspired to remould party policy in this sphere, seeking to offer a more balanced and less 'statist' governmental approach, while retaining its own distinct principles and a renewed focus on 'community' as a compromise concept situated between the rival poles of rampant 'statism' and libertarian 'individualism'. This desire to instil the importance of enhanced civic activity in relation to the power of the state would also have a significant and moderating influence over the New Labour approach to welfare and social policy provision from 1997 onwards.

New Labour's dynamic emergence from the mid-1990s onwards, followed by its accession to power in 1997, accelerated the need for the modernising elements within the Conservative Party to revisit the party's conventional, well-established position on low taxation and resistance to increased public spending, often at the expense of social policy innovation. This policy-making approach had been cemented during the 1980s, but was under increased scrutiny due to successive general election defeats and increasing evidence that the British public 'were increasingly willing to see increased public expenditure and improved public services rather than tax cuts'.[69] In reaction to such socio-political developments and as part of a more long-term strategic perspective to formulating a coherent social policy-making approach, from 2005 the 'Cameron Conservatives' implicitly challenged the Thatcherite legacy by further modifying and pragmatically revising their attitude towards the mainstream interpretation of social justice in the light of ongoing socio-political change and a shifting electoral landscape. This involved acknowledging the effectiveness of Blair's 'Third Way' agenda and accepting that that it had some positive political value as opposed to completely rejecting it out of hand, while also indicating an underlying admiration for Blair's approach as a political operator. In response to the New Labour socio-economic agenda from 1997, a revised Conservative approach became progressively evident in comments by some of the party's more prominent politicians of recent years, in particular Michael Gove who acknowledged that 'At its best, New Labour was recognition that the values of enterprise and aspiration could be fused with commit-ment to social justice and fairness. The party that best represents that fusion now is David Cameron's Conservative Party.'[70]

The significance of such fulsome praise for New Labour's clearer emphasis on the promotion of greater social justice was that it was voiced by Michael Gove, a 'modernising' Conservative politician viewed as a key ally of David Cameron and a member of the inner-circle of his leadership. Such sentiments appeared to transmit a clear message that the Conservatives would embrace many post-1997 social policy initia-tives when returned to national office, while seeking to instil their own enterprising agenda into the political formula. This revised stance in the sphere of social policy among the Conservative modernising tendency, ostensibly aligned with a more moralistic and communitarian outlook, had initially originated in a public context in mid-2005, when prior to becoming party leader Cameron stated: 'We do think there's such thing as society, we just don't think it's the same as the state',[71] a provoca-tive rebuke to the much-quoted remark of Margaret Thatcher in 1987. According to various commentators, such bold comments were 'a clear indication that he (Cameron) intended to mark out different territory for the party',[72] although Cameron's modernisers reaffirmed their oppo-sition to the more explicitly egalitarian implications and consequences of 'social justice' as viewed by the traditional left. This was primarily because the record of the previous Labour government in this key policy sphere has been condemned by the right as being 'greatly flawed',[73] reflecting a perception of the failure of the liberal-left's broad approach to achieving social justice. Cameron has subsequently been described as being 'more open than his predecessors to socially inclusive welfare policies',[74] and as a result both he and his frontbenchers have utilised variations of the political language and vocabulary associated with it. Such evolving and modernised Conservative attitudes have ultimately reflected a more 'social-oriented' political agenda since Cameron gained the leadership in 2005. Indeed, the use of such 'Blairite' and 'communitarian' language and the acknowledged policy fusion of enterprise with social justice have appeared to represent a resurrection of Cameron's previous (and rather controversial) claim when seeking the party leadership that he was 'heir to Blair'.[75] This explicit willingness to focus on and talk about the concept of social justice on Labour's territory as it were, appeared to signal a dilution of the Thatcherite tradition and a move away from the view of society as inspired by both F.A Hayek and Enoch Powell, both 'anti-collectivist thinkers... who were fundamentally opposed to this idea'[76] (of social justice).

This apparent repositioning on social policy issues has raised fundamental questions as to whether the modern Conservative Party has a markedly different approach to this subject matter than the last period of Conservative government between 1979 and 1997, or whether its policy proposals are more an example of style over substance. In this context, Cameron's greater willingness to talk about poverty and social issues since 2005 can be interpreted as an implicit criticism of the Thatcherite social agenda that was established during the 1980s, and an attempt to soften and redefine the Conservatives' image on social policies in the process. In doing so, the modern Conservative outlook relating to social policy has sought to promote a new model of Civic Conservatism for the 21st century and hence detach the party from the often negative interpretation of social justice that prevailed among many Conservatives of Thatcherite pedigree. In turn, the Thatcherite tradition has been fearful that the party's focus on what they perceive to be such vague social concepts has symbolised a retreat from traditional Conservative values in a time of shifting political attitudes and social–demographic developments. The Cameron leadership has sought to instil a communitarian emphasis together with a positive view of human nature, although there has been some caution as to what extent things have changed from the 1980s, with fears that 'The "Big Society" concept that Cameron is promoting is an attempt to reject Thatcherism in the eyes of the voting public, while reaffirming it in practice'.[77]

Despite the belief that Thatcherism remains a potent presence behind the scenes, such bold expressions of modernised 'new' Conservatism have appeared to unsettle the party's New Right and neo-liberal elements, who view this revamped interpretation of social justice and refreshed acknowledgment of 'society' as an unnecessary concession to the 'collectivist' left of centre political tradition in the UK, moulded by New Labour and departing from the more explicit elements of the free-market legacy of the 1980s. The New Right viewpoint fundamentally believes that social justice should not be about statist, egalitarian 'levelling' and intervention, but rather develop in line with more traditional Conservative values of 'incentives, self reliance and independence',[78] promoting meritocracy and embracing a downgraded and minimalist role for the state in the process. The alternative emphasis of a more regulated approach to the delivery of social policy and social justice from the centre, with a detachment from the more ruggedly individualist Conservative values of the Thatcher era, was often evident within New Labour's social policy agenda after 1997. It also influenced David Cameron's approach to this policy area after late 2005, and right-wing fears that Cameron has absorbed too much of New Labour's approach on this issue led to a subsequent revival of the New Right's critique of 'a social justice that ran counter to nature',[79] with its explicit rejection of statist, interventionist tendencies that seek to engineer 'artificial' individual social fortunes and conditions. In implicitly embracing a softer vocabulary, language and tone in this policy sphere (in rhetorical terms at least), Cameron's approach has been focused on making the Conservative Party more attractive to floating voters, but in doing so has threatened to alienate a specific faction of his own party.

Ultimately, Michael Gove's complimentary sentiments about New Labour and its influence on the evolution of modern Conservatism, while being provocative in terms of internal Conservative Party politics, are broadly consistent with the overall political agenda and 'detoxification' strategy of David Cameron since he became Conservative leader in December 2005. This has been further evident in his speeches, in which similar sentiments have been regularly expressed:

'The first of the policy groups I set up was Iain's, (Duncan Smith) looking at all the full range of social justice issues. For the Conservative Party I'm leading, social justice is a vital issue. The reason is simple: the degree of social injustice in our country'.[80]

Such vocabulary and rhetoric being deliberately used by both David Cameron and his key political allies, aligned with a background focus on the integral theme of 'society', have formed part of a sustained attempt to 'modernise' and reposition the Conservative Party's image on social policy matters, which in turn has consolidated a revived version of 'Civic Conservatism' from an early stage of his leadership.

In this subsequent evolution of its policy programme within this specific sphere, the party has indicated its willingness to address and embrace the social justice agenda, confronting a traditional area of Labour policy dominance while also seeking to retain its own distinct interpretation of the term and develop an innovative and distinct range of social policies accordingly. However, precisely how such theories, rhetoric and ideas have developed and been translated into practical policies has been an dynamic that has been further developed under the auspices of the Conservative–Liberal Democrat coalition government between 2010 and 2015, and such a process ultimately requires some more explicit analysis in terms of actual policy implementation.

4
Social policy case study 1: Modern Conservatism, practical social justice and welfare reform

Having assessed the theoretical and philosophical origins of the concept of social justice, we move on to focus on how the term has influenced the contemporary social policy agenda of the Conservative Party in practice, particularly in the sphere of general welfare reform. In the context of reframing the Conservative policy message in both image and rhetorical terms while aligning it with an appropriate ideological framework, the desire to mould a new and distinct 21st-century interpretation of 'social justice' has been a key challenge for David Cameron's leadership, both while in political opposition from late 2005 and in power from mid-2010. The narrative and analysis of Britain's 'broken society' has therefore been a central and developing theme of the Cameron era since his accession to the Conservative Party leadership; a mechanism to allow him to propose his own distinct political solutions.

A New social policy narrative

Cameron's approach involved a close focus on achieving a more 'just' outcome to British society's sustained socio-economic problems such as long-term poverty, poor living conditions, fragmented families, limited social mobility and rising levels of crime. One academic observer remarked that the approach was driven by an acknowledgement that when '[Cameron]became Conservative party leader in 2005 he recognized that something was badly wrong with the right, and a new radical conservatism was desperately needed',[1] instigating a new and innovative approach to 'society' and related social policy matters. This entailed a re-engagement with some aspects of the Conservative 'One Nation' legacy, an infusion of moralistic considerations into social policy development, and a pragmatic absorption of aspects of New Labour's social agenda. Indeed, the need for full-blown and significant 'change' appeared to be at the heart of Cameron's modernising agenda from the moment he made his pitch for the party leadership in the second half of 2005, as evident in his public affirmation that the Conservatives had to 'change and modernise our culture and attitudes and identity ... When I say change, I'm not talking about some slick rebranding exercise: what I'm talking about is fundamental change.'[2]

Given the established, historic Conservative philosophical acceptance of inequality as an inevitable consequence of a diverse and variable society, as well as considering the party's post-1979 tendency to prioritise economic policy over social policy issues, Cameron's strategy for 'change' was bold. It sought to create a consistent argument depicting the negative legacy of a sustained period of Labour government as having created a fragmented society that was 'broken' and ill at ease with itself in many social aspects, exacerbated by the excessive and often counter-productive interventions of a costly and inefficient welfare state and the associated high volume of welfare recipients.[3] While the outgoing Labour administration of 2010 vehemently disputed this critical analysis of its own socio-economic record and indeed attacked the Thatcher legacy for similar reasons, Cameron has displayed a degree of audacity and tenacity in pursuing this agenda, particularly given that he was encroaching on established Labour territory and venturing into an area of traditional Conservative weakness in policy terms. In seeking to move away from perceptions of Conservative indifference to social policy matters and to re-align both the party's wider image and its overall policy direction, Cameron has also created significant internal tensions in his party. Thatcherite figures such as ex-Cabinet minister John Redwood have been provoked into advocating a more 'dry' economic slant to the direction of party policy, focusing on tax cuts and fiscal retrenchment rather than an emphasis on society, social issues and the potential additional public expenditure and image of 'big government' traditionally associated with the socio-political perspective put forward by Cameron. It has been a specific challenge to Cameron to persuade party critics and sceptics that more attention to social policy does not automatically equate to a bigger state.

The Centre for Social Justice: Addressing the 'broken society' and promoting social justice?

Proceeding from this analysis of a fractured and unsettled British social model, Cameron has called for a fundamental reassessment of the welfare state, and has instigated significant, wide-ranging welfare reforms to tackle deep-seated causes of poverty and dependency, arguing that New Labour ultimately failed in this respect, despite making bold promises to pledging to 'think the unthinkable' on welfare reform when it was elected in 1997. Criticism of the established institutional structures of the post-war British state and advocacy of the need for radical welfare reform within renewed social policy initiatives lies at the heart 'of the Conservative Party's relationship with the post-war welfare state',[4] a relationship that has often been uneasy due to the desire of many Conservatives to preserve core public services by a process of radical reform in order for them to flourish in the long-term. Such reform often entails politically difficult implications (as evident in policies such as the controversial 'bedroom tax' or 'spare room subsidy' introduced from 2013 onwards), and pivotal to this approach has been the indefatigable desire of 21st-century Conservatism to reduce the prevailing 'statist' flavour of Labour's management of the welfare state. Instead there have been concerted attempts to develop a more diverse socio-political culture whereby 'Entrepreneurial innovation is to be extended to social policy (leading to) reform of the welfare state by enhancing the role of social entrepreneurs in the voluntary sector'.[5]

The provision of adequate, streamlined public service provision but without a 'big government' model of delivery has emerged as one of the fundamental challenges to have confronted Cameron's leadership from its earliest phase. In this context, Cameron sought to put extra force into the stuttering attempts to broaden and 'modernise' the Conservative Party's image on social policy matters that had taken place under his three predecessors as party leader – William Hague (1997–2001), Iain Duncan Smith (2001–3) and Michael Howard (2003–5). All of these figures recognised, to differing degrees and with varying levels of urgency, the need for the party to expand its electoral base and broaden its appeal after the 1997 electoral debacle, not just in relation to traditional social policy areas such as health, education and welfare provision, but also on modern policy spheres such as the 'green' agenda and alternative lifestyle issues. However, in order to provide greater substance and urgency to this movement, and as part of the development of his policy rhetoric while in opposition, Cameron actively prioritised the improvement of key public services. In this, he built on some significant 'modernisation' processes already initiated by his direct predecessor Michael Howard. He established six groups with a brief to formulate new policy ideas for a future Conservative government, which convened from late 2005 onwards. Perhaps the most prominent was the Social Justice Policy group, led by former party leader Iain Duncan Smith, whose burgeoning interest in poverty, welfare policy and social reform had led to his involvement in the establishment of the Centre for Social Justice (CSJ) in 2004.

The CSJ sought to develop innovative policies and distinct initiatives to deal with wider social policy and reform of the welfare system, identifying the root causes of long-term poverty, driven by a Christian, moralistic ethos. Although its initial work promoted 'an agenda that found little favour under (Michael) Howard'[6] and the party hierarchy at the time, its attention to this policy area won praise from other Conservatives; David Willetts stated that 'Iain Duncan Smith deserves a lot of credit for [bringing] social justice... back into Conservative thinking'.[7] Duncan Smith aspired to champion a revived model of 'Compassionate Conservatism' that acknowledged the failed social dimensions of Thatcherism. 'Reforming the public services and helping the "vulnerable" in society were to become his mission... [which] stemmed in part from his Christianity and sense of social justice'.[8] Indeed, such was Cameron's interest and focus on this policy area that he spent the first day of his leadership formally launching the Social Justice policy initiative at a youth project in East London in the company of Iain Duncan Smith, a development that can be viewed as a gesture symbolising his impending political priorities.[9]

Following over 3,000 hours of public consultation, and after receiving submissions from over 2,000 different organisations, Duncan Smith's 'Social Justice' group published two reports in 2006 and 2007,[10] reflecting a distinctive and revised emphasis to the Conservative Party's welfare policy agenda, evident in the document *Breakthrough Britain*:

> *Breakthrough Britain* advocates a new approach to welfare in the 21st century. We believe that, in order to reverse social breakdown, we need to start reinforcing the Welfare Society. The Welfare Society is that which delivers welfare beyond the State.[11]

The term 'welfare society', opposed to the more bureaucratic connotations of the 'welfare state', was an important differentiation of vocabulary which chimed in with the sentiments of the recently installed Conservative leader and his focus on addressing social injustice, tackling the 'broken society', and with his later focus on the 'big society', critically seeking to operate within a 'smaller state'. The renewed social agenda that focused on the importance of society but less so on the state, was, therefore, an attempt simultaneously to emphasise the renewed Conservative agenda in this policy sphere and revitalise the Conservative Party's broader public image, as 'under Cameron, the idea of the "broken society" was being used to help dispel the impression that the Conservative Party, by its own admission, was the "nasty party" of British politics'.[12] In summary, the findings of Duncan Smith's Social Justice Group were the clearest indicator in a generation that the Conservatives were embarking on a renewed, concerted effort to develop a distinct approach to social and welfare policy. Its findings could be broadly summarised as emphasising 'the importance of marriage and strong family values and the need to reverse the dependency culture'.[13]

The specific focus on the perceived stabilising influences of marriage and conventional family values raised questions as to how new or original this policy agenda was, particularly whether it was merely a reversion to neo-Conservative social values and traditionalist policies fused with distinct moral guidelines. This is an approach that can be ascribed to the influence of American-based thinkers such as Lawrence Mead,[14] whose work in this sphere over recent years has rejected the entitlement aspect of welfare benefit as a means of addressing long-term unemployment, questioning whether receipt of state benefit should be an automatic social right of citizenship. This approach seeks to introduce conditionality into receipt of welfare support, and has pursued an alternative model of benefits provision where the state seeks to actively promote enhanced values of citizenship, responsibility, obligation and the work ethic as a condition of the receipt of welfare benefit. Some observers have noted that this moralistic approach and its identification of an entrenched, poverty-stricken, dependent 'underclass' is an interpretation that has some parallels with the neo-liberal socio-economic analysis of American libertarian scholars such as Charles Murray.[15] Using contemporary US society as a model example, Murray has argued that welfare payments are harmful to both the individual recipients and wider society in the long term, and that it is desirable to remove welfare provision altogether, as an incentive for people to work. Such a morality-infused focus on conditionality has proved to be a controversial concept in the debate about British welfare recipients. This approach requires a degree of proactive reciprocity and civic obligation from the recipient, addressing the inadequacies and moral failings of those who are unemployed for a long period of time by motivating them to find work through the fear of losing their welfare support. It appears to have partially shaped and influenced the 'welfare to work' and 'workfare' agenda promoted by both New Labour and Conservative politicians from the 1990s onwards.

However, while no-one in the senior Conservative hierarchy has publicly or practically promoted such extreme examples of welfare conditionality either in opposition or since returning to power in 2010, there is evidence of limited conditionality within a more moralistic overall approach to welfare policy. It appears to be aligned with the agenda of the Centre for Social Justice. Whether this attitude is compatible with a heightened overall 'compassion' remains to be seen, and although the origins and originality of this agenda are a source of some dispute, Cameron's Conservatives have certainly focused closely on social policy and, within that, on a more individualistic, decentralised, less bureaucratic approach to welfare provision. Notably, in July 2008 David Cameron launched the Conservative Party's 'broken society' initiative into the practical political world at the beginning of the Glasgow East by-election campaign,[16] and this revamped and innovative socio-economic stance was certainly influenced by the general aims and values of Iain Duncan Smith's Centre for Social Justice.

The Conservatives in power: The welfare state, social policy and social justice from 2010

Although the Conservative Party continued to struggle to achieve any sign of electoral progress in the inner-city urban areas such as Glasgow East,[17] the target of much of this renewed social agenda, the party did return to national power in May 2010, albeit as the senior partner in a coalition with the Liberal Democrats. David Cameron's blossoming affinity with, and interest in, Duncan Smith's work on the welfare and social policy agenda stemmed from their shared focus on a revised vision of social justice, and this came to fruition in May 2010 when Duncan Smith was Cameron's choice as Secretary of State for Work and Pensions, an appointment described by one commentator as 'an incredible transformation for a man many had written off only a few years before'.[18] This political resurrection provided Duncan Smith with the opportunity to leave behind his ineffective spell as Conservative Leader between 2001 and 2003, and to put his thorough policy research and practical experiences while in opposition to the test by running a key government department that focused primarily on social policy. Some fellow-Conservatives have subsequently praised his knowledge and approach in dealing with this challenging policy area, heralding him as 'the champion of early intervention'[19] in sensitive aspects of social policy (broadly covering the welfare state and the long-term reform of associated policy areas). Vigorous and active interventionism has not been a trait of the Conservatives when dealing with such issues in the post-1979 political era; yet, from an early stage of his leadership, Cameron 'recognise(d) the importance of softening the Party's approach towards those experiencing poverty and disadvantage'[20] and embracing a more pro-active approach.

The reformist intervention of Cameron and Duncan Smith, set along-side a less ideological and apparently more 'compassionate' and flexible attitude towards the welfare state, was initially described by some commentators as a typical example of the re-emergence of Conservative pragmatism. It also acknowledged the need to utilise the power of a 'strong state' (as alluded to by Andrew Gamble[21]) in achieving a desired long-term political goal and removing the necessary obstacles to achieving such an outcome. However, while the government's position appeared on one level to represent a move towards the One Nation Conservative tradition as opposed to the neo-liberalism of the New Right, Duncan Smith's infusion of a 'moral' need to improve the welfare of the poorer members of society could also be said to reflect distinctly Thatcherite influences, for it has been argued that 'Margaret Thatcher was not a reductionist in that all that mattered was a free-market economy. For her, a free market economy operated within a moral and cultural framework ... largely shaped by her devout Christianity, which is much under-rated'.[22]

Although its moral and political compass derived from a fusion of influences, it became apparent that post-2010 social Conservatism did not envisage the state's role as being as universal and comprehensive as had been the case for the majority of the post-1945 era. Conservative expectations demanded more devolved and diversified public service provision as part of a strategy that offered new solutions and was aimed at ensuring a better-functioning social model and a version of civil society much more appropriate and credible for the 21st century. This outlook has been summarised by Robert Page as follows:

> Under David Cameron's 'Progressive' form of Conservatism the Party has adopted a more liberal approach towards the poor and those pursuing 'non-traditional' lifestyles. Whilst recognising that the state still has a role to play in funding and ... providing welfare services, greater emphasis is now being placed on the part that individuals and communities can play in meeting their own welfare needs ...

another illustration of the ... Party continu[ing] to adapt to changing economic and social circumstances.[23]

This revised contemporary form of Conservatism as promoted by the Cameron leadership and his inner-circle has been associated with the ambiguous and subjective term 'progressive'.[24] Its proponents have sought to emphasise the specific Conservative interpretation of this term. As part of this approach, Cameron has embraced and promoted the value of 'society' and 'community', yet continuing to stress the importance of individuals in achieving desired social outcomes and improved social justice, rather than an over-reliance on the hegemonic state. Indeed, advocates of a less centralised and more devolved approach to the organisation of the state have criticised the years between 1997 and 2010 as being a missed opportunity for more radical changes in the approach to national governance, as 'state growth without state reform has missed the opportunity to make structural changes'.[25] Cameron's general approach to welfare reform is therefore in accordance with the views of some commentators that the thirteen years of Labour rule 'saw the emergence of something of a new political consensus on welfare'.[26] It was a period that saw some initial political agreement about steadily rising levels of state investment in social and welfare policies, fuelled by Labour's significant public spending increases between 1997 and 2010, although Conservative criticisms of bureaucratic inefficiency lingered on. However the extent of such 'consensus' is open to debate, as by the autumn years of New Labour's period in office and the advent of economic slump from approximately 2008 onwards, a new consensus was evolving among 'modernisers' in both major parties that, after a period of significant state growth, major structural reform of welfare provision and a degree of 'roll-back' was now required. Indeed, the Conservative politicians of the 2010 administration have appeared to reject the governmental approach that prevailed for most of the New Labour era, which primarily focused on increased levels of micro-managed state investment from the centre. The revised Conservative interpretation about the nature of this 'welfare consensus' was thoroughly re-formulated in the aftermath of the 2008 financial crisis and the beginning of a deep economic recession. This has led to the re-emergence of a 1980s-style scepticism towards the pervasive role of the centralised state, maintaining a view that 'does not regard public spending per se as a necessary vehicle for the amelioration of social ills'.[27] However, such a bold vision for decentralised policy-making has again led critics to question how this approach equates to the practical achievement of enhanced levels of social justice, as despite promising greater efficiency and less bureaucracy, 'the flipside of decentralization is that it means fewer guarantees ... about the scope and quality of provision available in each locality'.[28]

Duncan Smith's first attempts to devise policies for the CSJ linked to a modernised and reformulated Conservative vision of social justice and associated policies stemmed from his renewed attention to Britain's inner-cities. This was notably evident following some well-publicised visits to the deprived Easterhouse estate in Glasgow,[29] and in taking this path that focused on the most vulnerable members of society, he sought to re-ignite and revive the Conservative Party's 19th-century Disraelian 'One Nation' legacy, an approach that emphasised a concern for poverty that had been eclipsed during the 1980s decade of individualistic 'New Right' dominance. This approach also sought to challenge the perception (fuelled by events in the 1980s) that the Conservatives were indifferent to the plight of deprived communities, and that genuine attention and effort was required in order to address those members of society that were 'dependent on the state ... [whose dependency] becomes a stigma and allows [their] demands to be disregarded'.[30] There was, therefore, the potential for political, economic and social benefits to flow from dealing with the stigmatised dependents, a problem that successive governments had acknowledged to be an issue needing to be addressed. The impulse was justified by the premise that 'the quality of your life and your morale is affected by how you do and are compared with other people'.[31]

This provided a moral impetus for some significant attempts by the Conservative-led government to radically reform welfare provision during the 2010–15 parliament. While reforms have emerged to varying degrees, the efforts have been affected by the fluid electoral and political priorities over this five-year period. In particular, the language of 'compassionate conservatism' has appeared to be progressively downgraded and replaced with more hard-nosed electioneering that focuses on the development of social policy that supports and bolsters 'hard-working families' as opposed to those dependent on welfare benefits. This message has supposedly been moulded by Conservative election strategist Lynton Crosby, who, since his reappointment as Conservative general election strategist in November 2012, has sought to replace much of the 'softer' rhetoric of the early Cameron phase with a 'tougher' message, designed to address the harsh reality of winning votes. This would suggest that by the tail end of the 2010–15 parliament, the Cameron project on social justice has been altered by electoral pressures and now lacks consistency in its broader social policy agenda as a result.

Labour's legacy of 'Social Justice'

The requirement for initiatives to challenge long-term social dislocation and political alienation emerged in the context of the Labour government's struggles to reform the welfare system and reduce long-term 'dependency' on the state. During thirteen years in power between 1997 and 2010 it has been claimed that 'they had done only slightly better than their Tory predecessor in liberating from welfare dependency the millions without good education or training'.[32] Indeed, according to critics of New Labour from the 'Big Society' wing of the Conservative Party like Jesse Norman, the successive administrations of Blair and Brown were ultimately unsuccessful in their desired aspiration of achieving greater social justice, for the prime reason that they failed to significantly reduce dependency on the state by welfare recipients, and this in turn led to a failure to reform, to instil a sense of morality, and to inject greater economic efficiency into the welfare system.

Such an unconvincing New Labour legacy prompted a Conservative rebuke that such statism 'actively undermined social justice',[33] along with academic observations that acknowledged that the New Labour era 'encouraged dependence on the state, while failing to meet the aim of reducing social inequality'.[34] Within the context of such criticisms, a more efficient streamlining and decentralisation of resources in this policy sphere were prime objectives of an aspiring Conservative government, particularly given that the scope of the welfare system had grown in both bureaucratic size and financial expenditure over thirteen years. Such challenges within this policy area during Labour's most sustained spell in office was readily admitted by new party leader Ed Miliband in late 2010, when he claimed that Labour 'did not do enough when it was in power to reform the welfare system'.[35]

The size and scope of the inflated welfare structure that emerged under New Labour was exacerbated by an increasingly complex and bureaucratic benefits system, which was expanded in scope by the introduction of 'statist' and administration-heavy policies such as the proliferation of tax credits and the broad extension of means-testing by Chancellor Gordon Brown (1997–2007). Welfare spending was said to have risen 40% in real terms (allowing for the effects of inflation) between 2000 and 2010, but the Labour government's performance in terms of effective and financially efficient policy delivery must be viewed in the context of welfare spending never having been kept under control by any post-war government,[36] so it is perhaps inevitable that public spending in this area would have risen anyway. However, Conservative critics of this policy have highlighted what they believe to be waste and excessive cost, with Iain Duncan Smith claiming that:

> In the years between 2003 and 2010, Labour spent a staggering £171 billion on tax credits, contributing to a 60% rise in the welfare bill. Far too much of that money was wasted, with fraud and error under Labour costing over £10 billion.[37]

Although the issue of 'waste' is open to political debate, such an allegedly profligate performance by the Labour administration relating to general welfare spending since 1997 formed the context for the socio-economic policy approach of the incoming coalition government, with prominent advocates of 'The Big Society' arguing that many of Britain's social and economic 'problems (can be traced) ... to the long-term growth and centralization of the state',[38] alongside the associated costs that this trend has generated.

In the context of such perceived failings by the previous Labour government, the concerted efforts to reformulate the Conservative Party's attitudes within the wider social policy arena and its revised view of how to make the state more effectively and efficiently function has led to political commentators observing that 'Team Cameron' has 'adopted a more ameliorative approach towards poverty and social injustice than their Majorite or Thatcherite predecessors'.[39] However, critics have argued that in the wake of the post-2010 austerity and retrenchment measures, practical policy has failed to match such rhetoric, focus and attention,[40] and despite this specific refocusing, at recent elections the Conservative Party has continued to struggle to win over key sections of the electorate that appear to remain sceptical of the party's social policy aspirations. Although there has been emphasis on developing policies that focus on addressing long-term poverty and maintaining good standards of social welfare delivery while also acknowledging the need to streamline public spending, an image remains of the Conservatives as a party representing the better-off members of society.[41] The contemporary Conservative concept of social justice remains hazy and open to interpretation. In 2012 the Conservative-led government, therefore, sought to clarify its understanding and promotion of what it meant in practice by releasing the document: *Social Justice: Transforming Lives*,[42] which offered an updated interpretation of this key concept:

Social Justice is about making society function better – providing
the support and tools to help turn lives around ... the most effective
solutions will often be designed and delivered at a local level ... [it]
is closely related to another Government priority: to increase social
mobility.[43]

Given the Conservative-inspired re-evaluation of the concept of
social justice, the development of the Centre for Social Justice (CSJ)
and its links to senior party figures such as Duncan Smith, this has
led to the inference by many political observers that there has been a
broad ideological re-alignment with the Conservative Party. The CSJ
appears to have played a significant role in re-moulding the party's
attitude towards social and welfare policy matters, with many observers
acknowledging that this policy sphere was neglected during the 1980s.
Bolstered by his involvement with this pressure group, Duncan Smith
has argued in vigorous 'One Nation' language that the Conservatives
have a duty to assist those in poverty and to promote their own
specific version of social justice in a 21st-century context, with a
specific emphasis on community-based self-help as the springboard
to enhanced social mobility. However, despite such perceptions of its
political role and affiliation, the CSJ denies being explicitly connected
to the Conservative Party, stating that it is 'unable to comment on the
evolution of policy within the Conservative Party [in its role as] an
independent think tank'.[44] This is despite the high-profile connections
to Iain Duncan Smith and the fact that the Head of the CSJ, Philippa
Stroud, stood unsuccessfully for the Conservative Party at the 2010
General Election and was subsequently appointed as an adviser to the
Department of Work and Pensions, headed by Duncan Smith following
the 2010 election result.[45] Nevertheless despite such connections, the
CSJ continues to confidently assert its status as a genuinely independent 'think-tank' that seeks to influence social policy of all parties 'across
the political spectrum and believe(s) that social justice should be a key
plank of any party's vision'.[46] It aspires to cultivate cross-party links in
dealings with social justice and welfare reform agendas.

In exploring the most efficient methods of delivering welfare provision, and composing a distinctive vision of the much debated concept
of social justice in a 21st-century political environment, the CSJ has
focused on the role of government in the delivery of welfare provision.
This has led it to a significant critique of the approach of both major
parties while in government. This in turn has inspired demands for significant reforms of the welfare system and the encouragement and promotion of innovative and devolved policy practices that have primarily

derived from community activities, voluntary groups, charities and other 'grassroots' social projects rather than the more traditional post-war funding streams from the monolithic state structure. In doing so, the CSJ has sought to promote the relatively novel proposition, endorsed by many Conservative modernisers in particular, that the state does not have the answer to every socio-economic problem and that 'localism' is a better option in the long term. Increased 'dependency' was claimed to be the end product of the exclusively 'statist' approach that has prevailed much of the post-war period, and it was this criticism that figures such as Iain Duncan Smith sought to attach to the Labour Party at the conclusion of its thirteen years in office:

> Labour's policies have left the poor even more dependent on the state for their incomes and the kind of public services they receive. And that, in the end, will be Labour's legacy to the poor. Dependence, not independence.[47]

Table 4.1 Public spending in UK as a percentage of GDP (1975–2012)

Year	Public Spending as % of GDP
1975–76	49.7
1976–77	48.6
1977–78	45.6
1978–79	45.1
1979–80	44.6
1980–81	47.0
1981–82	47.7
1982–83	48.1
1983–84	47.8
1984–85	47.5
1985–86	45.0
1986–87	43.6
1987–88	41.6
1988–89	38.9
1989–90	39.2
1990–91	39.4
1991–92	41.9
1992–93	43.7
1993–94	43.0

(continued)

Table 4.1 Continued

Year	Public Spending as % of GDP
1994–95	42.5
1995–96	41.8
1996–97	39.9
1997–98	38.2
1998–99	37.2
1999–2000	36.3
2000–01	34.5
2001–02	37.7
2002–03	38.5
2003–04	39.3
2004–05	40.5
2005–06	41.2
2006–07	40.9
2007–08	41.0
2008–09	44.5
2009–10	47.7
2010–11	46.8
2011–12	45.0

Information Source http://www.ukpublicspending.co.uk.

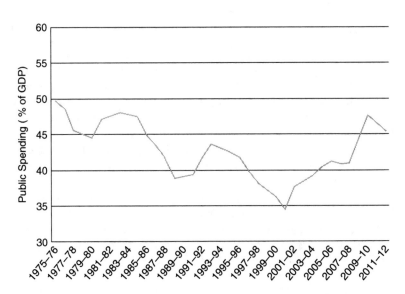

Figure 4.1 Public spending in UK as a percentage of GDP (1975–2012)

Such 'dependency' has, according to right-of-centre political critics, been reinforced by the progressively higher levels of public spending associated with social and welfare policies during Labour's tenure in office. This viewpoint argues that the widely acknowledged additional public spending of this era created and funded additional levels of bureaucracy and complex means-tested welfare schemes (e.g. tax credits), that led to a further reliance on the benevolent mechanism of the state for many individuals. In the long-term this contributed (along with the post-2008 economic slump), towards a record deficit which Conservatives were increasingly critical of while in opposition and which they identified as a key priority to be tackled once in power after 2010, and which has subsequently been a pivotal under-current to their social and welfare agenda since the global financial crisis of 2008.[48] Labour's difficulties in addressing this policy area while in office occurred despite the fact that a key aim of New Labour was to 'make work pay', a sentiment that has generated broad political consensus and which has been heartily echoed by Cameron's Conservatives in government from 2010. On the formal launch of the high-profile 'Universal Credits' policy initiative in late 2010, Iain Duncan Smith's ideas from opposition now appeared to be materialising in practical terms. This policy aimed to merge several different benefits into one single payment, with the significant aim of reducing government bureaucracy in the process. Duncan Smith alluded to the extreme economic conditions of the time as a specific reason to address this particularly expensive aspect of welfare provision, commenting that 'In prosperous times this dependency culture would be unsustainable but today it's a national crisis.'[49] On Labour's departure from office in 2010, it was evident that spending on public services had steadily risen during their tenure, particularly in contrast with the broadly declining rate of public spending as percentage of GDP between 1979 and 1997 (as evident in Table 4.1 and Figure 4.1). Conservative critics would claim that such public spending increases after 1997 had not always gone on frontline services, that such a long-term rising cost was unsustainable, and that the issue of 'welfare dependency' had not been addressed.

These accelerating fiscal figures and public expenditure trends after 1997 could justify the sentiments of Conservative politicians such as Duncan Smith, who have repeatedly and consistently lamented the progressive growth of 'statism' and its associated high levels of government spending and apparent failure to address 'dependency'.

Such trends have been exacerbated by the bureaucratic implications of 'targeted welfare' which was a prominent feature of Gordon Brown's welfare vision in particular, and which the Conservatives claimed provided further fuel to the overall culture of 'dependency' that remained in place under the sustained period of Labour government. In adopting this approach they revived calls for greater 'fiscal conservatism' and the rejection of excessive state provision of core public services, and instead have sought to develop a more individualistic, efficient and self-reliant range of public services aligned with an alternative version of social justice. This narrative has even been adopted by some more moderate reformist and chastened elements within the post-Brown Labour Party.[50] Such an emphasis on linking fiscal conservatism and a smaller state with the provision of social justice is arguably a difficult outcome to achieve (particularly within an era of significant austerity), and it raises questions both in terms of practical policy delivery and the true motives of the Conservatives' renewed focus on this policy area. This relates to the key issue as to whether this is a genuinely new and more compassionate approach to policy-making, or merely a return to the Thatcherite policy of retrenchment and cutting back on the size and scope of the state's provision and support, moulded by moral and financial pressures while being cloaked in less language.[51]

In the context of Conservative attacks on the 'dependency culture' that was alleged to have been exacerbated during Labour's thirteen-year period in power, it could be equally argued that 'dependency' was a prominent legacy of the Thatcher era during the 1980s, a consequence of its historically high levels of sustained long-term unemployment and the significant financial cost of subsequent benefits. Indeed, such dependency has proved to be a similar burden for the Cameron-led coalition, as unemployment rose on his watch, peaking at a 17-year high of 2.64 million in late 2011 (although the rise had begun under Labour prior to 2010), before steadily failing, though still hovering at the 2.1 million mark in mid-2014. In such a context, the comments below, while directly alluding to the 1980s, could be seen as a damning indictment of the cross-party administration of power that encompassed the 31 years between 1979 and 2010: 'instead of strengthening work incentives and reducing dependency, the government's policy of targeting created ... a dependency culture'.[52]

The fact that greater 'dependency' could be seen as a consequence of Thatcher's socio-economic approach was ironic, given her hostility to 'Welfarism' throughout her time in power. She and her New Right allies had consistently argued that the post-war years of consensus 'had spawned a dependency culture'[53] that 'had been allowed to take hold ... (and) become both dysfunctional and costly'[54] over a long period. Tackling this culture was, therefore, a fundamental political and socio-economic priority after 1979, yet it was not successfully dealt with during her long years in power, with unemployment levels and consequently welfare recipients higher when she left office than when she was first elected,[55] although public spending was reduced and streamlined (see Tables 4.1 and 4.3 and Figure 4.1). Thirteen years of Labour in power saw the country's levels of public spending as a percentage of GDP steadily increase towards levels not witnessed since the mid-1970s (also see Table 4.1, Figure 4.1), a trend that would justify long-standing right-wing criticisms of the profligate tendencies of Labour governments. There were significant increases in the levels of expenditure on some key areas of welfare provision and social policy (as outlined in Tables 4.2 and 4.3 and Figure 4.2), with notable increases following the economic slump in 2008, although it should be noted that Conservative social security spending during its 18 years in power was actually a higher percentage in real terms (see Table 4.3). Whether increased public spending on key public services successfully addresses society's core socio-economic problems as well as the fundamental issue of social justice is not clear, and it remains a matter of significant political debate whether the centralised state is the best and most efficient mechanism of delivering key public services.

Table 4.2   Government spending by key social policy areas as a percentage of GDP (2011 estimates)

Policy Area	£ Billions	% of GDP
Pensions	122.6	8%
Health	122.4	8%
Education	83.6	5%
Welfare Benefits	113.1	7%
Overall GDP	1539	

Information Source http://www.ukpublicspending.co.uk.

Table 4.3 Comparative government increases in public spending (by percentage, 1979–2010)

Policy Area	Conservative (1979–97)	Labour (1997–2010) Total	Labour (1997–2008) Pre- crisis	Labour (2008–2010) *Post- crisis
Social Security	3.8	2.2	1.4	5.3
NHS	3.2	5.7	6.3	3.7
Education	1.5	3.9	4.3	2.4
Total public spending increase (all policy areas)	0.7	4.4	4.6	3.5

Information Source: Institute for Fiscal Studies, *Public Spending under Labour* (2010), 2010 Election Briefing Note No.5, (Robert Chote, Rowena Crawford, Carl Emmerson, Gemma Tetlow), p. 10; http://www.ifs.org.uk/bns/bn92.pdf.

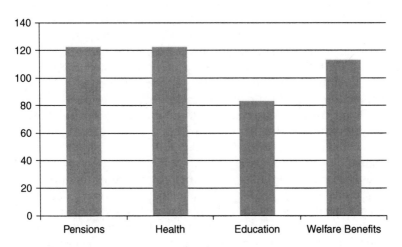

Figure 4.2 Government spending by billions (2011 estimates)

The influence of the Liberal Democrats on post-2010 social and welfare policies

The above figures and tables indicate considerable ongoing government expenditure on key public services at a structural level, representing a massive challenge to any administration intent on reforming the scope and streamlining the cost of social policy in the early 21st century. At the same time, the vocabulary of contemporary political parties has sought to create the necessary socio-economic conditions for addressing inequality, long-term poverty and welfare dependency within a framework of a revised vision of social justice, and it was such a scenario that faced the Conservative–Liberal Democrat coalition from 2010 onwards. It presented a particularly challenging scenario for a Conservative-led regime whose key political instincts and principles have historically (in modern times at least) been linked to retrenchment, welfare cuts and the need to keep levels of public spending under control, rather than using the powers of the state to initiate improved public policy options. It remains to be seen whether this combination of factors has remoulded the concept of social justice in line with the government's priorities and political agenda from 2010 onwards, and whether the political fusion of the Conservatives with a traditionally more interventionist political party has created original and lasting policy formulations in this sphere.

Given the political situation that arose from the uncertain outcome of the 2010 General Election, it is important to analyse the extent to which the Conservative Party's coalition partners, the Liberal Democrats, have influenced the narrative regarding welfare reform and overall social policy during this period, particularly as, since the party's official inception in 1988, they have been viewed as being more 'liberal' on social issues, more 'statist' in their approach to government intervention in the economy, and more profligate in terms of public spending than the Conservatives. However, the two parties appear to have moved closer together on such policy issues in recent years due to a combination of the parliamentary arithmetic from 2010 and the pragmatic reaction to it, coupled with a revised Conservative attitude towards social policy under the Cameron leadership from 2005, and the ascendancy of Nick Clegg's 'Orange Book'[56] (economic liberal) faction of Liberal Democrats from 2007 onwards. This sharing of political priorities was bolstered by a joint hostility to an unpopular outgoing Labour government and a growing level of co-operation at local government level, resulting in broad agreement in the form of the Coalition Agreement of May 2010[57] that emphasised the need for the 'greater use of private, social enterprise and voluntary organisations in the provision of (public) services'.[58] This indicated a likelihood of a more diverse approach to public service delivery within the context of retrenchment between 2010 and 2015, alongside a cross-party willingness to pursue a more 'localist' and decentralised approach to policy development and implementation.[59]

Since May 2010, Conservatives and Liberal Democrats have shared a greater emphasis on the importance of developing a healthy and more localised civil society encouraged to flourish away from the tentacles of a bureaucratic central state and its capacity to grow inexorably if given the opportunity to do so. Within this revised version of 'New Conservatism', a vigorous, decentralised civil society can be viewed as a more effective means of promoting social justice, with an over-powerful state perceived as an obstacle to achieving a more socially just society. This perspective espouses the vision of the 'big society' and its less bureaucratic structure as a socio-political model to aspire towards, being detached from and less controlled by the political centre and politicians who often seek to manipulate the state's activities in their own partisan interests. It is also not over-reliant on the deregulated markets promoted by neo-liberals, primarily driven by arbitrary economic profit motives, and perceived as undermining communitarianism and damaging to the social fabric. This alternative approach has emerged from a combination of political developments, philosophical overlap and electoral circumstances, and has culminated in the Conservative Party's 'coalition with the Liberal Democrats, [and] the possibility of developing a somewhat different social policy agenda than the Conservative governments of the 1980s and 1990s'.[60] These earlier administrations governed under different political, economic and social conditions, had larger parliamentary majorities and generally pursued a more ideological approach to policy development.

As part of the 2010 Coalition Agreement, Liberal Democrat MPs were expected to support Iain Duncan Smith's key policy initiatives in the important and politically significant sphere of social and welfare policy, the first high-profile example being his White Paper: *Universal Credits: Welfare that Works* (November 2010).[61] As previously discussed, this policy was notably influenced by the Centre for Social Justice. It aimed to cut costs and tackle the bureaucratic legacy of New Labour, primarily by streamlining and fusing a multitude of welfare benefits into a single payment, with the intention of providing a 'moral' incentive to move way from dependency on state benefits. However, it remains to be seen whether this will be successful[62] in social, financial or indeed political terms. Critics have regularly claimed that such a policy is 'practically unachievable' in terms of delivery,[63] fuelled by the assertion that its principal motive was not moralistic or anti-bureaucratic as has been claimed, but was in fact fiscal: essentially a means of reducing government expenditure and cutting the much-heralded deficit, the raison d'être of the coalition government's policy agenda established during its first year in office (2010–11). Other welfare-related policies such as the 'bedroom tax' (2013), and the £120 billion 'welfare cap' (2014) have been similarly motivated. In this context, critics of the Conservative Party's intentions in its post-2010 austerity measures claim that rather than offering a genuinely revived model for innovative social and welfare policy formulation, and by default an alternative vision of social justice, such financial cutbacks seem to represent the Thatcherite tradition reimposing itself on the party and reasserting the Hayekian agenda of 'rolling back the state', combined with the contemporary 'strivers vs. shirkers' narrative. The dilemma for those members of the coalition government with a genuine and long-held interest in the policy area of welfare provision (such as Iain Duncan Smith), who seek to address long-term social injustice and initiate radical and morally-infused reforms rather than wielding the blunt instrument of retrenchment, is that their aims are likely to be thwarted in an atmosphere of austerity. This scenario also creates potentially serious and destabilising tensions for the coalition, particularly given the more interventionist and fiscally expansive tendencies of the 'social democrat' wing of the Liberal Democrats. However, the coalition government's dynamics relating to this issue have initially proved to be fairly robust, and Cameron's determined focus to both decentralise the government structure and, as a corollary, to save money within the sphere of welfare provision, does appear to have been broadly accepted by the junior coalition partners.

However, the inclusion of the Liberal Democrats in the coalition government may have curtailed the more radical and reformist tendencies of some Conservative politicians regarding the broad area of welfare policy over the entire 2010–2015 parliament, and the often tense political relationship has had the potential to scupper various proposed welfare reforms. This political compromise at the heart of national governance has been a recurring threat to the stability of Cameron's administration. During the maintenance of the delicate balance between public spending cutbacks and innovative policy-making in this area, it has been a subject of debate as to whether external Liberal Democrat pressures or internal Conservative divisions have more decisively shaped the coalition's social policy agenda. In the early phase of the coalition government, at a time of Liberal Democrat discipline and loyalty to the May 2010 Coalition Agreement, it appeared that the tensions were internal to the Conservatives, with reported clashes over policy expenditure between Iain Duncan Smith at the Department of Work and Pensions (DWP) and George Osborne at the Treasury.[64] Such internal friction has been evident over a number of years, and it starkly indicates the long-term challenges faced by the incoming government of 2010 in relation to its attempts to deliver enhanced social justice via revamped social and welfare policies.

The Conservative Party has encountered a range of practical problems in implementing its own distinct social justice agenda since returning to office in 2010, with prominent obstacles being the need to tackle the national deficit, internal party conflict about its precise policy direction, challenges in distinguishing its policies from New Labour's legacy, difficulties in putting theory-based policy initiatives into practice as well as the compromises required to sustain coalition government. Such underlying disruptive pressures have been evident in various social policy areas since the Conservatives returned to power in 2010, which subsequent chapters will explore in further detail.

5
Social policy case study 2:
The 'Big Society' Policy Framework

This chapter seeks to fuse theory with practical policy examples, aiming to highlight links between developments in contemporary social policy-making and the theoretical issues discussed in earlier chapters. It seeks, therefore, to explain and analyse the development and evolution of the concept of 'The Big Society' as a specific strand of David Cameron's attempts to create a framework and sense of direction for a practical social policy agenda stemming from theories of social justice as well as broader ideological and political influences. Such an approach has been linked to his aspiration to modernise the Conservative Party's social agenda since he secured the party leadership in late 2005. In analysing Cameron's revitalised social policy agenda, this chapter seeks to address the role of the state in providing key public services, and in turn assess how realistic have been the attempts by Cameron's government to provide a comprehensive, stable range of public services and social policy initiatives within a smaller state model and a less bureaucratic structural framework. The socio-political term 'The Big Society' has evolved into a high-profile, emblematic element of the way in which Conservative Party 'modernisers' have strived to create a revised social policy agenda that promotes a fresh vision of social justice for the right-of-centre tradition of British politics; one that aspires to remain loyal to some core Conservative traditions while also pragmatically adapting to many of the significant socio-economic developments of the New Labour era from 1997 onwards. This policy approach is a culmination of Cameron's drive to regenerate interest in the broader sphere of social policy and 'society' since becoming party leader, and it came to fruition in the prolonged lead-up to the 2010 General Election, becoming a flagship Conservative policy proposal, which promised to put:

more power in people's hands – a massive transfer of power from Whitehall to local communities. We want to see community empowerment, the opening up of public services, and people encouraged and enabled to play a more active part in society.[1]

As the 2010 general election date loomed, opinion polls indicated an appetite for change among the dissatisfied electorate and the likelihood of a return to power for the Conservatives after 13 years in the political wilderness.[2] Cameron's specific remedy to deal with his identification of the country's social and welfare-related problems (originating from various policy reviews), subsequently materialised in the form of a policy agenda that was clarified and condensed into three words – 'The Big Society'.[3] This succinct, well-marketed title was part of a broader attempt by Cameron to instil some communitarian vision and direction, and an ethos of 'social justice', into his distinctive brand of socially infused Conservatism. Within this approach, in practical terms Cameron sought to 'boost social action and community volunteering'[4] as a legitimate and more flexible alternative to uniform state provision, while also instilling a moral streak of enhanced citizenship into the formulation of social policy in the process. However, in its evolution in the period that followed, the brevity of the title has created confusion and uncertainty, and for all the Conservative claims that 13 years of Labour rule resulted in 'big government' that failed to deliver a more 'socially just society', this social and moral vision has been somewhat blurred and misunderstood, both as a concept and practical entity, by significant sections of the media, the political classes and the wider general public.

The origins of 'The Big Society'

The specific political term had been developing and germinating from an early phase of David Cameron's leadership, with one prominent advocate of the 'Big Society' stating (in 2012) that 'David Cameron has been speaking about "Compassionate Conservatism", which is the governing philosophy behind the 'Big Society', for at least seven years'.[5] However, the idea was firmed up towards the end of 2009 at the Hugo Young Memorial Lecture, when the Conservative leader sought to explicitly create a distinct, alternative model for a better-functioning and more efficient civil society to replace the stuttering and 'broken' one his policy reviews had identified. In doing so he emphasised the need for a bottom-up approach to social policy, involving 'greater

citizen involvement and empowerment, and a bigger role for coopera-
tives, private service providers and voluntary groups',[6] all of which were
key components of his specific model of public policy provision that
rejected the dominance of the centralised and bureaucratic state had
been the core provider of public services for the majority of the post-war
era. In arguing for a radical review of how poverty and inequality were
to be tackled in the name of social justice, Cameron boldly proclaimed
that 'the recent growth of the state has promoted not social solidarity
but selfishness and individualism'.[7]

In essence, Cameron was arguing for a revised 'rolling back' of the
state from a 21st century perspective, which would in turn create localised communities with greater autonomy and the power to initiate,
influence and organise public activity, including the provision of key
social and welfare policies. However, he conceded that the state was
not to be eliminated entirely, but instead 're-imagined' and given a new
role in remaking society. Vocal supporters of the 'Big Society' agenda
argued that this policy sought to re-energise a 'strand of Conservatism
that has existed for over 200 years'[8] and which dated back to the 18th-
century Whig tradition of Edmund Burke, with its focus on individual
civil liberties, a vibrant civil society of 'little platoons' and effective civic
institutions, a strong sense of community and a limited yet paternalistic
state. Some contemporary Conservatives have lamented the reduced
influence of Burke's Whig tradition in the modern Conservative Party,
an outlook dating back to the early 19th century which was essentially 'optimistic about the ability of parties to make things better and
(which was) lost when the Whig or the liberal strand diverged from
the Conservative strand'.[9] Modern Conservatism from the Thatcher era
onwards has suffered from this absence.

This concept of an enhanced and more constructive role for political
institutions released from the ostensible shackles of an overbearing centralised state, which in turn would create the appropriate conditions for
a vibrant civil society and instil a creative and moralistic individuality
into local communities, was the basis of the new Conservative agenda
for social policy. In the months following the initial public declaration
of this agenda in late 2009, Cameron progressively formulated it as a
dynamic and indeed vigorous doctrine, which in its practical application would promote voluntarism and generate a wider collective social
conscience as a means of rebuilding Britain's cultural and social fabric:

> David Cameron's pitch is that British society is broken... and the
> underlying causes are cultural not economic. Taking his cue from the

Social Justice Policy Group, (he) argues that British society is broken because of what he terms the decline in 'responsibility' and 'social virtue'. Civil society has become a lot less civil. By extending the powers and reach of the state, and taking responsibility away from individuals and communities, the Labour government has added to this social fracture.[10]

This emphasis on 'social virtue' and on the reinvigoration of a 'civil society' associated with reconstituted 21st-century socio-political structures has been at the heart of the Conservative Party's social agenda in the Cameron era. This remodelled Conservative social and welfare policy outlook was at first encouraged by the party hierarchy on an internal party basis while in opposition, as evidenced by the 'self-help' social action projects that many Conservative politicians and parliamentary candidates were encouraged to develop in the build-up to the 2010 General Election (and to continue beyond in some cases), although political opponents dismissed them as gimmicks. Such schemes were deliberately targeted at a grassroots level to provide models of ways to respond to some genuine needs by means of a more communitarian welfare provision, while being as free as possible from 'statist' bureaucratic control and regulation. In political opposition they were used by the Conservatives to illustrate the effective role of voluntarist, non-state bodies in delivering vital areas of public policy. Indeed, in early 2007, Cameron was keen to 'indicate just how important the third sector and its workforce would be for a future Conservative government'.[11] Such an approach also sought to exploit new social media and technology, an approach influenced by Cameron's Director of Strategy, Steve Hilton, who enthused other modernising Conservatives with 'the creation of new forms of social action via advances in technology'[12] (as evident in the clean-up operation after the 2011 summer riots, when positive social action was instigated via Facebook). The involvement of the voluntarist 'Third Sector'[13] was also identified from an early stage as a key component to be encouraged in such schemes and initiatives, again as a means of finding more efficient alternatives to uniform, monolithic state provision, and as a rebuttal of the notion that the state has the answer to all of society's major socio-economic problems. While attacking the 'statist' agenda of Labour in office, and also implicitly accepting the charge of neglect by his own party of social policy innovation in the past, the policy's overall ethos can be summarised as seeking to 'empower civil society using the failed approaches of left and right (as they've clearly failed to broker a new solution'.[14]

There does, however, remain a persistent undercurrent of doubt and scepticism as to the viability of such an approach, with most opinion surveys indicating that the public retain faith in the power of the state to administer and deliver social and welfare policy most effectively. This has resulted in a quixotic public mood, given that for all the inflated levels of public spending yet questionable service delivery under 13 years of New Labour in power, there remains limited public support for the private sector replacing key state services and 'deep divisions over the delivery of services by other organisations in the voluntary and third sector'.[15] Nonetheless, and despite such public doubts, the 'Big Society' social policy ethos has remained on the political stage to argue that, by promoting and developing public service delivery schemes that fuse a reduced role for the state with voluntarism and greater community-level involvement, a sense of greater social responsibility and civic virtue will be instilled in those who participate, and the taxpayer and the government will get better value for their money. With a focus on a smaller state and enhanced civic and even moral benefit for those involved in community activities, Cameron's brand of Conservatism seems to offer a robust critique of, and a coherent solution for, Britain's 'broken society', through specific alternative policy approaches. This applies particularly to the funding of, and strategic approach to, welfare provision in the UK, widely recognised as a potentially rising expense for all governments now and in the future, and particularly so during a period of recession and austerity. Despite a greater emphasis on civic and community-based activity to deliver a distinctive Conservative vision of social justice, this agenda, however, is not supposed to mark a return to the 'rugged individualism' of the Thatcher era, but instead aims to provide a more diverse, responsive, compassionate and flexible range of decentralised, community-focused services and support structures for vulnerable members of society.

'The Big Society' during and after the 2010 General Election

During the 2010 General Election campaign there was much dispute and political debate as to what the rather ambivalent term 'The Big Society' actually meant,[16] with one political commentator describing the term as having the power 'to send voters into a state of catatonic indifference',[17] and some Conservative candidates citing confusion about its meaning as an issue on the doorstep when canvassing for votes.[18] Critical voices cited it as a factor in David Cameron's inability to secure an overall parliamentary majority despite Labour's failings in office,[19] accusing him of being unable to connect with his party or the wider public about the fundamental problems facing Britain. Coalition with the Liberal Democrats was an essential compromise to get the Conservatives restored to national power.[20] Cameron appeared undeterred by his incomplete success: as Prime Minister he continued to promote the values and agenda of 'The Big Society', albeit within a coalition framework tinged with political expediency. Following the coalition's formation in May 2010, in one of his first high-profile press conferences alongside his Liberal Democrat Deputy Prime Minister Nick Clegg, Cameron indicated how the concept was central to the party's coalition agreement and aims for coalition government.[21] Clegg endorsed this position. The official Cabinet Office document that supported the policy affirmed its essence as follows:

> Our Conservative–Liberal Democrat Government has come together with a driving ambition: to put more power and opportunity into people's hands. We want to give citizens, communities and local government the power and information they need to come together, solve the problems they face and build the Britain they want. We want society – the families, networks, neighbourhoods and communities that form the fabric of so much of our everyday lives – to be bigger and stronger than ever before. Only when people and communities are given more power and take more responsibility can we achieve fairness and opportunity for all.[22]

Despite such cross-party support for this localist and decentralised political agenda being proposed to run through the heart of the coalition government's decision-making and policy process, debate over the precise meaning of the term has continued in the election aftermath. Some political observers claimed that despite Cameron's buoyant rhetoric, during the first six months of his premiership from May 2010 onwards, his high-profile policy stuttered along and hovered on the brink of collapse.[23] In response, David Cameron has consistently and vigilantly argued that this policy agenda represented a remoulding of a more compassionate form of Conservatism for the post-bureaucratic political era, replacing Labour's 'big government' model with the Conservatives' 'big society'[24] alternative. Within such a framework, Cameron has sought to utilise figures such as the academic, Phillip Blond, and the social entrepreneur Baron Wei, with his focus on enhanced 'social capital' and innovative decentralised social activity, as prominent supporters of his agenda. In turn, they have been dubbed Cameron's 'Big Society gurus', broadly endorsing the coalition government's critique of Labour's state-heavy approach during its 13 years in power, and, bolstered by the emergence of bodies such as 'The Big Society Network' (now defunct), they have sought to generate greater social energy and community activity by applying a bottom-up rather than a top-down model of socio-political action.

Blond has been a key influence behind the 'Big Society' blueprint, and, as the founder of the tank-tank 'Respublica'[25] (from 2009), he has emerged as the architect of the 'Red Tory'[26] vision that espouses a more compassionate and less individualistic form of Conservatism, yet rejects a powerful state. It has been succinctly summarised as follows:

> A commitment to the progressive merits of tradition and social conservatism and the need to build ethos-driven institutions, and a new Tory economics that distributed property, market access and educational excellence to all.[27]

A Conservative-minded, original thinker, Blond has echoed the sentiments of David Willetts in arguing 'that the fundamental objective of Conservative politics should be a healthy civil society',[28] with a more explicit emphasis on the importance of community and 'mutualism',[29] yet featuring activities and services that are not the sole preserve of an all-powerful bureaucratic state. Blond's argument is both anti-statist and focused on community cohesion, rejecting the bureaucracy of New Labour and the post-war model of welfare delivery, while also desiring '"red Tory" communitarianism, socially conservative but sceptical of neoliberal economics'.[30] Such a viewpoint rejects both the dominance of the state as an agent of delivering standardisation, which Blond describes as the 'the great destroyer of wealth and opportunity',[31] and the New Right's ideological prescription of an inflated status and supremacy for the free-market in influencing policy-making. Blond has repeatedly offered a scathing critique of the modern New Right agenda as having produced 'an argument for free markets but a failure to deliver them',[32] or provide a fairer distribution of wealth and resources. He prescribes instead a paternalistic and community-led approach to shaping social policy, and he views the emergence of this policy approach as:

> A response to what I think is an historically unprecedented situation, which is the destruction of both the standard left and standard right positions. We're now in a situation where both are busted flushes.[33]

This vision is aligned with enhanced levels of government efficiency alongside a more streamlined state which, combined with a more diverse and innovative range of service providers, aims to deliver wider social policy improvements and stake-holding opportunities for ordinary citizens, for, as Blond has argued:

> we have followed the standard model for, goodness knows, some sixty years that the state can deliver all, and the state has failed. During the time under New Labour we pumped more money into the state than ever before and actually all the indices fell – social mobility fell, the ability of people to transform their lives dropped, poverty increased. What the Big Society is saying is that the state hasn't been working, how can we make it work? It is a pro-poor, pro-society agenda.[34]

In further developing his argument, Cameron has proclaimed that this new political approach would represent a 'big advance for people power', and that 'my great passion is building the big society... (to) turn government completely on its head',[35] due to the creation of a less 'statist' model of government as a consequence. This line of argument has been described by another leading proponent of the 'Big Society' as a rejection of 'a diet of top-down prescription and centralised government'.[36] Blond has gone on to argue under the aegis of his think-tank that the role of collective and 'community' action should be an important feature of modern and rebranded Conservatism, and this focus represents an implicit rejection of the Thatcherite 'New Right' individualist analysis of society. In claiming that the policy is 'pro-poor', this appears to challenge post-1979 Conservative policies that promoted a free-market model of government featuring a 'rolled-back' state and low taxation, yet which created a socio-economic climate which broadly appeared to favour the better-off members of society.[37] This 21st century approach, moulded on the back of three successive general election defeats, aspires to broaden the party's electoral appeal while maintaining the general Conservative rejection of the state's ability to provide the answer to society's problems, broadly adhering to the right-of-centre viewpoint which maintains an 'embedded scepticism about the benefits of public expenditure'.[38] Nevertheless, the viewpoint of Blond explicitly argues that both the neo-liberal 'market-state' of the 'New Right' under Thatcher's guidance and the more socially liberal and interventionist tendencies of 'New Labour' under the Blair–Brown axis, have ultimately failed to meet the needs and demands of the wider population:

> Under the auspices of both the state and the market, a vast body of disenfranchised and disengaged citizens has been constituted... stripped of their culture by the Left and their capital by the Right, and in such nakedness they enter the trading floor of life with only their labour to sell. Proletarianised and segregated, the individuals created by the market–state settlement can never really form a genuine society: lack(ing) the social capital to create such an association and the economic basis to sustain it.[39]

From an academic perspective, therefore, Blond has sought to consolidate and bolster Cameron's attempts to shape a Conservative political agenda that has an ideological anchor and an enhanced social policy focus and emphasis, promoting a framework for policy-making that values the importance of society and community, yet is not exclusively dominated by the power of the state, and which seeks its withdrawal from everyday life:

> The Big Society, let me put it at its most simple, is helping people to help each other so we can help our neighbours, our communities and renew the places where we live and rebuild our society... the Big Society is saying something is wrong with the traditional approaches... what's happened is we've taken away power and opportunity from more and more people and put it in the centre... it is about putting ordinary people in the driving seat.[40]

Public response to 'The Big Society', austerity and a smaller state

Conservative Party activists have appeared to acknowledge the appeal of this concept in rebranding and remarketing some core Conservative values, with one lay party worker arguing that this policy agenda is 'extremely complementary to Conservative Party traditions of the "small state", "localism" and the "empowerment of the individual"'.[41] However, despite claims of the 'Big Society' having an ideological coherence and consistency with the Conservative Party's overall 'localism' agenda of recent years, parts of the media, the political commentariat and indeed the wider general public have continued to be frustrated and confused at the perceived 'fuzziness' of what it actually means in practice, continually asking for further. In this context, two opinion polls in mid-2011 – approximately a year after Cameron became Prime Minister – suggested that 'the public are increasingly confused by the concept'.[42] One persisting public belief, as expressed in opinion polls and British Social Attitudes surveys, is that, despite a short-term growth in concern about the level of government spending as the New Labour era progressed, certain key social and welfare policies should remain the fundamental responsibility of the state:

> ... it is apparent that a large proportion of the public nevertheless feel that welfare provision is mainly the responsibility of the government. This may call into question the level of likely support for the Conservative idea of the 'Big Society'.[43]

Along with a sceptical public, even 'Big Society' supporters such as David Willetts have appeared to acknowledge that this strategic policy approach faces practical problems in terms of implementation, as well as risks for the Conservative Party's image. They argue that the emphasis of the 'Big Society' on community-led voluntarism reveals an ignorance of practical realities in terms of policy delivery and implementation, and so generates a negative reaction towards the Conservatives by leading people to 'think that Conservatives hate the state'.[44] One commentator has observed that there doesn't appear to be 'any coherent means by which efforts to mend the broken society can be co-ordinated'.[45] A key cross-party report published exactly one year after the launch of 'The Big Society'[46] subsequently claimed that the government 'has failed to properly explain it... amid fears it will be concentrated in wealthy suburbs and leave the poorest parts of the country behind'.[47] Such apparent failings of communication and delivery have exposed the Cameron-led government's inability to transmit effectively its message in relation to this high-profile policy – a particularly notable failure given that it was the poorer parts of society that 'The Big Society' was supposed to focus on, and that Cameron highlighted it as one of his government's potentially most enduring legacies. Amidst such ongoing public confusion, Cameron was forced to promote what was claimed to be the fourth relaunch of this flagship policy in May 2011,[48] again emphasising the need for greater voluntarism and charitable activity stemming from community level rather than the unerring control of the hegemonic state. In doing so he offered a brand of Conservatism that presented a fresh image; a break from the past in rhetorical emphasis at least, being detached from both the New Right's individualist neo-liberal focus and the perceived bureaucratic tendencies of New Labour in government. In reaffirming his support for this policy, Cameron referred to his ongoing faith in it, and described it as his 'passion' and 'mission'[49] in politics.

However, further criticism of 'The Big Society' policy emerged in autumn 2011, when the House of Commons Public Administration Committee restated practical concerns, declaring that the proposed devolution and decentralisation of power would not work without radical structural reforms to the civil service in order to meet the demands of the new policy.[50] Further critical comments came from the same committee at the end of 2011, when it declared that the public and voluntary sectors remain confused about the implications of the Big Society, with the Chair of the Committee, Bernard Jenkin, adding that the government's ongoing focus on greater localism and devolution of political decision-making would take a period of time to impact on broader public perceptions of its policy:

> This was never going to happen overnight. To make a change of this magnitude successfully will take a generation. It represents a whole new way of government. However, so far, the government has not been clear enough about what the Big Society means in practical terms.[51]

Such concerns followed claims from both political opponents and erstwhile allies that government spending cuts were further hampering the implementation of this policy ethos, and that, indeed, the whole political approach was a smokescreen to mask the significant public spending cuts being pursued from May 2010 onwards. This was partially acknowledged by a key instigator of the policy, Philip Blond, who in early 2011 stated that 'the cuts as administered I think risk damaging the infrastructure of the Big Society',[52] and who later in the year claimed that the policy was 'failing' and being undermined by the sheer depth and scale of the government's retrenchment agenda, amidst rumours of a cooling of his relations with, and influence over, the Prime Minister.[53] Similar critical conclusions were reached by an independent analysis of the policy a year later (mid-2012), with the think tank Civil Exchange concluding that the flagship policy had been 'undermined by cuts and distrust'[54] in the eyes of the wider public. Cameron's response to claims that public spending cuts were undermining the 'Big Society' ethos was to launch the 'Big Society Bank' in the spring of 2012 as a public-private source of funding that aspired to provide 'start-up capital for social enterprises'.[55] Such a pro-active move, which appeared to reaffirm a notable role for the state in this revised model of society, has formed part of a vigilant response by the Prime Minister in response to the viewpoint that austerity has undermined the whole concept of the 'Big Society'. This argument has been heightened as the government's spending cuts have impacted from 2010–11 onwards and on the remainder of the parliament up to 2015.

Nevertheless the concerned and pessimistic outlook has been further articulated by a prominent figure from the charity sector, Dame Elisabeth Hoodless, who claimed that the coalition government's slashing of public expenditure in pursuit of deficit-reduction, the re-invigoration of voluntarism and the reduction of reliance on the state would, paradoxically, erode the very principles of voluntarism that such a devolved, communitarian political agenda sought to encourage, claiming that 'there are other ways of saving money without destroying the volunteer army.'[56] This allegation followed reports that the charitable sector, the 'supposed vanguard of the Big Society',[57] and central to the delivery of its agenda, was facing massive cuts in government funding and subsidies as part of the coalition government's determined attempts to drive down the national deficit from mid-2010 onwards, with an estimated 7,000 such bodies having to close during 2011–12.[58] Many otherwise civic-minded citizens are also too busy either maintaining or seeking employment during a difficult economic period to have the time or commitment to engage in the community-based voluntarism envisaged by the Big Society's approach to public policy,[59] as well as having less money to donate to charity due to the adverse economic climate. Some critics and bodies such as 'Volunteering England' have even claimed that charities are being exploited, and the unemployed targeted, in the name of work experience within a 'Big Society' narrative, both being expected to provide their services free of charge as a means of reducing the costs of private work programme providers.[60] Such developments strike at the heart of the argument inherent to the Big Society's agenda, that a smaller state will encourage greater levels of citizen engagement and charitable activity. Optimists, however, have continued to argue that there are innovative means of getting round such challenging socio-economic realities, as outlined below:

> When times are tough hardly anything is protected, and amongst the victims of any recession are voluntary giving and voluntary activity and we have to be realistic about that. However what the likes of Steve Hilton has brought David Cameron's Conservatism is ..... using social media for new forms of community action and volunteering.[61]

Whether utilisation of new technology will fill the charitable void remains to be seen, given such an unconvinced wider reaction towards the policy in an environment of public spending cuts. The government has been regularly forced on the offensive to advocate this overarching policy direction, with further attempts to clarify the precise sentiments of the 'Big Society' made by Cabinet members on a regular basis. For example Baroness Warsi, then Chairman of the Conservative Party, sought to define it in a concise manner in the House of Lords in February 2011:

> The big society is defined by many in this House as being what most of them have done for most of their lives. It is a volunteering, social action, philanthropic approach to life, but it is also about the opening up of public services to local control and devolution of power.[62]

However, the policy's inability to capture the wider public and indeed Conservative imagination could perhaps be seen in its failure to make the formal agenda of the 2011 Conservative Party Conference,[63] while there was only one limited mention of it during David Cameron's conference speech in 2012, when he aligned it with the voluntarist spirit of the 2012 London Olympics workforce: 'And those Games-Makers. You know, I've spent three years trying to explain the Big Society... they did it beautifully in just three weeks.'[64]

David Cameron sought to re-ignite its relevance by linking the 'Big Society' as a key driver and narrative behind the New Year's honours list of 2011/12,[65] suggesting that he was not willing to totally abandon the concept despite the setbacks affecting its overall evolution and progress. He was supported in retaining some faith in this policy agenda by the prominent commentator Anthony Seldon, who has argued that the policy, despite being unfavourably likened to Tony Blair's vague and uninspiring 'Third Way', still had the potential to act as the 'pro-active' driving force, the moral compass and the sense of political coherence for domestic policy that Cameron had so far struggled to articulate.[66]

The reaction to the 'Big Society' from left and right

Left-of-centre figures have been critical of this new Conservative-led agenda and sceptical of claims that the policy does not have right-wing or 'neo-liberal' implications. This viewpoint also expresses fears that the Big Society's emphasis and reliance on voluntarism and localised schemes could affect the provision of key public services. In its rejection of the hegemony of the state as a public service provider, such a policy agenda, it is feared, could initiate a return to the mentality of the Victorian era when state welfare provision, the effective regulation of standards and the assurance of 'safety nets' for recipients of key social benefits were limited, and both public and charitable welfare provision was more arbitrary and less uniform and universal in nature.[67] In practice, there is fear that such an approach would mark a dismantling rather than a restructuring of the post -war welfare state. Voluntarism has, therefore, been lambasted by many political and academic figures on the centre-left who claim that the term 'Big Society' is merely a vague euphemism for the justification of savage public spending cuts and a considerable shrinking of the state's size, egalitarian scope and remit, regardless of David Cameron's soothing vocabulary and renewed focus on the concept of 'society'.[68] Indeed, some leftist commentators have issued explicit warnings of the dangers of this approach, arguing that the Cameron regime threatens to bypass the goals of the Thatcher era, claiming that 'Where she privatized state-run industries, the Cameron government would dismantle the state itself' and that Cameron 'retains the misleading aura of a pragmatist, disguising the fervour of his anti-state dogma'.[69]

However, despite such media, academic and broader public scepticism about the nature of the concept, following the 2010 General Election result Labour politicians were forced to adapt and respond to the agenda of the 'Big Society' and its associated vocabulary, with concerted efforts being made to mould rival, distinct political messages in order to both contribute to and challenge Cameron's revived Conservative narrative about social justice and the welfare state, all tinged with a left-of-centre political hue.[70] This has been evident in the appearance of alternative, though similar, concepts based on localised co-operative activity, namely 'Blue Labour',[71] 'The Purple Book'[72] and the 'good society',[73] the last phrase, was utilised by Labour's arch-revisionist Anthony Crosland in the 1950s.[74] All of them are responses to the perceived growth of an overbearing state. These developments reflect the traditional teleocratic emphasis of Labour policy and its focus on aiming for devised or utopian ends based on some form of planning for a future socio-political settlement. However the 'Big Society' approach does not attach such an explicit plan or specifically determinist outcome to its agenda, although it does align itself with some elements of New Labour's repeated focus on 'rights and responsibilities' within society. Such reactive developments from the Labour Party have been evident under Ed Miliband's leadership from September 2010 onwards, as he has sought to promote a vision of government (initially influenced by Lord Maurice Glasman), that also offered a reduced reliance on the role of the state, an embracement of more responsible capitalism and a return to the pre-1945 focus of Labour governments, with emphasis on utilising voluntarist and co-operative activity to deliver public services where appropriate.[75] Although the Labour left can cite the various failings of pre-1945 Labour governments as a reason not to hark back to an illusory 'golden age', this reciprocal development on the political left-of-centre mat be evidence for a degree of success in Cameron's promotion of more innovative social agenda for the Conservative Party and the need for political opponents to adapt accordingly, appearing to embrace a less 'statist' agenda in the process. This has been a clear indicator that Labour has been forced to rethink its approach to public service delivery along more pragmatic, flexible and creative lines within the specific context of an economic slump and joined to an austerity agenda.

Other figures from the modernising wing of the Conservative Party have also attempted to sharpen the term's vague meaning into a more penetrating political entity with the potential to maximise government performance. This has been based on the premise that it will work in the party's favour by providing enhanced clarity to the wider electorate, although there have been suggestions that it does not have to become an explicitly partisan or 'party political' entity in the process:

> The big society, which is ultimately about creating and releasing latent sources of social energy, is an extraordinarily ambitious conception of how this underperformance occurred, and how to address it... The big society is not itself either a left- or right-wing idea.[76]

Such sentiments clearly imply that in an ostensibly 'post-ideological' era of less adversarial politics, the 'Big Society' project could be comfortably pursued by either a Conservative or Labour administration in a restructured political paradigm. In the autumn of 2011 and again in 2012 the Respublica think-tank lobbied the Labour Party Conference amid claims that some senior Labour figures wanted to 'save the Big Society agenda'.[77] As a corollary to this, in late 2012 influential Labour MP, Jon Cruddas, claimed that Labour had 'missed a trick'[78] in failing to embrace its own version of the 'Big Society', and in his role as Labour's policy review co-coordinator he stated that 'We want to build our own version of the big society. That's going to be a big part of our policy review over the next 12 months'.[79] This approach endorses the view that the 'Big Society' transcends traditional left–right politics, but many reformers and advocates of this agenda within the Conservative Party remain wary of Labour embracing and effectively trying to 'hijack' this policy approach, primarily due to the belief that it is essentially in conflict with the 'Fabianist' and centralising instincts of Labour governments. As one of its leading advocates on the Conservative parliamentary benches has argued, the 'Big Society' idea fundamentally rejects:

> the state-first Fabian dogma that is the specific political target of the big society ... (but rather) emphasises the renewal of social capital, localism and greater personal empowerment. However, the big society also contains a robust critique of neoliberalism... critical of the fundamentalism of free market uber-libertarians, who see no role for the state at all... (and) is ultimately derived from the ideas of Edmund Burke and Adam Smith, who emphasized not rampant but limited markets; not the over-mighty state but free and independent institutions; not personal greed but trust and sympathy.[80]

This viewpoint argues that the essential localism and personal empowerment of the 'Big Society' rejects both the statism of the left and the neo-liberalism associated with the free-market Thatcherism of the 1980s, and is essentially a modern, original and mainstream idea in tune with traditional Conservative philosophical instincts (as well as the 'localist' agenda of the Liberal Democrats), and aligned with the natural, instinctive communitarian tendencies evident across broader society. In advocating the 'Big Society' agenda, its key supporters have described it as representing an original fusion of political concepts and structures, reflecting 'not the two-way opposition of state vs. individual, but the three-way relation of enabling state, active individual and linking institution'.[81] Other Conservatives with interests in the Big Society agenda do, however, acknowledge some potential for Labour to exploit its key themes, principally due to the 'communitarian strand in Labour... going back to the Methodist tradition of dissent'.[82] From another ideological angle, however, there has been some right-wing criticism of David Cameron's apparent abandonment of the economics-driven, individualist, neo-liberal focus of the Thatcher era, which has consolidated the mainstream criticism that the policy is vague and unclear.[83] One backbencher has appeared to reflect the sentiments of many more 'traditionalist' Conservative MPs, in describing it as 'intangible and incomprehensible... odd and unpersuasive',[84] while a prominent Internet-based Conservative commentator has labelled the policy 'as intellectually interesting as it is useless on the doorstep. It's so far removed from working families' current concerns that polls find, over time, that it is understood less rather than more'.[85]

Such wide-ranging criticism has generated concerns that the post-2005 Conservative agenda of David Cameron has abandoned the hard-won political territory that the party seized after 1979, as well as becoming detached from the clear and coherent identity associated with it. This has been due to the emphasis placed by Cameron on an enhanced and revitalised social policy agenda that stresses the importance of co-operation and the benevolent 'mutualism' of relationships within 'society'. The nature of this revised agenda has raised suspicions from the right that the 'dead hand' of the state will continue to be unerringly and prominently present within such an approach. Such suspicion has perhaps been justified in policy terms in the form of Cameron's reluctance to cut taxes or make savings in key public services such as the NHS, which the Conservatives pledged during the 2010 General Election would be ring-fenced from any future spending cuts, despite a common right-wing complaint that it is an inefficient and excessively bureaucratic organisation. Although there is fierce political debate about the true nature of Cameron's controversial NHS reforms (see Chapter 7), Cameron's counter-argument to internal critics from the right is that his own specific vision of an increasingly 'rolled-back' yet benevolent state model is actually consistent with one of Thatcher's greatest political and philosophical inspirations, for as Hayek himself argued: 'The virtues these people possessed (British)... were independence and self-reliance, individual initiative and local responsibility, the successful reliance on voluntary activity... and a healthy suspicion of power and authority'.[86]

The above language of Hayek is notable for its explicit rejection of the 'collectivist' state whose growth was said to unerringly accelerate under left of-centre governments, and which established what has been described by Phillip Blond as 'the rotten post-war settlement of British politics'.[87] Hayek's sentiments can therefore be said to be wholly consistent with the support for this voluntarist emphasis and the vision for reduced statist welfare provisions as espoused by both Cameron's 'Big Society' gurus and bodies such as the Centre for Social Justice. Cameron's revised welfare and social agenda has sought to maintain a delicate balance of preserving some inherent Conservative traditions while simultaneously developing a new and more refined social dimension to the party's contemporary image, calling for 'greater citizen involvement and empowerment... (resulting in) the amplification and development of earlier ideas of compassionate Conservatism and post-bureaucratic politics'.[88] Such desire for a more compassionate Conservative image has been reflected in Cameron's rhetorical focus on 'society', which appears to be an implicit rejection of the tough yet

somewhat uncaring reputation the party became associated with in relation to its social policy attitudes during its sustained period in power
between 1979 and 1997,; this has formed part of Cameron's wider strategy to 'detoxify' the brand.[89] His renewed focus on a refreshed approach
to social policy and its associated issues can be linked back to the period
when he was striving to establish himself as an effective Leader of the
Opposition, when he promised to adopt a distinct policy focus and
stated that he was: 'going to be as radical a social reformer as Margaret
Thatcher was an economic reformer'.[90]

However, despite some on the right of politics speaking about a 'post-
bureaucratic state'[91] and pushing for a perceived logical conclusion that
entails a radically reduced level of reliance on state-provided welfare
and the need for greater 'marketisation' of its core services, there has
been a broad acceptance among the modernising 'Cameroons' that
the state is required to retain a co-ordinating, if less cumbersome, role
in the delivery of social provision. So, whereas the Thatcherites of the
1980s desired a 'strong state' yet limited government intervention as
a means of delivering the necessary conditions for the 'maintenance
of a free economy'[92] with a reduced emphasis on social and welfare
policy, 21st-century Conservatives acknowledge that markets alone
are not sufficient to tackle the country's 'broken society' and wider
welfare needs. Their 'Big Society' analysis argues that a reformed and
streamlined state's framework can be effectively used in instigating and
formulating generic social policy goals and then devolving the process
to allow innovative and 'localised' policies to flourish in a way most
appropriate to tackling challenging social conditions and associated
problems in the long-term, with the state ultimately stepping back from
such policies' direct implementation. By supporting and promoting the
different, variable dimensions of government-initiated activity, a more
detached state role can therefore be fused with 'third sector' charities
and localised bodies to provide a 'creative', diffused model of policy
delivery that fragments the role of providing core public services while
also consolidating individual social ambition, saving money and liberating individuals from excessive and centralised 'statism' in the process.
In this respect the politics of Cameron's modern-day Conservatives
ultimately appear to be distinct (but not totally detached) from the
more explicitly libertarian, free market and ideological agenda of the
neo-liberal Thatcherites, with Cameron's essential argument being that:

> Whatever talk there is of a post-bureaucratic state... State action, not
> limited government, is necessary because there is recognition that

however important market-led growth is to fixing the broken society, it is not enough. There are real problems of poverty and social breakdown that a political economy based on the incentives of market forces cannot fix.[93]

However, given the focus on austerity and financial savings as the strategic driving force behind many key government decisions from May 2010 onwards, some critics from the Labour Party and the centre-left of the political spectrum have questioned whether Cameron's vision of a more devolved and 'enabling' welfare state, with an increased focus on self-help and voluntarist providers as opposed to direct state provision, is actually a genuine and original post-Thatcherite policy development or merely an extension of the economic and social priorities of the 1980s and the mood of economic austerity often associated with this historical period. Replacing direct state provision with greater voluntary and charitable involvement is by no means guaranteed to provide a more solid basis for innovative and sustainable social policy development, and indeed, in the worst-case scenario it could create serious risks to both the sustainability and the comprehensive and regulatory aspects of the British welfare state and its historic focus on protecting society's most vulnerable citizens. Therefore, by reducing the hegemonic nature of the state's role as part of the 'Big Society' agenda, yet at the same time pursuing fiscal retrenchment that adversely impacts on the charitable bodies that often bolster state provision (and which were expected to have an enhanced role under the original 'Big Society' model), there is a potential increase in the probability of vulnerable individuals being excluded from 'non-universal' and fragmented welfare provision. Such a prospect has led to high-profile interventions from prominent religious figures also, with the retiring Archbishop of Canterbury Rowan Williams condemning the policy in the summer of 2012 as 'aspirational waffle designed to conceal a deeply damaging withdrawal of the state from its responsibilities to the most vulnerable'.[94] In this context, some critics have claimed that such policies represent a significant movement towards the socio-political trends of the pre-1945 era, when the role of the state was much smaller and the provision of welfare services was sliced between a range of different and more localised providers including charities, friendly societies and voluntary groups. Such a scenario directly conflicts with the more generous and statist 'social democratic' welfare model that has prevailed for the majority of post-war British history, and it is in this respect that the 'Big Society' proponents have struggled to convince the sceptical public.

The influence of 'The Big Society' on Conservative social policy

In the context of developing a critique and a background narrative to the evolution of the Conservative Party's new social policy agenda and its approach to a streamlined and genuinely reformed welfare state provision, David Cameron has specifically sought to reframe the image of contemporary Conservatism in relation to its neo-liberal socio-economic agenda of the past, revising and modifying its relationship with the party's Thatcherite legacy in the process.[95] This has led to a more 'compassionate' Conservative analysis of a 'broken' or 'atomised' society that needs to be genuinely healed in the long term, and such 'compassion' appears to have been a distinct contrast to the short-term punitive outlook and broad lack of sympathy aimed in the direction of long-term recipients of the welfare system, as was the tendency of some right-wing Conservative politicians during the 1980s.[96] Yet Cameron's distinct approach to dealing with such a fractured society has not been to call for more state intervention, but instead to argue that the state needs to do less and that other agencies should absorb some of the strain so that 'the active citizen as philanthropist and volunteer'[97] can emerge to take some burden off the state. However, it must be conceded that changes like these will tend to marginalise some of the more vulnerable members of society. In adopting this stance, Cameron has explicitly rejected the state's 'accompanying ideology of centralisation, managerialism and intervention'[98] that has prevailed for most of the post-war period.

Cameron has faced significant difficulties in 'selling' his analysis of society to both his political party and the wider public, as well as struggling to overcome some scepticism about how his less 'statist' solutions can be practically implemented. He has been further hampered by the fact that many politicians, including some Conservative ones, have rejected the blanket and perhaps simplistic 'Big Society' analysis that implied that all aspects of British society were 'broken' and required such a radical overhaul when the Conservative-led coalition came to national power in 2010. For example, London Mayor Boris Johnson has openly questioned the mantra,[99] rejecting its arguably simplistic conclusions as 'piffle'. In his continuous affirmation and determined emphasis on how 'broken' Britain was when the Conservatives returned to national office in 2010, it could be legitimately claimed that 'the Conservative leader is in danger of exaggerating the social problems facing Britain today'.[100] Certainly there are significant enclaves of poverty and deprivation throughout British society, (exacerbated by rising levels of unemployment as a consequence of the prolonged economic recession), many of which are long-established and have persisted under different governments that have administered state welfare provision during modern history. However, critics of Cameron's notion of 'broken Britain', from both the left and right of British politics, argue that its analysis is too primitive and its message too gimmicky, and that it needs to be grounded in greater practical realism, without distorting or exaggerating the state of contemporary society in order to generate party political benefit. Political opponents have also questioned whether such 'compassion' and focus on greater efficiency is in fact illusory in nature, and is a mere rhetorical device to justify significant public spending cutbacks and an ideology-driven reduction in the size of the state.

Ultimately, if this new socio-economic policy approach by the Conservative Party is to be constructive and effective in the long term, able to carry the necessary weight and subsequent public support, it requires intellectual rigour and practical reality behind it. Iain Duncan Smith's experiences with the Centre for Social Justice and his subsequent focus on proposed socio-political remedies appears to have the potential to instil a greater degree of realism and credibility into this overall hypothesis of British society, although the nature and effectiveness of his detailed proposals in this key area of public policy are open to conjecture. Thus, in the context of the search for a distinctive post-Thatcherite identity, David Cameron's leadership has aligned itself with the desire for a speculative post-bureaucratic model of governance as identified and alluded to by contemporary academics and political thinkers. There has subsequently developed significant further analysis of the key socio-economic issues and problems that exist within contemporary Britain and how best to address them. The 'Big Society' is a prominent example of how an innovative and revised critique of social justice can best be formulated within a reconstructed state, coupled with a revised social and welfare policy agenda which acknowledges the communitarian tendencies within modern society. In promising a renewed and changed approach to the social policy sphere, David Cameron has been a central figure in this high-profile socio-political debate since his accession to senior political office, but both in opposition (2005–10) and in government from 2010 onwards, his arguments for a genuinely 'changed' post-bureaucratic vision of government for the future, as well as its capacity to effectively and practically deliver key and innovative social policies, have struggled to convince much of the political community, let alone the wider British public.

6
Social policy case study 3: The Free Schools policy

This chapter focuses on one of the most prominent elements of social policy pursued by the Conservative–Liberal Democrat coalition government since May 2010, namely education, and specifically the Free Schools agenda. As a high-profile component of the 2010 Conservative Party manifesto,[1] the proposal came to practical policy fruition within the coalition agreement with the Liberal Democrats in seeking to 'promote the reform of schools in order to ensure that new providers can enter the state school system in response to parental demand (and) that all schools have greater freedom over the curriculum'.[2] This initiative has subsequently provided a pertinent indicator of how Conservative social policy has evolved and developed since the party lost national power in 1997. As a policy area with extensive public impact, education has also illustrated the Cameron leadership's interpretation of what 'social justice' entails in contemporary society, while seeking to maximise its impact in the process. The development and evolution of this agenda and its associated aims and socio-political principles provide, therefore, an effective means of assessing how the modern Conservative Party has sought to adapt and infuse its own ideological heritage and distinct political traditions into social policy formulation. The actual policy outcome that has emerged also reflects a pragmatic reaction to both coalition government and the realities of a political landscape moulded by 13 years of a Labour administration. The Conservatives' educational initiative demands appropriate analysis and evaluation as to the extent to which it resembles the dominant political traditions that preceded it, namely the New Labour period of government (1997–2010), or the Thatcherite and Major era of Conservative rule over its 18-year duration from 1979 onwards.

The Free Schools policy provides an insight into the approach of 21st-century Conservatism towards public educational provision in the UK, exposing the specific influences that have shaped the policy while also comparing and contrasting the extent of continuity and change in the outlook of the contemporary Conservative Party leadership. Exploring comparisons with the approach of previous governments of the modern political era regarding this policy sphere opens to scrutiny the nature of mainstream British Conservatism's reformulated, 'modernised' and much-heralded compassionate attitude towards social justice and associated policy-making in the 21st century. In particular, it enables us to assess the perspective held by the Cameron Conservatives that the left's conventional vision of social justice has fundamentally failed to deliver in its desired aims over recent periods of Labour government, and indeed for most of the post-war 'consensus' era between 1945 and 1979. Within this context, according to one contemporary Conservative moderniser, there has been an 'internal difficulty on the left in that many of the things that were designed to support social justice... actually ended up hurting it'.[3] This rejection of such conventional left-of-centre 'statist' and bureaucratic solutions to issues connected to social justice has been evident in the post-1979 Conservative focus on education as a key policy area that can actively improve social mobility and generally enhance the quality of life of British citizens, but with a greater focus on individualism as an alternative framework in which to operate.

Modern Conservatism's approach to educational policy has been fuelled by a prevailing, influential political ethos of the post-1979 period, namely the 'belief in markets and a minimal state... (and the) view that the route to tackling poverty and educational underachievement lies in greater responsibility',[4] rejecting the state-knows-best ethos in the process. This acceptance of a greater degree of autonomy in education has been accepted, to differing degrees, by all governments since 1979, encouraged by external bodies such as the OECD that have claimed that 'countries that delegate managerial discretion to head-teachers and school governing bodies often have higher educational attainment'.[5] Indeed, it is a valid, important area of discussion as to whether this socio-political viewpoint – instilled into the public policy agenda after the Conservatives came to power in 1979 – was altered by the long period of exile from national office during a sustained spell of centre-left government that moulded its own distinct political agenda and culture, and whether a genuinely original brand of 'New Conservatism' emerged as a result. From another angle, this policy also provides a means of indicating how the party's political aspirations have been affected and influenced by the formation of a coalition government in alliance with a junior partner (the Liberal Democrats), who traditionally have a different ideological outlook on such matters, and whose conventional position on education has appeared to rely on the dominance of the state, based on the premise that 'liberalism could only be delivered by "big government solutions"'.[6] However, as the coalition has been formed and evolved since May 2010, some key areas of common ground in educational policy have emerged, namely a common focus on a more localist outlook, as well as specific policies such as the 'pupil premium', a Liberal Democrat policy which the Conservatives have also enthusiastically supported, and which has been claimed to represent the 'freeing up and empowerment of disadvantaged individuals... as much a Conservative as a Liberal Democrat policy'.[7]

The Origins of the Free Schools Policy

Following the Conservative Party's ejection from national office in 1997, the subsequent years of political opposition led to a period of sustained introspection and review of the party's broader political identity and purpose. One of the many policy areas that the party sought to address in terms of formulating a revised and refreshed agenda was educational provision within the wider sphere of social policy. Education is a policy area that has the potential to impact on a significant proportion of the electorate, and its identification as a key issue was part of a specific strategy of the Cameron leadership to 'decontaminate' the party's brand by focusing on issues that had a more 'communitarian' emphasis, with the party keen to project a more 'compassionate' image. In doing so, Cameron sought to attach to such policy areas a distinctly Conservative perspective, and the contemporary Conservative Party has therefore sought to develop a contemporary social policy agenda that has aspired to the achievement of enhanced social justice coupled with improved social mobility, implying a reduced role for the state as part of the process. This would be a challenging target for any political party, and the fusion of these motives at the heart of educational policy-making were the crux of the party's attempts to devise an alternative viable counter-narrative to the approach of New Labour in office.

Arriving in office after an unprecedented 13 years of Labour government, the Conservatives inherited a state of affairs that had seen New Labour under both Blair and Brown, despite some initial caution, invest significant amounts of public spending in core educational provisions. The average increase in education spending was 3.9% a year during Labour's period in office,[8] with funds steadily pumped into the service's buildings and infrastructure by a largely centralised and interventionist 'command and control' style of government. However, the New Labour approach to key social policy areas like education also retained some aspects of local autonomy in pragmatic recognition of the significant educational reforms of the Conservative administrations between 1979 and 1997,[9] and in the words of one academic commentator 'New Labour took the Conservative infrastructure (on education policy) and gave it meat and teeth'.[10] There was a gradual build-up by the post-1997 Labour administrations of programmes and educational initiatives which entailed major capital investment from the centre, a prime example being the 'Building Schools for the Future' (BSF) policy, which emerged during Labour's third term from 2005 onwards; it had the lofty ambition of rebuilding or refurbishing all of England's 3,500 secondary schools, at an estimated cost of £55 billion. This policy clearly adhered to the party's 1997 high-profile focus on 'education, education, education', and it was characteristic of the trend towards increased bureaucratisation and educational documentation that had appeared in the modern political era from 1979 onwards, with 'the pace of reform being especially frenetic after the victory of New Labour in 1997'.[11] However, in an acknowledgement of the neo-liberal trends of the 1980s, while a significant degree of centralised funding was a consequence of this policy, the use of PFI[12] to deliver many such educational projects appeared to indicate some degree of 'neo-liberal' market-driven influence on the traditional model of state intervention and investment in public services. However, the steady emergence of such significant centralised planning and bureaucracy that accompanied this policy initiative appeared to downgrade the focus and emphasis on schools autonomously and responsibly managing their own organisational affairs alongside the enhanced educational choice for the individual that had been established by the modern (post-1979) Conservative Party.[13] It was the extent of alleged bureaucratic expenditure from central government that generated criticism from the then Conservative opposition, who claimed that a future Conservative government would be committed to tackling such statist tendencies which stemmed from 'New Labour (being) excessively managerial in its conception of both the private and public sector'.[14] As a consequence, the axing of BSF was one of the first major decisions taken by Michael Gove after becoming Secretary of State for Education in May 2010, with the costs and bureaucracy cited as the key reason why the programme could no longer be justified in a period of austerity.

As innovative and original policy-making in all spheres became more in demand as the economic downturn bit from 2008 onwards, a revived emphasis on fiscal conservatism led to a desire within the Conservative Party for the development of social policies that would provide enhanced value for money for the taxpayer, yet which would also offer the prospect of strengthening the traditional Conservative ethos of individualism alongside the more recent emphasis on compassion and social justice within social policy provision. One commentator has observed that the economic crisis was a key turning point and arguably a major disruption to the Conservative modernisation project, when 'an era of austerity and serious economics had dawned'.[15] This development would initiate a more frugal approach to government and impose greater flexibility, enterprise and a more fragmented model of government on the whole.

Within the generally expensive sphere of social policy matters, educational policy has traditionally been an area of heavy public spending, and this motivated a significant surge of Conservative interest in an educational policy with a more efficient and cost-effective aura that originated on the European continent, namely the 'Free Schools' initiative. This policy derived from the socio-political experiences of Sweden from the early 1990s onwards. The Swedes elected a non-socialist government for the first time since the 1930s, and as a result of such a radical political swing the country's long-established centralised welfare model and bureaucratic educational system came under governmental scrutiny. One academic observer has described such a development as an acknowledgement that the global influences of 'Neo-liberal politics (had) come to Sweden',[16] somewhat belatedly compared to the New Right hegemony that had infiltrated Britain and the USA during the 1980s.

'Free Schools' were devised as a decentralised alternative to universal policy delivery by the centralised and bureaucratic state, and as a model of educational provision the policy has been described as offering 'state-independent schools' whose functions would be delivered by 'independent providers of different sorts'.[17] The localised role and focus of such bodies would, according to supporters, remove the cost and inefficiency of the centralised state, respond to local needs and ultimately provide better value for money for the hard-pressed taxpayer in the long-term. This model of education has experienced significant growth since its inception in Sweden, as 'the number of pupils in free schools has increased from 20,247 in 1995/96 to 95,948 in 2009/10'.[18] A system based on the premise of an enhanced degree of freedom and autonomy from state control was viewed by those on the political right as an attractive, effective and efficient mechanism for increasing overall educational standards, social mobility and individual choice. One academic observer has described such policy trends emerging in Britain as marking a departure from 'a more managed Labour response' in relation to educational policy-making after 1997, and instead moving towards 'a more libertarian Conservative one'.[19] Such schools could utilise a wider, more diverse range of mechanisms to raise standards while enjoying enhanced efficiency and dynamic detachment from the state, with private and community sector interests having increased opportunity to access and influence the delivery of educational services. This educational model seemed, therefore, to have the potential to deliver better long-term value for money for the taxpayer, while in the process challenging what had traditionally been a state-dominant approach in this policy sphere.

Arguments for the Free Schools Policy

The Free Schools policy attracted Cameron from an early phase of his leadership, as the Conservative Party sought to reinvent its social policy agenda in the wake of a demoralising third successive electoral defeat. From the outset, his primary aim as leader was to develop innovative policies that would generate wider public and electoral support to avoid a potentially fatal fourth general election defeat in a row. As the policy's formulation developed, Cameron's Shadow Education Secretary, Michael Gove, emerged as a key figure in its evolution. In pushing the Free Schools agenda, he justified his support by attacking Labour's record in this policy area after over a decade in power. Apparently damning statistics that 'almost half of children from deprived backgrounds leave school without a single good GCSE',[20] provided some evidence that broader social, and specifically educational, inequality had been maintained and even exacerbated under New Labour's 'statist' public service agenda – such a prominent feature of its period in office. This bolstered Gove's faith in decentralised and devolved Free Schools as a solution to the problem. He envisaged such institutions as a means of delivering the vital socio-political assets of greater social mobility and enhanced social justice for traditionally disadvantaged parts of society, with such specific terms forming key elements of the vocabulary of 'modern' Conservatism. As Gove himself argued:

> Schools should be engines of social mobility ... the education system isn't delivering social mobility at the moment... we wanted to

overturn that injustice (and) we looked to social democratic Sweden for reform. Fifteen years ago the Swedes decided to challenge declining standards by breaking the bureaucratic stranglehold over educational provision and welcome private providers into the state system. Since they introduced their reforms, 900 new schools have been established in Sweden, a country with a population one-sixth the size of England. Those new providers have not only created schools with higher standards than before, the virtuous dynamic created by the need to respond to competition from new providers has forced existing schools to raise their game. There is a direct correlation between more choice and higher standards; with the biggest improvements in educational outcomes being generated in those areas with the most new schools.[21]

Michael Gove's confident assertion that greater competition and choice instilled by an influx of enterprising private involvement would raise standards was a controversial one. It challenged some fundamental conventions of the post-1945 welfare state, notably its absolute belief in enhanced localism and decentralisation as opposed to the entrenched 'state knows best' ethos. However, Gove could cite some evidence from Sweden to support his claims that such schools improved overall standards by enhancing competition in the system,[22] and in adopting this stance he appeared to be seeking a return to an era when the state was less comprehensive and controlling in its remit, and where a greater diversity of public service provision existed, offering enhanced choice for the citizen. In doing so, Gove seemed to embrace the legacy of the 20th-century Conservative scholar Michael Oakeshott,[23] who was critical of the left's utopian vision and state-centred approach to shaping and moulding civil society into a more engineered and manipulated direction, which he referred to as an 'enterprise association'. Oakeshott ultimately rejected such an artificial and state-induced society as he saw it, and instead envisaged the alternative development and distinct evolution of a more natural and traditional 'civil association' that would be 'organised as a communal enterprise or undertaking in its own right'.[24] This approach focused on greater individual choice and input at a grassroots level, with the fundamental raison d'être being citizens naturally obeying the rule of law rather than a desired socio-economic outcome being imposed from central government. Such a model of society entails that citizens have roles, values and autonomous social goals within their communities which they are fully conscious of and which are detached from the state's explicit control, direction and instructions. This approach can be aligned with the Free School agenda's emphasis on greater autonomy for key public bodies rooted at community level, such as schools, although the extent to which this could occur due to natural local enterprise and autonomy without the state's guiding hand is a major practical challenge.

The driving-force behind the Free Schools policy is the notion that that providing more varied choice of schools and instilling an enterprising emphasis will create improved standards and address areas of genuine educational need – a policy agenda that has been a dynamic area of modern political debate and dispute between the two major parties, and which has continued to influence the evolution of educational policy since 2010. Cameron's strategy has appeared to want to utilise this and other social policy initiatives as a means of depicting the Conservatives as a forward-looking political party, equating such policies with the dynamic political values of 'progressivism… modernism and the future, as opposed to (Labour's) statism and egalitarianism, (and) to portray New Labour as the party wedded to a backward looking repressive centralism'.[25] Gove visited Sweden in early 2010 to see how such schools worked in practice, and, supported by academic research,[26] developed an enthusiasm for a more diverse selection of educational provision with an enhanced role for the private sector and a consequent greater range of choice for parents and pupils. This culminated in the policy's inclusion as a prominent feature of the 2010 Conservative Party manifesto. Its explicit focus on promoting individual choice and wider social responsibility certainly appeared to have the desired effect, and created a distinct area of 'clear blue water'[27] between the Conservatives and the outgoing Labour government. In pursuing this policy the Conservatives were seeking to establish a sharp 'political contrast between the centralisation of the Brown era and the decentralisation that is characteristic of the philosophy of the (alternative) Cameron government'.[28] The policy's practical form materialised following the return to government in May 2010, and after a period of planning and preparation that entailed 323 bids for Free School status, the first wave of 24 Free Schools opened in September 2011. One of the most prominent of these new educational institutions was the West London Free School,[29] whose high-profile creation was instigated by the author and journalist Toby Young[30] and other local parents.

The policy has been rolled-out at a fairly rapid rate, and in November 2011, the coalition government announced an extra £600m to be used for building 100 new Free Schools in England over the next three years. A further 55 Free Schools were confirmed as opening in the autumn of 2012,[31] tripling the number in England alone,[32] and reaching 79 in total. This further expansion was part of a rolling process, with a further wave of applications for Free School status having been established by the government from February 2012 (for opening in the autumn term of 2013). Among those applying for the distinctive status in 2012–13 were Christian charities, former soldiers, football clubs[33] and existing private schools.[34] Within this rolling programme of Free Schools, of the provisional proposals for 102 new Free Schools approved in the summer of 2012,[35] a third had a religious ethos,[36] and, following on from his initial foray into secondary education, Toby Young applied to open a further primary institution attached to his original West London Free School in the next phase of proposed Free Schools announced in mid-2012,[37] primarily due to the apparent popularity of his first educational venture:

> Over 1,000 children applied for our second batch of 120 places (in (2012)... making us the most over-subscribed secondary in the London Borough of Hammersmith and Fulham... The teaching unions warned us that free schools would increase social segregation, but ours hasn't. On the contrary, it's a genuine comprehensive.[38]

The popularity evident in the number of applicants has formed the basis of Toby Young's viewpoint that such schools generate social and community integration rather than segregation, and that a diverse range of grassroots bodies expressing a committed interest in this policy area offers major advantages to the country's education system, for, in bringing a variety of experiences, they offer the prospect that 'the groups responsible for free schools are likely to be better at setting up and running schools than politicians and bureaucrats, with a firmer grasp of what a good education looks like'.[39] This argument is clearly aligned with the devolved and localist sentiments and theories at the heart of the policy's formulation and direction.

The challenges facing Free Schools

The first wave of Free Schools was established amidst a degree of hostility and opposition from some local authorities and politicians on the left, largely fuelled by fears (supported by the teaching unions), that in adopting a more fragmented and diverse approach to educational policy delivery, the Conservatives were undermining the broadly egalitarian principles of education that provide and protect minimum, uniform standards, and which are administered and regulated by the central-ised state and its devolved local education authorities. Toby Young, the Free Schools advocate, has described such hostility from left-wing politicians, commentators and teaching unions as akin to 'rabid oppo-sition'.[40] The left of the political spectrum has been broadly critical of the 'free schools revolution', as it is often termed by both proponents and opponents, particularly in relation to its deregulated nature, which appears to bypass aspects of the state's bureaucratic structure and its accompanying mechanisms and prescribed procedures. A potential negative consequence of this policy could be seen in the chaotic closure of one proposed Free School in Yorkshire just days before it was due to open in the autumn of 2012.[41] A further example of such deregulation and potentially harmful avoidance of government bureaucracy emerged in early 2013 when the LGA voiced critical comments that Free Schools do not have to adhere to national food standards when providing school meals,[42] while other Free Schools have been criticised for poor standards and a number have been forced to close permanently during 2013. As a further significant criticism, in the spring of 2014 the Labour opposition claimed that 70% of places at the first wave of Free Schools were not filled after two years of opening,[43] although Conservative advocates claim that such schools will grow in popularity over time.

Such adverse developments appear to confirm one of the funda-mental criticisms of this new educational policy, namely that far from raising standards and improving quality and social justice within the education system, Free Schools actually create greater inequality and social divisions in their arbitrary methods of educational provision, primarily due to their essentially neo-liberal, free market approach to meeting educational demand, with fears being raised that such schools 'are being funded by money taken from other schools ... (with) no account of how the schools will be joined up with other local schools and services ... (with the possibility of a) free-for-all undermining other schools'.[44] Indeed, one critical commentator has gone as far to say that the approach of the Conservative Party to this area of policy-making after 2010 is to 'break up and privatise English education'[45] within a wider deregulation of welfare and social policy delivery, while other critical comments have warned that by replacing uniform central state-driven provision 'with local voluntary providers, the claim of rights is reduced to an act of charity'.[46] Such a negative interpretation of the policy appears to suggest an undermining of people's rights to the full range of welfare state support. Convincing the broader political spectrum of their value is certainly a significant challenge. However in a similar vein to other spheres of social policy since 2010, the left has reacted in varying ways to Free Schools, and, despite some notable opposition, the prominent Labour peer Lord Adonis is a particularly strong advocate who has argued that his party should fully support their development.[47]

The Swedish experience of Free Schools has also raised further potentially negative implications, in that, according to some academic analyses, there has been a decline in educational standards and an increase in social division, with similar negative social patterns said to have emerged in another Scandinavian country, Denmark, since it also rolled out a programme of devolved yet state-subsidised Free Schools in recent years.[48] While individuals such as Toby Young dispute this argument and highlight more positive conflicting data,[49] this debate goes to the heart of the Cameron government's educational agenda, with critics arguing that Free Schools and their neo-liberal focus on market-driven individual choice will actually create greater social injustice, segregation, increased selection and ultimately discriminate against poorer members of the community who will be less likely to utilise the opportunities offered by their establishment than the middle classes with their higher levels of 'social capital'. During 2014 such trends were cited as a development that has now also occurred in the UK, according to research by London University's Institute of Education.[50] This would appear to be the exact opposite of the desired outcome of the policy as outlined by Michael Gove, and indeed suggests the replication of social policy failures that Gove sought to attach to many of the educational policies of the Labour government between 1997 and 2010. A key long-term challenge for advocates of the Free School agenda is, therefore, to create genuinely enhanced educational choice for citizens, while negating the likelihood of greater social and educational segregation. If this can be eventually achieved, it should nullify the criticisms of the policy.

Re-invigorated Conservative education policy

Despite such vehement, concerted criticisms, the confident, re-invigorated Conservative educational agenda demonstrates that as well as raising educational standards, the Free Schools seem to be popular in meeting the needs of parents and the communities in which they are located, as, according to one government minister, 'Parents are voting with their feet. Around two-thirds of Free Schools were oversubscribed for their first year. The West London Free School has just reported more than 1,000 applications for 120 places in September 2012'.[51] Such figures would appear to vindicate the Conservative Party's faith in this policy as an alternative and populist alternative to the universalised state-led approach favoured for much of the post-war era. Free Schools, it is argued, must seek to adhere to the following core principles: they are 'all-ability state-funded schools set up in response to what local people say they want and need in order to improve education for children in their community'.[52]

At a basic level Free Schools are still under the ultimate control of the state, albeit in a more arms-length relationship. This policy for more 'innovative' and flexible educational provision aims to provide a more localised service and autonomous curriculum which is, in theory, accessible to the whole community and which offers a service model that devolves centralised state funds in order to provide Free Schools with greater independence in terms of prioritising core functions and key decision-making on an operational basis. Such freedoms are particularly important in relation to staffing, facilities management, curricular options and specific local requirements, and they allow schools to tailor their appeal in order to make educational choice available to parents in a consumerist style. In this respect the approach has some parallels with the prevailing Conservative neo-liberal attitudes of the 1980s and the broad focus on improving parental options, reducing government intervention and bureaucracy (both central and local), enhancing the role for the private sector, instilling greater levels of competition within mainstream education and the broad decentralisation of the state's educational scope and provision. This ethos was previously evident in the period between 1979 and 1997 in flagship policies such as grant-maintained schools, school league tables and city technology colleges, and which established elements of a more 'individualist' culture within educational policy that was maintained to a degree by New Labour policy from 1997 onwards, notably through the academy programme.[53] In many ways, the policy ultimately aims to strike a revised balance between uniformity and diversity in the provision of state education in Britain, with an underlying inference that there has not been sufficient diversity over recent years.

However, David Cameron and Michael Gove have emphasised what they believe is a radical and innovative edge to such a policy, one that transcends previous administrations and which genuinely reflects a form of 'New Conservatism', specifically in the way that groups of parents, community activists and local charities can operate as the ultimate instigators of such schools to meet local educational needs and demands – an option that has not previously been available and which appears to instil a more competitive and dynamic aspect to the delivery of such a vital social policy. Conservative politicians who have actively promoted and supported this policy have also explicitly sought to integrate the ethos of Free Schools within the ongoing narratives of the 'Big Society' and 'localist' policy agendas since returning to power in 2010. This approach focuses on decentralised, community-led activity across a range of social policies, promoting greater individual responsibility detached from bureaucratic state control, seeking, in the view of advocates of this brand of Conservatism, to instil 'variety, experimentation and local innovation'[54] yet remaining 'within the taxpayer-funded education sector'[55] as part of a more diversified public service delivery. As a consequence, those who promote Free Schools dismiss the fears of the political left that the enhanced competition caused by these new schools will cause greater segregation among and between neighbouring schools. Instead, Free Schools should act as a catalyst to generate enhanced choice, egalitarian outcomes and the raising of 'standards all round... (with such) new schools (acting) as a spur to their neighbouring maintained schools',[56] and instilling an ethos that will 'make sure middle-income and low-income families benefit as much from those choices as high income families'.[57]

In its approach of seeking to raise standards by offering educational provision that benefits all social classes and which derives from genuine grassroots demand, this policy is, therefore, distinct from what has gone before, and in turn it appears to offer a radical glimpse of the potential of post-bureaucratic politics in action. It adheres to the basic premise that 'there is a difference between public services and state provision'[58] in the sense that neither is mutually exclusive to the other, and that effectively functioning public services can be delivered away from the monopolistic control of the state. On a negative level however, there is anecdotal evidence from those involved in the application process to establish a Free School that the procedural preparations are so challenging and complex that 'there is a real danger that free schools become the sole preserve of those with the resources and capacity to take on such a huge undertaking, such as faith groups or independent schools'.[59] This would suggest that the notion that everyone has equal potential to establish such a school is questionable, and that middle-class communities capable of 'exploiting (their) social capital'[60] are at a major advantage over poorer and more deprived groups.

This approach to educational provision can also be said to be coherently aligned with the Conservative vision for education that has been established since 1979, whereby 'individuals, families, school staff and communities will be given "freedom" to "take responsibility" for the education system'[61] within a less regulated and decentralised model of policy delivery that allows schools to have greater choice and flexibility in the type of educational provision on offer. The enhanced ability of Free Schools to emerge and develop without a prior organisation being in place is viewed as one of the most radical aspects, something that transcends the Conservative policy agenda of the 1980s, as does its more explicit use of commercial and non-public bodies as sources of funding and service delivery. Many right-wing think-tanks such as the IEA have argued that the eventual outcome of this policy will be an inherent profit motive that will be influential in the delivery of state education, and which will ultimately raise overall educational standards,[62] particularly for the lower social classes who have been guaranteed a proportion of places due to the proposed non-selective nature of such bodies,[63] in social terms at least. Indeed, Free Schools pioneer Toby Young has offered the powerful example that at 'the West London Free School... 25% of our first cohort are on free school meals',[64] as a clear indicator of the diverse social composition of its initial pupil intake. However this socially inclusive aspect of Free Schools has been challenged by figures that suggest that first-phase Free Schools have taken a lower proportion of pupils who qualify for free dinners[65] than other schools in the same area or borough, which appears to undermine their status as being vehicles for greater social mobility and raises questions as to whether they are fully representative of the wider community they claim to serve.

Some notable right-of centre think tanks and policy lobbyists, such as Policy Exchange, were active in lobbying for reform of key social policy spheres. Michael Gove was significantly one of this body's key founders in 2002, representing an obvious and practical link between the origins of social policies such as Free Schools and contemporary political developments. Prominent educational charities such as The Sutton Trust have also consistently argued for enhanced opportunities to be provided for bright students from disadvantaged backgrounds,[66] and Free Schools have been identified as a vehicle for providing such access. Bodies such as the Sutton Trust want to ensure greater social mobility and opportunity for those from deprived backgrounds, seeking to ensure that schools are able to 'serve disadvantaged pupils to give preference to pupils from low income homes in their admissions criteria' and that '"free schools" are established primarily in disadvantaged localities'.[67] The role of such charities alongside various right-of-centre pressure groups and think-tanks such as the IEA, Policy Exchange, Civitas and the New Schools Network in broadly supporting Free Schools and in seeking to influence distinct initiatives and innovative policies in the educational sphere has been viewed by some as evidence of a thriving civil society existing within a separate sphere between the individual citizen and the state. These independent bodies that drive and benefit from the establishment of devolved Free Schools, are viewed by advocates of a decentralised post-bureaucratic state structure as symbolising 'the heart of the Big Society'[68] in practice.

In a pluralistic model of government and society, these advisory groups are viewed positively as prominent and pro-active civic stakeholders, who are 'authoritative voices... undertaking further commissions to deliver initiatives'.[69] Indeed, the educational charity The New Schools Network (established in 2009) is run by Rachel Wolf, a former adviser to Michael Gove and is viewed as a particularly significant organisation in having an initiating, enabling and co-ordinating role in the process of establishing Free Schools.[70] Such apparently diverse influences on policy formulation are viewed by those who share this new Conservative outlook as beneficial to the contemporary educational and wider social policy sector, and a further advantageous asset to be credited to the Free Schools policy, essentially promoting an ethos that revives the vibrant and pro-active civil society that arguably preceded the post-1945 'big state' era. After 1945 and the extension of universalised, 'statist' public service delivery, it is claimed by some sympathetic to the 'Big Society' agenda that autonomous and localised bodies were 'largely pushed to the margins'[71] when it came to the practical implementation of government policies, and it is this aspect of policy influence that modern Conservatism seeks to restore.

Does the Free Schools policy represent a new type of Conservatism?

It has already been alluded to that the Free Schools policy in many ways reflects a consistent strand of Conservative thinking on educational provision that dates back to the advent of the New Right, and particularly the evolution of the Thatcher administration from 1979 onwards, namely the emphasis on devolving power away from the centralised, bureaucratic control of the state to meet local demand in a broadly neo-liberal model of governance. Conservative Party interest in educational policy was tentative during this period, as from the outset the government had a more economically-oriented agenda, and 'education was not a priority of the Government in 1979'.[72] However, even the Thatcher administration had its own internal tensions in terms of moulding the country's educational policy during the 1980s, with internal conflict evident within the New Right political faction itself, between on the one hand the radical neo-liberals who favoured even greater deregulation of the economy and the centralised state, and on the other the distinct brand of neo-Conservatives who were 'interested primarily in upholding 19th-century notions of tradition, hierarchy and social order',[73] and who sought to retain a significant degree of centralised control of policy from the centre. It can be ultimately argued that despite Thatcher's own neo-liberal economic instincts and broad aversion to state intervention, it was Conservative politicians such as Education Secretary Kenneth Baker who favoured maintaining a 'strong state'[74] – acknowledged by Gamble as a key tenet of the overall political doctrine of Thatcherism – and which sought to retain significant social controls at the centre of government, along more authoritarian lines.

It was this more centralising and 'strong state' variant of modern Conservative thought that sought to instil and impose greater moral standards from a strong and co-ordinated centre which appears to have won the day, as domestic-orientated 'neo-Conservatism' appeared to have triumphed over more 'neo-liberal' influences during the period of government. Such tendencies became evident in the emergence of key 'centralising' educational policies contained within the 1988 Education Reform Act,[75] which notably delivered the National Curriculum[76] that has remained in place to the present day, and which as a piece of legislation has been likened to the 1944 Butler Act in its long-term significance. To the dismay of contemporary neo-liberals this Act represented an avowedly bureaucratic element of government educational policy-making, taking up 'nearly 370 hours of parliamentary time and (giving) the Secretary of State 451 new powers'.[77] Over 20 years later its centralised co-ordinating role and content came under the scrutiny of Michael Gove, as it appeared to conflict with his decentralising policy agenda. With Free Schools only adhering to the core elements of this centralised curriculum, and with greater flexibility in terms of the range and diversity of their subject provision as a result, Gove launched a formal review into the purpose and functions of the National Curriculum in early 2011,[78] with significant and potentially more flexible developments expected on this front before the end of the 2010–15 parliament.

In returning the party's attention to this key area of social policy while back in national office after 2010, the Conservatives sought to revive the debate of the 1980s, yet with a greater degree of decentralisation, alongside an enhanced philanthropic emphasis, heightened paternalistic compassion and a sense of communitarian zeal. Within this context, one of the Conservative ministers in charge of the implementation of the Free Schools policy from 2010 onwards has described the policy in radical terms as 'a grass-roots revolution',[79] and some of the policy's most enthusiastic supporters have argued that it has transcended the 1980s policy agenda in its genuinely more radical connotations, with the nature of its 'grassroots', bottom-up approach its key innovative aspect: in theory anyone is able to instigate a Free School if the appropriate localised organisation and funding can be put in place. Prominent media commentators from the libertarian right of the political spectrum, such as Fraser Nelson, have proclaimed the establishment of Free Schools as a 'triumph',[80] particularly in the rapid pace of their introduction and the fact that they may even struggle to keep up with demand fuelled by population growth and increased pupil numbers in some parts of the country. This radical vision of educational provision therefore advocates an ethos of genuine post-bureaucratic individualism, meeting local needs while also diluting, yet not eliminating entirely, the previously dominant influence of the centralised state. Key regulatory bodies such as OFSTED maintain a monitoring role of Free Schools, while the Secretary of State retains the power to suspend any school that appears to be in breach of the terms of its 'Articles of Association'.[81]

Yet from another less supportive angle, it has also been suggested by sceptical political commentators that far from freeing schools from the tentacles of centralised state control, such regulatory controls of a financial and bureaucratic nature will continue to be an inevitable aspect of government intervention in the British education system, despite such an essentially decentralised approach to educational policy.[82] This it is claimed, has been the fate of all such attempts to devolve educational provision in the modern political era, as it is argued that pure and genuine 'devolution' of this social policy is extremely difficult to achieve in practice due to the need for basic minimum standards and regulations to be adhered to, e.g. the continued application of the centralised national school curriculum (since 1988) or the regulatory monitoring of standards by OFSTED (formed in 1992), as obvious examples. This has led to criticism that in practical terms the policy on Free Schools is unrealistic in its deregulatory aspirations, as a genuine and credible educational policy simply cannot be as radically decentralised as has been claimed by its advocates, and is therefore something of a paradox in practical terms:

> Tory ministers claim to be decentralising power in our education system (yet) they are doing the complete opposite... they have been

quietly accumulating power in the centre... (academies and Free Schools) are reliant on central government funding, are accountable to ministers and civil servants, and are monitored through seven-year finance agreements decided in Whitehall.[83]

This particular line of criticism therefore suggests that despite the radical rhetoric associated with Free Schools. and their links with the broader vision of 'The Big Society', the reality is somewhat different in terms of disentangling such localised institutions from the centralised state and its bureaucratic labyrinths of Whitehall. One commentator has gone as far as commenting that such is the extent of government central control that 'Michael Gove's centralism is not so much socialist as Soviet'.[84] It is indeed the central Whitehall machine that controls the funding for such educational bodies, in many ways simply bypassing and transcending the role previously held by democratically account-able local education authorities in the traditional funding process, and this would appear to conflict with the localist thrust of the policy. The post-2010 government has been accused by the Labour opposition of prioritising financial investment in Free Schools, in contradistinction to their centralised and more comprehensive 'catch-all' policies such as the abandoned 'Building Schools for the Future' programme. This has allegedly led to poor value for money and low student numbers in some Free Schools, with one commentator describing them as part of a '"free" (meaning expensive) state school movement',[85] which lack genuine experiment and liberation, and whose creation has brought about a two-tier and segregationist structure whereby Free Schools will face difficulties integrating with existing local authority bodies.

The impact of coalition government on the Free Schools policy

The internal political pressures of coalition government can be said to have blurred the policy's focus and dulled its radical edge, with the Liberal Democrats, who did not advocate the policy and have been more hostile and sceptical to its agenda, appearing to restrain its more radical neo-liberal elements. As a consequence it would appear that a significant degree of state bureaucracy and restrictions will continue to be imposed from the centre, limiting the scope of commercial free-dom, with specific limitations and conditions applying – apparently demanded by Nick Clegg – in relation to whether such schools can make a profit, although existing fee-paying private schools can apply for the status of Free School and continue to charge for admission. Such limits and restraints being applied to the radical model of Free Schools have been retained throughout the period 2010–2015, although the vision of establishing Free Schools run for profit is clearly a desired policy for the more vehement advocates, who aspire to a scenario whereby 'after the first batch of free schools have been judged a success, the government will allow for-profit Education Management Organisations to set up, own and operate Free Schools, as they can in Sweden and some American states'.[86] Such a scenario will almost certainly depend on the outcome of the General Election in 2015, representing a source of significant policy difference between the three main parties, with Labour and the Liberal Democrats broadly sceptical of such a development, while some Conservative modernisers are openly enthusiastic about a profit-led agenda.

The coalition government's divisions over the competitive, commercial and selective implications of the nature of educational provision and the financial arrangements for Free Schools chimes with a long-standing political debate within British politics, namely how to improve and reform educational provision in the UK. This centres on whether delivering core public services on a comprehensive, uniform basis is preferable to the alternative of allowing greater diversity within public service provision in order to meet specialist individual and finance-driven requirements, which supporters of Free Schools claim are the decisive dynamics behind government policy-making in this policy sphere. The devolved status of such schools opens up the long-term prospect of business and community groups behind Free Schools to have commercial interests and profit incentives as a driving force in their involvement.[87] This was evident in Michael Gove's decision to approve the opening in autumn 2012 of IES Breckland in Suffolk, a Free School run by a Swedish private company (IES), who run several schools for profit in Sweden. While limited in their capacity to make profit under the existing British model, such a development potentially heralds a significant breakthrough for private involvement in the state education system. However, it is by no means certain that a desire for profit automatically equates to either improved public services or aligns with the communitarian emphasis of the broader Big Society agenda.

The most enthusiastic advocates of 'The Big Society' view educational policy as a key testing ground for the implementation of the socio-political freedoms that the Big Society's framework as 'a governing idea'[88] seeks to instil across all of society, and they envisage that reforms such as Free Schools will ultimately alter the way that the public views the provision of public services. This in turn might enable 'a drastic scaling back of the national curriculum... (and) the creation of new schools, be they publicly or privately funded, and in corporate, trust or co-operative form',[89] which will create an educational model featuring a diffusion and diversity of different types of state school, an explicit aspiration of the Free Schools education agenda in its role in asserting a new brand of Conservative social policy.

The future direction of the Free Schools policy

There are those of less ideological and visionary tendencies who adopt a more pragmatic socio-political outlook, and who would claim that state bureaucracy and private commercial restrictions are inevitable when dealing with public administration and the need to guarantee a minimum national standard. This latter point is consolidated by a sociological theory promoted by Max Weber in the early 20th century:[90] he observed and argued that a more 'bureaucratized society' steadily develops due to the growth in size and complexity of states and communities, which therefore suggests that the contemporary aspiration of creating a wave of post-bureaucratic Free Schools is not based in practical reality given the significant demands and varied complexities of 21st-century British society. In the sphere of education, this is a particularly pertinent argument given that during 'the 20-year period from 1979 to 2000... (there were) over 30 separate Education Acts, together with large numbers of accompanying circulars, regulations and statutory instruments'.[91] Such persistent bureaucratic and socially complex trends appear to undermine the 'radical' post-bureaucratic tenets of this policy as propounded by its principal advocates such as Michael Gove, and to erode and suppress the apparent 'freedoms' that it creates. However, it remains to be seen as to whether the ability of Free Schools to hire teachers without formal teaching qualifications, the lack of need for conventional educational buildings, the progressive appearance of a more flexible curriculum and the potential emergence in future of greater commercial freedoms will improve Free Schools, and make them more able to resist the bureaucratic tide.

In its focus on decentralised, localised policy making, reduced bureaucracy and a greater emphasis on individual choice and needs, the Free Schools education agenda appears to chime with the wider 'Big Society' narrative of the Cameron leadership, but its steady evolution as a policy has gone to the heart of the Conservative Party's delicate identity issues following its return to national office. The policy does appear to embrace some traditional Conservative political priorities that could be said to hark back to a pre-1945 model of society, where mutualism, localism and enhanced local autonomy thrived before the comprehensive and universal welfare state was constructed. From a later political era, such 'neo-liberal', New Right principles that then demanded a reduced role for the centralised state also suggest that such a policy would not have looked out of place if it had been initiated during the heyday of Thatcherism in the 1980s. Indeed, it has been argued that this flagship policy has maintained the neo-liberal outlook of the 1980s, but has been given a sharper focus on 'society' and 'incorporated elements of communitarianism' within a 're-imagined state',[92] an approach that fundamentally affects the structures of both central and local government. Despite its enhanced focus on 'society', the Free Schools policy, some argue, is part of a wider, more radical political strategy from the right of the political spectrum that seeks to erode the structural basis of the post-1945 model of the British state and its inexorable tendency to grow and expand, and in the process challenge what this perspective views as a fundamental error at the heart of the post-war political consensus that 'a large state was a guarantor of good public services and social well-being'.[93] The critical counter-argument to the positive view of the Big Society (as espoused by the likes of Jesse Norman MP), would instead claim that such policies of New Conservatism are potentially 'dangerous... In its genuine belief that charities and volunteers, rather than the state, can and should provide numerous, core public services'.[94]

However, there is an alternative interpretation: the 'collectivist' and 'mutualist' influences on the 'Big Society' and its associated goals and key policies such as Free Schools, have in fact represented a dilution of the 1980s Conservative 'free-market' agenda, and this distinguishes it from the more individualist emphasis and arbitrary outcomes of pure neo-liberal policies. From this viewpoint, the policy appears to acknowledge some aspects of the more paternalistic 'One Nation' Conservative tradition, particularly in response to criticism from the left that Free Schools are elitist and designed to cater for a largely affluent and middle-class market,[95] with the government insisting that all such bodies are not for profit and must guarantee that a significant proportion of their intake comes from poorer sections of society, not exclusively from wealthier, middle-class families with enhanced levels of 'social capital'.[96] This, again, indicates an interventionist, bureaucratic element in the policy, and would appear to suggest that completely decentralised, deregulated and devolved decision-making is not feasible or desirable in meeting wider social and community needs. Here is the paradoxical element that lies at the heart of the Free Schools initiative: a localist policy requires the state to initiate the decentralisation and devolution of power and to maintain an influence, albeit a streamlined one, over the functioning of the policy. The policy is, however, consistent with the focus of past Conservative governments in at least striving to minimise the state's control and to extend opportunity in a meritocratic manner to all pupils regardless of social background, as evident in previous Conservative policies such as the assisted places scheme and the long-standing affinity with grammar schools.

This much-heralded emphasis on ensuring quotas of specific socio-economic groups in Free Schools' intake in order to tackle the cycle of social inequality and injustice in parts of the country, would appear to reflect an approach to education policy that derives from a goal-based vision, with enhanced elements of compassion instilled within a quasi-regulatory structure. This 'determinist' aspect of the policy goes to the heart of why initiatives like 'Free Schools' illuminate a key philosophical debate, central to the whole 'Big Society' agenda: the Oakeshottian conservative approach of a 'natural' or instinctive sense of community activity and responsibility among ordinary citizens,[97] which rejects the rationalism of 'ideology... and (moves) towards pragmatic principle'.[98] This is in contrast to the 'rational' and planned approach to governance as espoused by various (often left-wing) ideologies that place a greater emphasis on theory and which seek to impose such values on citizens through the state's influence and intervention. Such a traditionalist Conservative rejection of utopian ends can be aligned to the philosophical debate on the fundamental nature of government, namely whether 'nomocratic' (rule-based) governance featuring a broadly neutral end or aspiration, is preferable to a 'teleocratic' model of government, which focuses on a governmental approach designed to achieve specific ends or which has a desired outcome.

In applying such theoretical approaches to a specific policy such as the Free Schools programme, a key practical question arises which equally applies to the overall 'Big Society' agenda and the evolution of a 'New Conservatism': does such a political narrative have specific ends or is it neutral and merely legalistic in its aspirations in line with the traditional and 'natural' Conservatism of Oakeshott? While the Big Society's cloak around the Free Schools policy does seek to shield it from the explicit ideologies of both the traditional left and right, this stance has been rejected by many teaching unions, who argue that 'although the Government may indicate that they are introducing this programme to reduce disadvantage, the reality is that it is wholly an ideological move'[99] with its focus on a more diverse utilisation of private educational provision. Nevertheless, the policy does appear to have a clear focus on addressing fundamental socio-economic problems with a degree of state intervention, and although it is unclear how success and progress will be measured, advocates of the policy claim that as an eventual outcome 'this agenda may do more to improve equality than straight tax and spend',[100] and its underlying centralising tendencies. This would suggest that the Free Schools agenda ultimately adopts an approach that emphasises social outcomes that are linked to key political goals and values, regardless of how vague such socio-political targets may be. The policy could, therefore, be aligned with the teleocratic model of governance where the various mechanisms of the state are utilised to guide public policy towards broad and imprecise goals, although their utopian nature is likely to be limited in scope.

Given this fusion of variable Conservative traditions and ideological influences within the policy's formulation, it remains a matter of conjecture as to which aspect or nuance of influence has been the dominant one in driving the Free Schools agenda forward and shaping its distinctive evolution so far. There appear to have been some tensions between pragmatism and ideology within this policy sphere, with Michael Gove's more dynamic ideological emphasis being moderated by the caution of the Liberal Democrats alongside some more pragmatic Conservative figures, adjoined to the practical necessity of retaining state control of educational bodies, and such factors restrained Gove's, and the policy's, reforming drive. Gove having left the Department for Education in July 2014, it remains to be seen which dimension or influence will take the more prominent role in moulding the policy in the long term, and as a result whether a genuinely populist educational agenda can legitimately be said to be at the forefront of a credible and new model of social Conservatism. The removal of Gove raised some significant questions in relation to the policy's further evolution, with ongoing debate as to whether his replacement, Nicky Morgan, will adopt a different tone and approach. Within this context it can be debated whether the reforms represent 'common sense and a new perspective (as opposed to)... more ideological commitments',[101] and competing personalities and influences suggest some scope for flexibility in relation to the dynamics of the policy's identity and future direction.

However as a rebuke to the various critics of the policy who would prefer it to fizzle out, it has been claimed that its innovations have created a 'competitive education quasi-market',[102] which has already brought about fundamental changes that cannot be quickly altered. Such developments suggest that a distinct new political consensus will emerge on this issue, with 'free schools continu(ing) to be set up regardless of who wins the next election (as) the policy is irreversible, as the Swedes discovered in 1992'.[103] This will spawn yet another distinct feature or type of unit within the UK's educational structure, nestled alongside comprehensives, grammar schools and academies, providing more diversity of schools via a broader range of providers as opposed to a hegemonic state monopoly, and creating something of a 'patchwork quilt' appearance for the country's state education provision in the process. The number of Free Schools remains relatively small, and the question of whether their creation proves to be beneficial for wider society has not been answered. It has been claimed that policies that generate devolved, quasi-private bodies do not always automatically equate to benefits for all of society, as in practice 'parental preferences over education are not fully aligned with the public interest'.[104] This would suggest likely tensions between the dynamics of individual parental choice, the communitarian instincts of civic engagement and the desire to encourage and enable commercial profit-making within such institutions. Alternative propositions for what drives the Free Schools policy are that it can be viewed as a remarketed reversion to the individualist, neo-liberal agenda of the 1980s, or that pragmatic Conservative 'statecraft' and its associated populist tendencies have responded to local needs, and for primarily electoral purposes have flexibly moulded the formulation of a key social policy within national governance. The benefits or failings of the policy will only be identified over a long period of time, and while it has certainly delivered change, it remains a matter of conjecture as to whether such change has been positive or negative. There is a significant debate to be had as to whether this policy can genuinely deliver a 'post-bureaucratic' educational utopia as its advocates desire, and also whether such contemporary socio-political developments are part of a long-term, broader shift towards the emergence of a distinct, radical brand of 'New Conservatism' for the 21st century.

7
Social policy case study 4: Reform of the NHS

This chapter focuses on a further area of contemporary and topical social policy that, like Free Schools, has been aligned with the 'Big Society' agenda, has aspired to address the 'broken society' and sought to consolidate levels of social mobility and social justice across the wider population. It deals with attempts by the Conservative-led coalition government to effectively manage and, simultaneously, reform the key institution of the National Health Service. Like educational policy, this area of welfare provision is an important aspect of modern British governance in the 21st century, and as an integral high-profile component of the British welfare state it has been said to have 'no parallel in terms of its resilience, its longevity and its abiding appeal to the citizens of the United Kingdom'.[1] The sheer size and complexity of the NHS as an organisation[2] provides a significant political challenge to any administration in terms of making it function efficiently and effectively along the organisational or functional lines that it desires. As a pivotal feature of British welfare policy provision, it therefore provides a clear opportunity for the modern Conservative Party to demonstrate just how original and innovative its approach is in dealing with a significant and increasingly expensive area of social policy. Parallels can be drawn with education policy: both are high-profile aspects of governance with a 'compassionate' policy edge that affect large numbers of people, and so both are potent electoral issues. We should also hope to find out if the party's proposals in this area of social policy present any evidence of a revised attitude since its last period in government during the 1980s and 1990s.

Historical Conservative attitudes to the NHS

On its face, the refreshed and rebranded approach of British Conservatism towards the NHS in the early years of the 21st century puts to the test the dynamic principles of the decentralised and localised aspects of the party's broader social policy agenda, the 'Big Society', which has been at the forefront of much recent rhetoric on social and welfare issues. This in turn raises the key question as to whether this social agenda's focus on 'self help, entrepreneurship and community energy'[3] can be appropriately transferred into the monolithic and bureaucratic structure of the National Health Service. Even those who believe in the values of this decentralised socio-political approach have acknowledged the difficulties of this challenge, describing it in analogous terms of 'taking five or ten years of reversing the supertanker to try to get it heading in the other direction'.[4] Such comments imply the need for a long-term strategy in the pursuit of the new socio-political agenda, and the Conservative Party's approach to this policy sphere raises important questions regarding the extent of its recent modernisation and revised identity. The question arises as to whether the party's emerging attitudes and policies in relation to the NHS represent a more compassionate and distinctive approach compared to the ideological mood and neo-liberal political agenda that prevailed during the last period of Conservative rule (1979–1997), and therefore whether the party is offering continuity or change in its health policy.

The prime aim of the National Health Service since its inception in the aftermath of World War Two has been to provide a quality service based on need, and not ability to pay, and its central ethos has been to provide quality healthcare 'from the cradle to the grave'. It has always been a particularly challenging area of policy to address for the Conservative Party, for the principal reason that the party originally opposed its creation when it was established by the reforming post-war Labour government in 1948, primarily due to its expensive burden on the taxpayer and its symbolic appearance as a vestige of bureaucratic, socialist government. Such opposition created a lingering and at times 'toxic' image that has adhered to the Conservative Party in relation to this issue, to a variable extent, ever since. The NHS has remained broadly popular since its creation in the collectivist aftermath of World War Two, with British people placing great emphasis on the value of the service and the need for investment in it in both social and political terms, and this has made it a political challenge for politicians of all parties aspiring to be in government. Over the years, governments of all parties have been faced with a 'never-ending public clamour for improved state health services',[5] and this historic legacy has meant that the NHS has been significantly intertwined with politics and public opinion, principally due to the fact that it is ultimately a public body, directly funded by the taxpayer, and this has resulted in a continuous political battle between rival parties to provide an appropriate selection of specific social and welfare rights to a demanding population.

The fundamental problem in seeking to address such elements of demand and supply within the NHS is that demand has appeared to be unlimited and has grown inexorably from the service's inception. However, in practical terms the supply of service has clear financial limits, and at times since 1948 this has led to a rationing and streamlining of resources in general, with some aspects of service having to be prioritised over others. The NHS, therefore, carries hugely significant implications for politicians, their electoral fortunes and their ability to govern effectively. In this context – significant public interest in the service and the general perception of the NHS as a pivotal aspect of welfare provision – it has become a key responsibility of government to determine 'how best to manage the gap between healthcare demand and supply'.[6] If the wider population comes to believe that politicians are not managing this key area of social policy effectively 'they will legitimately demand that their elected representatives press for changes to be made. Thus politics and the NHS are rightly inseparable'.[7]

As a corollary of the historical development of the NHS, as a policy area it 'has long been regarded as a core Labour issue... especially so since the 1980s,'[8] when it came under pressure from the Thatcher government's focus on retrenchment, reform and neo-liberal marketisation. During this period the Labour Party campaigned to preserve and defend the organisation's original aims and structure amidst claims that its core was being eroded. This resulted in a political battle characterised by ideological intensity, creating both a social and political scenario where 'a strong body of public and official opinion... saw the NHS as underfunded and ill-equipped to meet the legitimate expectations of its consumers',[9] a factor that blighted the Conservative Party's image in relation to this facet of the welfare state, with many critics questioning the party's 'compassion' and commitment in its governance of the service. In subsequent years, healthcare has become of even greater significance for the wider electorate, and can indeed be identified as one of the key issues that influenced the electoral mood from the mid-1990s onwards, as 'between 1995 and 2007 opinion polls identified healthcare as one of the top issues for voters'.[10] Such a socio-political development in turn provides a partial explanation for the Conservatives' political unpopularity during the approximate decade after 1997: many voters were suspicious of the party's initial reluctance to match the New Labour government's increased investment in the service during its first two terms (up until 2005).

Following a third successive general election defeat in 2005, the Conservative Party under David Cameron explicitly acknowledged the need to maintain and consolidate Labour's public expenditure in this policy area, and this represented a 'fundamental rethink of strategy and policy'[11] with regard to the NHS. However the Conservatives faced a difficult scenario whereby despite concerted attempts to improve the party's image on this issue during the early years of the 21st century, the harsh reality was that 'most people never trusted them (the Conservatives) on it (the NHS) in the first place',[12] and this has hampered the party's political progress in relation to healthcare ever since it left national office in the late 1990s. This explains why there have subsequently been concerted attempts to detoxify the party's brand, a reflection of this lingering suspicion and hostility from the wider public towards Conservative attitudes towards the NHS. Such attempts at creating a more compassionate image in relation to health policy have also been undermined by a perception that many Conservative politicians remain critical of the NHS and its essentially statist principles and bureaucratic implications, with occasional outbursts on the issue from figures such as Daniel Hannan MEP, who in 2009 described the NHS to an American TV audience as a 'sixty year mistake'.[13] Such views do not appear to correlate with the broadly favourable view of the NHS held by much of the wider British public, nor indeed the more moderate public 'line' of the modern Conservative Party leadership. Public opinion of the Conservatives' attitude towards the NHS has become a vital barometer of wider public perceptions of the modern party, its intentions for this integral British institution that impacts on all of the population at some point of their lives constantly under scrutiny.

David Cameron's focus on the NHS as a key socio-political issue

The Conservatives' sustained exile from national governance between 1997 and 2010, the longest period of continuous Labour government in history, saw the NHS gain further significance as a high-profile area of public policy. Its positioning at the top of the political agenda was instigated by Tony Blair as part of Labour's electoral strategy from the mid-1990s onwards, with the NHS prioritised as an election issue during the 1997 general election campaign, and the New Labour leadership declaring emotively that there were only 24 hours to 'save it' on the eve of the party sweeping to power. This approach and policy agenda resulted in a significant wave of financial investment in the country's health service after 1997, with the rate of NHS spending steadily accelerating the longer that Labour was in power (see Table 7.1). The Labour government therefore appeared to adopt a clear political and electoral strategy of progressively investing in this key public service while markedly pointing the finger of blame for failings in the service's administration and the associated apparent under-investment directly at the previous Conservative regime. This approach created a political narrative that attracted and engaged important socio-economic groups within the electorate, and it sought to contrast the perceived under-spending of the Conservative years in office with 'a relatively long period of sustained real terms growth in public spending'[14] on key public services such as health over the course of the Blair/Brown administrations after 1997, with significant public funds made available after 2002 in particular. Within the broad focus on enhanced investment were specific fiscal trends and intricacies, an example being 'particularly large average annual increases in spending on the NHS (5.7% a year)',[15] a factor that exposed Conservative vulnerabilities in both its NHS policy and broader approach to public services, while it also chimed with a broadly supportive public mood towards such explicitly inflationary trends in government expenditure on public health (see Table 7.1).

NHS policy was, therefore, an important contributing factor to New Labour's three successive general election victories over the demoralised and disjointed Conservatives between 1997 and 2005). The Blair/Brown approach to health policy after 1997 was somewhat ambiguous in its overall tone and direction, as alongside its significant additional spending the incoming government did not abandon the Thatcherite 'internal market' in its entirety, and indeed maintained many of the market-driven, 'consumer'-focused NHS reforms of the 'choice agenda' of the 1980s and 90s. This acceptance of a degree of private influence within the NHS was evident in the further use of private funding of NHS facilities in the form of the Private Finance Initiative (PFI), the extension of the autonomy of hospital trusts into foundation hospitals, enhanced managerial responsibilities for doctors, as well as private non-state providers delivering aspects of NHS provision. This degree of bipartisan continuation of policy direction appeared to reflect a broad consensus that there would be a likelihood of variable levels of service

Table 7.1   Public spending on health as a percentage of GDP in England (1993–2009)

Year	Public Spending on Health as % of GDP
1993–94	5.5
1994–95	5.6
1995–96	5.6
1996–97	5.4
1997–98	5.3
1998–99	5.3
1999–2000	5.2
2000–01	5.5
2001–02	5.8
2002–03	6.1
2003–04	6.5
2004–05	6.8
2005–06	7.1
2006–07	7.0
2007–08	7.2
2008–09	7.7

Information Source: House of Commons, Hansard, 9 September 2009, Health Minister Mike O'Brien MP in response to Peter Bone MP about NHS expenditure in England, Column 1989-1990W, http://www.publications.parliament. uk/pa/cm200809/cmhansrd/cm090909/text/90909w0021.htm.

and performance within an essentially state-run institution traditionally based on 'universal' principles, and this represented a pragmatic 'Blairite' acknowledgment of the realities of the existing system and its focus on patients as 'consumers' that was a legacy of 18 years of Conservative rule. As well as an awareness of the difficulties caused by massive organisational upheaval if such structures were totally abandoned, this more blended policy direction was followed because it was consistent with New Labour's potent tactic of 'triangulation', its desire to outflank the political opposition by adopting some of its policies, and its embrace of aspects of choice and marketisation within the NHS. This consequently appeared to blur the focus of New Labour's NHS agenda and tilt its policy direction slightly 'towards the policies pursued by the Thatcher and Major governments'[16] in the process. Despite aspects of the Conservative Party's NHS legacy being embraced by the incoming Labour government after 1997, a weak and untrustworthy Conservative image in relation to the NHS continued to persist in the wider public psyche, and this presented the party 'with a significant problem, creating pressures for policy change'.[17] Such a scenario could be seen as an opportunity from the perspective of party modernisers, particularly so after the modernisers' candidate, David Cameron, seized the party leadership in 2005.

Changes in relation to Conservative Party NHS policy and rhetoric began to evolve from an early stage of the Cameron leadership as the significance of a third successive general election defeat struck home. The newly-installed party hierarchy acknowledged the unpopularity of its manifestly market-friendly 'pro-private' instinctive approach on this issue, with the key 2005 election policy 'The Patient's Passport' that advocated state subsidies for private healthcare, rapidly discarded within the first month of Cameron's leadership.[18] Policy reform accelerated further as the Conservatives began to steadily regroup and threaten a return to national office from 2008 onwards in the wake of the onset of financial recession. Cameron's deliberate attention to this policy area from the outset of his leadership was an explicit aspect of his attempts as a party leader from a new generation to seek to achieve detoxification of the negative memories of past Conservative governments' treatment of such social policy matters. It quickly appeared to be an area in which Cameron and his political allies were considered to be more liberal-minded and reformist, and this was initially evident in public comments from an early stage of his leadership, notably when he stated in his first party conference speech as leader that 'Tony Blair explained his priorities in three words: education, education, education, I can do it in three letters: NHS.'[19] Cameron's personal connection to the issue was bolstered by to the NHS's treatment of his son's serious illness,[20] and this factor reinforced NHS policy as his 'number one priority'[21] should he be elected to lead a future government, further consolidated by his significant declaration that the creation of the service was 'one of the greatest achievements of the 20th century'.[22]

This bold approach of promoting a modern brand of Conservatism that was steadily reassuring in relation to the maintenance of the NHS appeared to directly confront a sceptical wider public, and attempted to suppress the electorate's general suspicions of Conservative intentions towards the popular public service. It also served to address internal Conservative policy tensions relating to a policy area with a high level of public interest and electoral potency. In adopting this approach Cameron was determined to give the party a more caring and compassionate image, which formed part of his broader political strategy of seeking to promote an enhanced and distinct Conservative-oriented version of social justice, albeit one with a less interventionist role for the state in practical political terms. In pursuing this more apparent 'socially just' agenda, therefore, Cameron sought to reflect the distinctiveness of his health agenda by establishing that his social policy formulation would avoid the dominance of the centralised and bureaucratic state, instead seeking to provide opportunities for devolved levels of service provision and delivery via a more diverse range of non-state providers and various devolved structural elements within the NHS.

In undertaking such an ambitious reformulation of his party's image regarding the NHS, Cameron swiftly acknowledged the need to seek the middle ground on such social policy issues, adopting an almost Blairite degree of flexibility that 'brought the party much closer to Labour's position'[23] in the build-up to the 2010 General Election, primarily in terms of matching spending commitments and investment in the health service. This revision and prioritisation of health policy took on more significance as the general election approached, with Cameron explicitly promising to 'back the NHS... (and) increase health spending every year',[24] a manifesto promise subsequently reinforced in the 2010 coalition agreement with the Liberal Democrats, which pledged that 'funding for the NHS should increase in real terms in each year of the Parliament'.[25] This was a notably inconsistent position, given that it appeared in the wake of a Conservative manifesto programme that focused on securing significant public spending cuts in order to tackle the national budget deficit.[26] Despite this, Cameron's brand of New Conservatism appeared to assert that the required investment could be achieved by ensuring that funds were more efficiently delivered to frontline services, ideally within a less bureaucratic infrastructure. However there was a cautious condition added to this ambitious fiscal pledge: promises to increase spending on health were tempered by the crucial addition that 'the rate of increase under Labour would not be continued'.[27] This was an acknowledgment that the rate of NHS spending had been on a dramatically upward curve and more cautious rates of growth were in prospect, evident in Cameron's acknowledgment that 'In the past two decades, NHS spending has more than doubled in real terms from £38 billion to £103 billion.'[28]

The NHS under Conservative governance since 2010

On re-entering government in 2010 as part of a coalition administration with the Liberal Democrats, Conservative ministers were keen to emphasise the party's much-heralded pre-election pledge of increased financial investment in the NHS, a stance that would fulfil An important manifesto commitment and which broadly aligned itself with the more expansive health policy of the junior coalition partners. This prominent commitment to substantial NHS investment had been a consistent policy stance throughout the Cameron leadership era and also aligned itself with attempts by party modernisers to mould a more compassionate public image as part of the broader strategy of embracing the ethos of vigorous, dynamic and innovative public service provision in the 21st century. Cameron himself made such sentiments as clear as possible a year into his premiership: in mid-2011 he reaffirmed his commitment that 'We will not cut spending on the NHS, we will increase it.'[29] However, this modern expression of social Conservatism and its focus on maintaining government investment into a core public service has appeared inconsistent and incoherent in the light of the party's high-profile rhetoric on deficit reduction, and this has left the policy's intellectual and philosophical basis open to criticism. In practical terms, such ambitious spending pledges have become vulnerable to scrutiny, particularly given media claims that NHS spending was actually cut in real terms by £25 million in the financial year 2011–12 when inflation is taken into account,[30] leading to one academic observation that 'the NHS is not immune'[31] from the era of economic austerity that has prevailed since the Conservatives returned to national office in 2010.

Despite this pro-investment rhetoric being such a prominent feature of NHS policy-making under the Cameron leadership since 2005, some on the right of the Conservative Party have lamented the party's perceived capitulation to the New Labour agenda and have challenged the apparent consensus that relatively high levels of public spending are desirable and automatically equate to an improved level of service. This was evident in the broad thrust of the televised comments made by the MEP Daniel Hannan in 2009, and such sentiments were at least acknowledged at a more senior level in comments made by Health Secretary Andrew Lansley, who in 2010 remarked in a post-election TV interview that 'Britain now spends European quantities of money (on the NHS) without achieving European standards of treatment',[32] which was a strong re-emphasis of a recurring Conservative criticism that Labour's NHS investment after 1997 had failed to reach frontline services due to alleged bureaucratic obstructions. This viewpoint has arguably shaped the Conservative critical narrative of the centralised and statist approach of Labour over 13 years in power, and which influenced Cameron's emphasis that the party's post-2010 NHS programme had to be accompanied by a long-term programme of reforms which he argued should seek to 'modernize the NHS – because changing the NHS today is the only way to protect the NHS for tomorrow'.[33] Such comments emphasise that Cameron's brand of social Conservatism aspires to create a more streamlined, diverse and efficient state structure that can deliver a modernised health service while always being aware of rising and arguably unsustainable financial costs, which appears to indicate that enhanced financial investment alone is not the Conservative Party's answer to ensuring a viable and effective NHS in the long-term.

This emphasis on greater economic and organisational efficiency can be connected to the fact that, since 2010, the government has been operating a stringent austerity agenda that has sought to drive down the national deficit and achieve better value for money in the process, and this has been a central dimension of post-2010 government's actions. Deficit reduction was identified by the Conservatives in particular as a fundamental issue during the 2010 General Election campaign and in subsequent coalition negotiations.[34] As an integral, high-profile theme that appeared to derive from the heart of government and which sought to control and direct the coalition government's overall policy agenda, the focus on deficit reduction was consistent with the alternative model of a more streamlined and less bureaucratic structure of public service delivery, the Big Society, which aspired towards 'a significant reshaping of public services... empowering front-line staff and allowing them to get on with the job'.[35] This would entail a more cost-effective and autonomous ethos and a clear reduction in centralised state control, perhaps symbolised in the NHS by the scheduled abolition of primary care trusts (PCTs) by 2013. Within such a socio-economic context, the incoming government's approach to NHS policy could be summarised as seeking to make a significant commitment to sustained financial investment alongside long-term organisational reform focused on managing and controlling the bureaucratic costs of this expensive public service. However, a key challenge that would be created by this approach would be to keep a sceptical and suspicious public opinion on board, alongside the large 'client state' attached to the service, namely the trade unions and the almost two million NHS employees, all of whom are voters at election time.

In its role as the senior partner of the coalition, the Conservative Party leadership has approached NHS policy since 2010 with an acute awareness of its responsibility for the management of the service in the short term, along with the associated sensitivities of reassuring the public about its long-term future viability, given the party's negative past image of the past. Within this context, Cameron's Conservatives have also had to acknowledge the growing socio-economic pressures on the service, and as a result have ambitiously sought to steer NHS policy direction towards targeting its considerable, escalating long-term structural costs as part of a focus on deficit reduction. Costs have been fuelled by the long-term demographic trends of a growing and ageing population; figures in support of this analysis include a 61% projected increased in those aged over 65 in the UK by 2032, as well as an increase in life expectancy in the UK of 30 years over the course of the 20th century.[36] In many ways such demographic variants have been a clear indicator of the NHS's post-war success: it has considerably prolonged average life expectancy via the promotion of 'improvements in health, diet and preventative care',[37] but with this have come significant financial costs relating to NHS infrastructure and service viability in the long-term. This trend in the UK's demographics has been identified as a specific cause of 'the inexorable growth of welfare spending'[38] and the ongoing extension of social rights in the post-war era. Such trends have provided an escalating and evolving challenge to most governments. While the incoming government from 2010 appears to have prioritised improved levels of efficiency, service and performance within the NHS, it remains a valid issue to consider as to whether NHS policy is ultimately both shaped and hampered by the considerable structural and economic constraints resulting from the UK's long-term, significant demographic changes. This has the potential to undermine government policy intentions in the healthcare sphere.

Such a scenario strikes at potentially conflicting Conservative motives for NHS policy-making, and in tackling this demographic reality the party's primary focus during the 2010–15 parliament appears to have been on enhancing the provision and quality of service within the NHS by a combination of financial investment and a simultaneous programme of organisational reforms intended to ensure improved value for money for the taxpayers and a guarantee of a quality public service in the long-term. The Conservative Party's focus on providing enhanced levels of choice within the service also appear to be fuelled by the post-2010 government's desire to employ a greater range and diversity of proposed healthcare providers, and alongside this development is a programme of structural reform as a further means of achieving an improved service in practical terms. These rival demands of simultaneous investment, reform, retrenchment and eventual service delivery have generated a maelstrom at the heart of modern Conservatism's social policy agenda; a collision of conflicting pressures and tensions which make a clear and coherent policy direction a challenge, difficult to predict in terms of planning, implementation and eventual outcome. This multi-faceted approach might be viewed as an effective political strategy reinforcing a key aspect of the party's traditional political identity and playing to some historic strengths, the Conservatives being perceived as flexible and pragmatic, financially prudent, in control of public spending and, at the same time, social policy innovators.

However on a more radical and innovative level, the party's NHS agenda has aimed to instil a modern variant of Conservatism into the policy mix, namely by promoting it as a core emphasis of the government's 'Big Society' narrative, focusing on overseeing the creation of a dynamic social policy within a decentralised and localised policy-making model. In adopting this approach, the new government has sought to distinguish itself from the allegedly profligate fiscal tendencies and bureaucratic, centralising instincts over public policy-making that were associated with the previous Labour regime. The outcome has seen the emergence of a scenario where there is evidence of the coalition government's commitment to the maintenance of healthy levels of investment in a key public service while simultaneously attempting to radically restructure and reshape it; and this has appeared to be an extremely challenging balancing act to fulfil. The attempt to reform the NHS was a major challenge faced by the Thatcher government in the 1980s, and even during the New Labour period there were difficulties in reorganising the service while also investing in it, particularly due to Labour's close links to the public sector trade unions and the resistance this movement generally expressed towards public service reform. Such historic parallels suggest that similar proposed reforms from 2010 onwards were always likely to be laden with a series of significant political and economic difficulties.

Within this increasingly expensive broad policy arena of wider welfare provision, and specifically health policy, the emphasis on streamlining costs and bureaucracy has encapsulated many Conservative criticisms of the previous Labour government.[39] However, whether such a reduction in bureaucracy and overall cost is practically possible within a credible social policy agenda that seeks to maintain established levels of service for an ageing society is highly questionable, particularly given the added aspiration of a devolved organisational structure and localised service delivery. This complex challenge of governance has been evident in the aftermath of the global economic crisis of 2008 and the increasing pressures on social and welfare policy expenditure caused by rising levels of unemployment. Such socio-economic crises have historically required a strong centralised state to co-ordinate an appropriate response, a factor which appears to undermine the coalition government's localist agenda. It is a fundamental question as to whether Cameron's administration has both the political desire and practical ability to be 'radical' enough to achieve its explicit aims in healthcare, namely to achieve significant retrenchment in expenditure while at the same time creating a more decentralised health service structure in line with traditional Conservative principles of freedom and marketisation, without damaging the fabric of British society and destabilising a key public policy in the process.

Linked to such socio-economic influences and structural organisational pressures, there have also been moral imperatives behind this policy. The Cameron-led administration has sought to infuse a greater sense of Conservative–orientated social justice into British politics and society, whereby a less centralised state structure exists to provide a regulatory framework to ensure the necessary quality of public service delivery, but which is less active and interventionist in policy provision, giving the individual greater personal responsibility and so less directly reliant on the state for support. Under this idealised vision of modern Conservatism, citizens are encouraged to embrace a model of public service provision that delivers enhanced levels of choice, personal responsibility and opportunity within a more independent and autonomous framework, operating in a broader political structure that features a diverse range of service providers, and which ideally entails a slimmer state – one more hospitable to personal autonomy. Within this context, increased choice is viewed as a positive means of enhancing the service, not eroding it, with the Prime Minister affirming that 'We will ensure competition benefits patients.'[40] Some Conservatives and right-of-centre commentators have embraced this perspective of enhanced choice and individuality within the service and developed it along a further dimension, making it the basis for arguing, in a neo-Conservative and morally infused position, that a logical conclusion is to question the universal ethos of NHS provision and to favour the availability of specific NHS services only to those who 'deserve' them, and that a form of desert-based rationing should result. Such an argument, seeking to instil a morality-based conditionality, has concluded that aspects of NHS provision should be withdrawn from people who do not take care or personal responsibility for their own health due to smoking or poor diet.[41] The party leadership has not offered public support or formally embraced this hypothetical proposal.

Cameron's approach to NHS policy has also come under pressure from a variety of right-of-centre think tanks such as the Centre for

Social Justice (CSJ), the Centre for Policy Studies (CPS), the Taxpayers' Alliance[42] and the Social Market Foundation (SMF), who, in a similar vein to their actions in the educational sphere, have sought to influence government health policy within a more libertarian, pluralistic framework. While such groups have sought to steer this area of policy towards a more individualised, marketised and streamlined organisational direction, the CSJ in particular, with particular emphasis on its distinct variant of social justice, has reinforced a sense of moral pressure by stressing the importance of enhanced self-help and autonomy in public healthcare as a means of improving an individual's self-worth and value to society. Cameron has had to balance the somewhat incongruous pre-election promises of enhanced levels of investment in the health service against the achievement of national deficit reduction, as well as reacting to the realities of coalition politics and external think-tank and pressure group activity in framing NHS policy after 2010. The challenging issue of reshaping and restructuring the pivotal public service that is the NHS, therefore, provides a number of variables to the largest party within the coalition government, offering the Conservatives a chance to fulfil their expressed commitment to improving the service via the devolution and debureaucratisation of public policy-making. However even the trailblazing and more ideologically assertive Conservative administration of Margaret Thatcher in the 1980s struggled to deal with the fundamental issues relating to the management of the costs and size of the wider extensive welfare state, for the principal reason that 'it affects the lives of so many people'.[43]

The NHS and 'The Big Society'

This key social policy area was therefore identified as a dimension of governance that would allow both traditional Conservative principles and innovative new ideas to be imposed as part of the party's new social agenda from 2010 onwards, while in the process promoting more efficient use of taxpayers' money. It would also offer enlightenment as to how Conservative social policies correlated and aligned themselves with the architecture of 'The Big Society', with its focus on greater 'localism', enhanced social responsibility and a remodelled state. Advocates of the 'Big Society' agenda have subsequently proclaimed that when its principles are attached to specific areas of social policy such as the NHS, its approach to governance is 'pragmatic and non-ideological in character... (providing) more freedom to innovate... and more freedom to act in accordance with simple common sense'.[44] Such an apparently practical and liberating political approach to the delivery of key public services would suggest that pragmatism and 'statecraft' prevailed over ideological dogma in social policy-making, and this practical political nature is consistent with a label that has been attached to Cameron by observers and biographers.[45] However, as a counter to this viewpoint, critics from both the political and medical world have claimed that the proposed NHS reforms of the Cameron government are tainted by explicit ideological tendencies that clearly and deliberately advocate a smaller state which seeks to make greater use of what Conservative supporters believe to be a more efficient private sector[46] to offer a balance to the state's previously hegemonic influence in public service delivery. Such an organisational model has been espoused by supporters of the post-2010 NHS reforms.

The government's focus on deficit reduction, eliminating excess bureaucracy and streamlining the functionality of key public services has generated controversial policies and proposed reforms to the existing health service structure,[47] with a particular emphasis on seeking to liberate the service from an overbearing and bureaucratic centralised state, as Conservatives perceive it. Advocates of the 'Big Society' agenda have argued that a universalised national health service, controlled from the centre of government since its creation in 1948, does not necessarily provide a better quality or more efficient service:

> Nobody wants a patchy health service, but the point is that we already have a patchy health service, we already have a health service that is delivering massive inequality, we already have a world where some people live thirty years longer than someone else.[48]

In the sphere of health policy (as in other policy areas since 2010), the principles of the 'Big Society' have been fused with the austerity agenda, and this combined pressure has led to an enhanced focus on the 'efficient' market ethos and the generation of 'greater competition in the NHS',[49] which in many ways has echoed the debate of the 1980s. In this sense history has seemed to repeat itself, with Labour leading the objections to such policy reforms from opposition, and many health professions joining the chorus of disapproval, with key groups such as the BMA excluded from government-organised summits to discuss proposed NHS policy changes after 2010.[50] The pursuit of such policies has suggested that the Conservatives possibly have some unfinished business in this socio-political sphere from their last sustained spell in government between 1979 and 1997, despite the fact that New Labour embraced private involvement and funding within the NHS while in office between 1997 and 2010. However, New Labour's pursuit of private sector involvement was not as radical or extensive as the coalition government's, with the potential limit on private patients in the NHS rising from a 2% maximum imposed by Labour in 2003, up to a 49% maximum to be obtained by private funds as outlined in the 2012 Health and Social Care Bill.[51] This scenario has resulted in the Conservative–Liberal Democrat coalition encouraging and indeed legislating for non-state providers and private companies to have access to a bigger share of the NHS and provide specific health and broader welfare services that have traditionally been under the remit of the state. In adopting this approach the Conservative-led government has sought to expand the opportunities for the private sector in order to diversify provision in the name of enhanced value, reduced administrative bureaucracy, greater choice and a more diverse public service, as has been the case with education policy.

This variable fusion of pressures and influences of an economic, social, moral and political nature has meant that proposed NHS reform, addressing an organisation that is complex, extensive and entrenched, has been an integral aspect of the revamped Conservative social policy focus since the party regained national office, absorbing significant amounts of government time in the process. The 'Big Society' approach to the health service has resulted in some core principles of the post-1948 NHS and its 'universal' provision coming under significant scrutiny and revision from private, localised and non-state elements, and this outlook has been fuelled by the dynamics of economics, demographics and communitarianism in particular. In pursuing a policy approach that promises investment alongside organisational reforms and restructuring, the Cameron government has developed what its supporters claim is a flexible and pragmatic premise which embraces the mantra that it is 'a perfectly reasonable question to ask whether you would get better public services by employing other organisations than merely the instruments of the state'.[52] This is a major gamble for Cameron's administration, and given that such reforms have associations with neo-liberalism and privatisation, he has rekindled connotations of the Thatcherite ideology and its impact on the NHS during the 1980s, which significant swathes of voters have viewed as being negative. This has risked 'retoxifying'[53] the party's precious brand and image in this 'compassionate' sphere of policy-making, in spite of Cameron's extensive efforts to achieve the opposite outcome.

Intellectual and other influences behind Conservative NHS Policy since 2010

As Michael Gove became the prominent figurehead for Conservative educational reforms after 2010, so Andrew Lansley took on a parallel role in relation to health policy until he left the post following a Cabinet reshuffle in September 2012, to be replaced by Jeremy Hunt. Lansley had been one of the longest-established Conservative politicians in their particular policy role, having held the Shadow Health position since 2004, therefore preceding Cameron's accession to the party leadership in late 2005. During this time he subsequently built up a considerable depth of knowledge of his policy portfolio, and Cameron appears to have deferred to such policy experience by keeping him in the same position for such a long period of time. Given his substantial pedigree in the field, Lansley will have been influential in shaping the commitment made by the Conservative–Liberal Democrat coalition in May 2010 that as far as NHS policy was concerned, the new government would seek to 'free NHS staff from political micromanagement... (and) stop the top-down reorganisations of the NHS'.[54] This pledge was a high-profile one and sought to epitomise the apparently distinctive approach of the new government from 2010, with its emphasis on patient empowerment and the liberation of the broader NHS as an organisational structure with reduced levels of government bureaucracy. However, it has been the source of much political debate in the months and years since 2010 as to whether the Conservatives have adhered to this aspect of the coalition agreement with its emphasis on greater devolution and autonomy within the service, as opposed to significant organisational restructuring imposed from above.

Such top-down reorganisations were identified as negative features of NHS policy-making that were associated with the previous Labour administration, and they were deemed as being undesirable from a Conservative perspective. The principal reason for this was that they were highlighted as an apparent cause of generating increased levels of organisational bureaucracy. From an early stage of the Conservative–Liberal Democrat coalition government's existence, reducing the levels of bureaucracy was identified as a key priority in terms of addressing a structural aspect of the NHS monolith that Labour's 13 years in office had failed to address, despite rhetoric to the contrary. An early specific target that was identified for bureaucratic cutbacks was the need to achieve a minimum of £20 billion in spending cuts over 3–4 years, as highlighted by the NHS Chief Executive Sir David Nicholson in 2009 during the final phase of Labour's period in government.[55] Achieving 4% spending cuts within the NHS for four successive years alongside the development of greater levels of integrated healthcare were therefore seen to be specific, essential elements of this prudent, cost-cutting agenda, and this approach has been broadly endorsed by the Commons Health Select Committee, chaired by former Health Secretary Stephen Dorrell (1995–97). This financial target was subsequently dubbed the 'Nicholson challenge', but, in the short-term at least, the government failed to reduce the bureaucratic costs in the NHS, according to National Audit Office estimates in 2011–12,[56] and this upward public expenditure trend undermined its health policy agenda from an early stage of its time in national office.

Within this broad context of seeking to control the long-term upward spiral of cost and bureaucracy within the NHS, spending on the service has increased tenfold from its original level in real terms since 1948,[57] although this has been generally in line with most other developed nations. However, since 2010, clear attempts have been made to steer policy formulation in a more explicitly Conservative-orientated direction, with a greater focus on traditional principles such as improved patient choice, enhanced devolution of responsibilities to GPs and medical professionals (more clinical leadership), alongside greater accountability and the attempted elimination of superfluous organisational structures. This has been bolstered by a background political narrative of debureaucratisation and tougher fiscal guidelines for government expenditure on the service, creating better value for the taxpayer in the process. Despite Cameron's post-2010 claims to have ring-fenced NHS spending, some critical voices have declared that the practical implication of this approach amidst cuts in overall government expenditure is that NHS spending levels (in real terms) could steadily slip below the Thatcher period of the 1980s. This is due to the developing scenario that despite the NHS facing less severe cutbacks than other departments in the post-2010 austerity drive, the health department's budget is set to rise by just 0.1% annually until 2014, compared to a 4.5% annual average for most of the service's lifetime since 1948.[58] Such challenging spending levels have been put into a stark historical context by NHS Chief Executive Sir David Nicholson, who has stated that proposed spending levels on the service after 2010 are 'generous when you look across the rest of the public service. [But] there has never been a time where we have had four years of flat real growth. It is unprecedented'.[59]

Such an 'unprecedented' background has generated renewed fears of 'rationing' within the service among political opponents, raising question marks against the Conservative Party's pre-election commitment to the NHS. Such fears will not be able to be accurately assessed until the end of the 2010–2015 parliament. The culmination of NHS policy in the early years of the coalition government was the high-profile Health and Social Care Act (2012),[60] which the then Secretary of State for Health, Andrew Lansley, praised as being:

> part of a broader vision of health and health services in this country being among the best in the world... a service where national standards and funding secure a high-quality, comprehensive service available to all, based on need and not the ability to pay; and where the power to deliver is in the hands of local doctors, nurses, health professionals and local communities.[61]

In its fundamental shake-up and restructuring of the NHS, this Act has been widely criticised by many on the left of British politics, primarily due to its apparent contradiction of repeated coalition pledges not to engage in a top-down reorganisation of the health service and its long-standing institutional elements. Its implications have indeed entailed some significant restructuring of the service, with an enhanced focus on imposing greater competition via a wider range of NHS service providers.[62] As junior coalition partners, the Liberal Democrats have been sceptical but have been gradually persuaded to support the general thrust of such reforms. However there have been internal tensions and divisions within the party amid claims from political opponents that the NHS was being privatised in all but name by such policy measures, with Deputy Prime Minister Nick Clegg offering reassurances that 'If I felt it was privatising the NHS or tearing it limb from limb, it would never have seen the light of day.'[63]

This policy proposal endured a prolonged and controversial passage through parliament in 2011–12, with significant amendments and concessions secured by Liberal Democrat peers in the House of Lords, primarily in relation to the nature of the proposed devolution of powers and financial decision-making to GPs, alongside the scale and range of private healthcare providers that suggested the resurrection of a more full-blown 'choice' agenda.[64] In this sense it can perhaps be argued that, as in educational policy, the Liberal Democrats have acted as a braking mechanism on the more ideological tendencies within the Conservative Party, although Andrew Lansley has been keen to further underplay the ideological implications of the policy, saying that 'choice, competition and the involvement of the private sector should only ever be a means to improve services for patients, not ends in themselves'.[65] The Prime Minister and Deputy Prime Minister have also sought to align such health reforms with their broader attitude to public service provision, namely that:

> a new approach to delivering public services is urgently needed. The principles that inform our approach, and the policies we will enact to give it force, signal a decisive end to the old-fashioned, top-down, take-what-you-are-given model of public services. We are opening public services because we believe that giving people more control over the public services they receive, and opening up the delivery of those services to new providers, will lead to better public services for all.[66]

However, one high-profile media critic has still claimed that the thrust of the reforms is aligned not with practical necessity or the mood of the 'Big Society' as the above quote suggests, but instead with an inherent market ideology with links to the neo-liberal agenda of the 1980s, and which therefore has the negative potential to 'finish the Health Service – and David Cameron'.[67] This implies a potentially adverse political consequence for the Prime Minister in his pursuit of such NHS reforms, which was perhaps a factor in Andrew Lansley's sideways move from the Department of Health in autumn 2012, amid media suggestions that he was bearing the brunt of criticism of the post-2010 NHS reforms.[68] Such a negative fall-out from the policy has resurrected images of retoxification of the Conservative image, a bleak prospect for a Prime Minister who in restructuring this core public service has sought to redefine his party's reputation in relation to it.

A central influence behind Cameron's NHS policy has therefore been the concerted effort to drive down the extent of government bureaucracy, a fundamental theme of the post-2010 'Big Society' agenda. Within such a context, a philosophical and practical desire to turn the clock back to the pre-NHS era of more localised and less bureaucratic control of the service is therefore perhaps apparent. However a particularly ironic aspect of the government's specific programme for NHS reform has stemmed from the Labour opposition's claims from 2012 onwards that despite this much-publicised focus on reducing the hegemonic role of the state in NHS provision, the practical implications of post-2010 NHS policy has been the creation of more structural bureaucracy and reliance on the centralised state within this area of

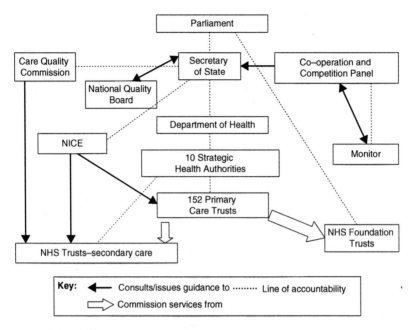

Figure 7.1   NHS structure (pre–2010), Adapted from: http://offlinehbpl.hbpl. co.uk/NewsAttachments/PG/Previous%20NHS%20structure.pdf GP Online, 5 July 2011, *'How clinical commissioning groups will work'*

social policy[69] (see Figures 7.1 and 7.2). This is the opposite of what the Conservatives had aspired to achieve via their 'Big Society' approach, and rather than it being a case of mere political point-scoring, it matches academic arguments that removing accountability from ministers actually increases, rather than decreases, bureaucracy.[70] David Cameron has repeatedly voiced this aspiration for NHS governance with recurring comments such as 'We're wasting too much money on empty bureaucracy when it could be spent on the frontline',[71] yet, despite such rhetoric, the warnings of bureaucratic growth have been re-emphasised from more unlikely quarters, with the right-of-centre, libertarian think-tank Civitas expressing similar comments in 2010 about additional organisational bureaucracy being created by government proposals to transfer NHS purchasing power to GPs, supposedly to save costs. Civitas argued that the outcome of this proposal could be counter-productive, primarily due to the NHS 'facing the most difficult financial times in its history (and) now is not the time for ripping up internal structures

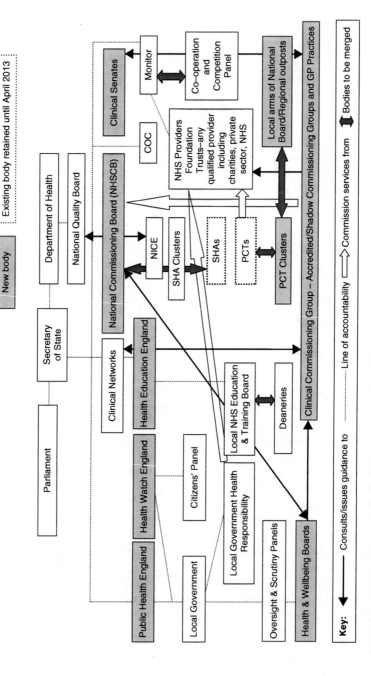

Figure 7.2 David Cameron's new NHS bureaucracy after 2010, adapted from: http://offlinehbpl.hbpl.co.uk/NewsAttachments/PG/new%20NHS%20bureaucracy.pdf, GP Online, 5 July 2011, 'How clinical commissioning groups will work'

yet again on scant evidence base',[72] with the contradictory consequence that such organisational reform has created another structural layer in the process, as instigated by the 2012 Health and Social Care Act.

Such arguments appear to undermine one of the prime influences behind the flagship Health and Social Care Bill's introduction, and this specific criticism ultimately suggests that the new NHS policy approach since 2010 has indeed instigated a top-down organisational restructure despite coalition government promises to the contrary. This has predictably brought its own distinct layer of associated bureaucracy and 'red-tape' that will potentially be difficult to eliminate in the long-term. This is further evidence to vindicate the Max Weber analysis[73] from the early 20th century, which argues that society becomes more bureaucratised over time, reflecting increased social complexity that transcends government attempts to stem the bureaucratic tide. This view has been concisely aligned and identified with specific contemporary problems by one political commentator as follows:

> Taking the development of local empowerment seriously could involve massive expenditure to set up the necessary infrastructures, and that may not be possible in the aftermath of the world financial crisis.[74]

A similar charge has been laid against the Free Schools policy, namely that any significant structural reorganisation in a key public service always carries its own bureaucratic and financial baggage in addition to existing structures, with entrenched and existing organisational layers difficult to eliminate entirely and new ones often more complex than initially envisaged. So, despite Conservative pledges to the contrary prior to 2010, it can be argued that top-down bureaucracy is very difficult to reduce in a vast and complex public service such as the NHS, for the principal reason that the practical running of the organisation is heavily influenced by political pressures to meet insatiable public demands and ensure adequate service delivery. The fact that it is 'a taxation-based economic system (which)... will always to an extent have to be managed in a top-down manner',[75] also generates further bureaucracy, and as the earlier quote suggests such pressures on the NHS have been exacerbated by the global financial crisis from 2008 onwards, which appears to have put further strains on the funding and management of this key public service.

Such explicit aims and influences focusing on the need for greater organisational efficiency and improved levels of performance have brought difficult practical implications with them, as public opinion figures have indicated the lowest recorded health satisfaction figures for 30 years,[76] with a 12% drop in public support between 2010 and 2011. This has prompted critics to make a link between the contemporary direction and focus of the NHS policy agenda since 2010 and a steadily worsening service that is likely to come under further strain due to the impact of the government's reforms and ongoing austerity agenda. Prime Minister Cameron expressed his awareness of the rising levels of political and public opposition and criticism to his NHS reforms, declaring a willingness to 'take a hit' (at least in the short-term) from the wider public over the issue, adding that the reforms were those of a 'brave government' and offering reassurance that the NHS was 'in the party's DNA and that's not going to change'.[77] Those who support the reforms have argued that, after the Health and Social Care Bill formally became law in Spring 2012, the new policy needs appropriate time to prove its worth and fulfil the coalition government's claims that the reforms will improve the service, particularly in the light of significant amendments in the House of Lords ostensibly intended to enhance the legislation and reflect concerns from the medical profession.[78] Former Health Secretary and Chair of the Health Select Committee, Stephen Dorrell, subsequently commented on the passing of the bill that the government should now be given 'opportunity to apply it (the new policy) and to demonstrate the value it can create.'[79]

A further negative feature of the formulation and implementation of NHS policy since 2010 has been the apparent influence of lobbyists and business interests who stand to directly benefit in financial terms from the enhanced competition and private investment created by NHS reforms, an accusation supported by media coverage in early 2010 suggesting that 'Tory MPs in charge of health policy had accepted donations from private healthcare companies'.[80] While lobbyists seeking to influence public policy is a regular, indeed inevitable, aspect of any pluralist political system, this particular example has raised critical concerns in relation to a fundamental commercial motive at the heart of Conservative healthcare policy, and this would appear to undermine the party leadership's morally infused compassionate rhetoric and its agenda to restructure the NHS supposedly in order to ensure its long-term survival as a thriving public service. Such doubts about motives strike at the heart of the Conservative Party's aims for NHS policy since returning to national office, raising the question of whether intellectual and philosophical factors really are ascendant over purely political and even commercial influences.

One further intellectual factor worth considering when assessing the Conservative Party's motives and influences in this area of policy is the relevance of 'nudge theory',[81] which argues that governments have the ability to influence and shape wider social behaviours in a more positive and beneficial direction that aligns with their overall socio-political agenda, particularly in seeking to mould the long-term mentality of the wider population towards its specific policies over a sustained period of time. This theory focuses on behavioural traits and social influences across society, and its core emphasis is that a government's consistent, active, overall direction, alongside a recurring message about acceptable or desirable 'social norms',[82] can produce 'positive economic and social outcomes without resorting to bans or increased regulation'.[83] This approach has been dubbed 'libertarian paternalism',[84] and it is within this context that the government has set up a 'Behaviourial Insights Team'[85] as part of the 2010 Coalition Agreement to try to facilitate various socio-political outcomes linked to its own political agenda, yet without seeking an excessively active role for the central state, a conclusion consistent with the 'Big Society' agenda. This team has identified certain aspects of public health policy in particular that can be influenced and shaped in such a way, notably by providing an enhanced and somewhat manipulated 'choice architecture' to the wider general public in a bid to influence its behaviour and specific lifestyle choices.

Examples of this approach to public policy-making can be seen in initiatives such as anti-smoking and healthy eating strategies, principally aimed at altering and moulding the public's mood and attitudes in line with a central government public health agenda, yet without the government appearing too authoritarian or interventionist in the process. Applied to the Cameron-led government's post-2010 health reforms, it is hoped, the public can be 'nudged' towards gradually accepting the necessity of more devolved and diversified provision within the NHS without the need for further interventionist legislation (as part of a smaller state). It has been a matter of fierce political debate as to whether such devolution is a practical means in itself, or whether it is part of a long-term process of creating a less statist, quasi-privatised, health service. It can be argued that such an approach bears some of the hallmarks of the pragmatic reformist Conservatism of Edmund Burke,[86] whose 18th-century works accepted the necessity of cautious government reform in order to preserve key institutions and allow them to evolve in a preferred way, Burke being 'optimistic about the ability of parties (and politicians) to make things better'.[87] This outlook firmly rejects revolutionary upheaval but instead embraces the need for steady, evolutionary political change initiated and controlled by the government. The Burkean parallel with recent NHS reforms can be made on the basis that the service arguably needs to reform and adapt in order to survive, and that 'a sequence of nudges of sufficient strength amounts to a push', with the government's role in such key reforms based on the overarching premise of 'Big Society' thinkers 'that interference is in principle a good rather than a necessary evil'.[88] This argument would seek to counter the critical viewpoint that the government's post-2010 approach to NHS policy-making is ideological, and it appears to suggest a detachment from the traditions and principles of the New Right in accepting a proactive role for the state. However, the direction in which the reimagined state is pushing the health service, or the eventual organisational form that is envisaged, has not yet become fully apparent.

The post-2010 government has sought to create a choice-based framework for socio-economic activity in key social policy areas such as the NHS, but in order to achieve this goal it has embraced an approach that includes a notable role for government in seeking to 'steer people's choices in directions that will improve their lives',[89] without being excessively overbearing. This is particularly evident in the sphere of contemporary healthcare policy and the way that the NHS is organised and run on a practical basis. Given that government health reforms from 2010 contain individualistic and neo-liberal choice-based elements that are controversial and provocative to some prominent members of the medical profession, the political classes and the media, the post-2010 government has been conscious of the need not to provoke unnecessary opposition, particularly given its coalition status. It has therefore approached this policy-making dynamic with some caution, establishing a House of Lords Committee to look into the nature of 'nudge'-originated policy in 2011.[90] This specific approach to governance has adopted a libertarian ethos in its core message, seeking to limit the need for additional legislation and excessive government intervention to achieve its desired outcome, as a strategy of changing people's attitudes 'cost(s) little or nothing... impos(ing) no burden on taxpayers at all'.[91] Therefore, while the nature of the post-2010 NHS reforms may endure some short-term hostility, in practical terms this emphasis on addressing and analysing wider social behaviour aims to 'nudge' popular culture and the mood of broader society in a specific long-term direction in order to bolster the socio-political outcome that the government wants, namely a more streamlined, marketised and autonomous policy vision for the health service. This approach aspires to erode the structural constraints and social obstacles attached to the health service in its current guise that have in the immediate term limited the scope of reform, and it aims to achieve this without resorting to interventionist, coercive or expensive government activity. However, it remains to be seen as to whether this approach will eventually create a scenario that will create the type of service structure that the Cameron-led regime desires, as well as increasing the levels of popular support for such reforms and their associated outcomes. This approach seeks to persuade people that the reforms to the NHS are effective and necessary measures on both a practical and financial level in the long term, and it may require a further term in office to fully suppress the high degree of opposition and controversy that such proposals have generated.

The influences and aims that have driven the Conservative-led government's reforms of the NHS after 2010 are therefore varied and multi-dimensional, with competition and tensions evident between vigorous ideological factors, the pressures of cost and economic aspects as well as pragmatic statecraft and cautious, gradual 'Burkean' reform, all acting to shape the evolution of this social policy. In pursuing its policy agenda the party has also faced institutional and structural limits within the NHS organisation itself, as well as commercially driven external lobbying and the recurring New Right desire to reduce and remove statist and managerial bureaucracy and instil greater choice in a monolithic state service – a desire which has lingered from the 1980s and has again been evident since 2010. The more radical elements of the New Right legacy have not been wholly abandoned, but they have been tempered by the Conservative leadership's strategic desire and electoral need to emphasise its compassionate credentials and to appease its junior coalition partners in social policy matters. All these influences and factors have led to the 21st-century Conservative Party making explicit and unprecedented pledges in government to maintain investment in the NHS, and this has alienated many within the party's New Right tradition. However, in a quixotic manner that indicates a lack of coherent short-term political direction on this issue, the Conservative-led government has also sought to use the powers of the state to 'nudge' public opinion towards accepting a more marketised, diversified and devolved organisational structure as a price for securing the long-term future of the NHS in some form.

During this process of organisational and institutional reform there has been considerable debate as to whether the post-2010 coalition government is genuinely committed to devolved decision-making within the NHS or whether it will revert to the tendency of many governments to impose policy from the centre in order to meet its key political aims, while also adhering to austerity measures aimed at reducing overall costs. Again, as with educational policy, there have been clear movements and gestures towards a changed social policy, but it is open to conjecture as to whether the Conservative-led government's approach to NHS policy and its desire to radically transform the nature of service delivery will eventually emerge from the shackles of austerity to construct a clearer and more streamlined, decentralised and rationalised version of the current organisational model, able to deliver quality public healthcare for the 21st century. This challenging task is further complicated by the desire of Conservative modernisers to maintain some adherence to an enabling and co-ordinating (yet far from hegemonic) state structure, which in its comparatively limited role will be required to encourage an ethos and functional framework within the NHS that promotes and extends the communitarian tendencies of the 'Big Society' socio-political agenda.

Conclusion: The nature and evolution of contemporary Conservative social policy

Key concepts: Debureaucratisation and 'progress'

In seeking to identify and address the extent of change in the formulation of Conservative Party social policy since the party emphatically lost national office in 1997, it has been necessary to assess a range of theoretical, ideological and practical social policy developments to reach a concluding overview which draws together all the factors and components. A clear and coherent concluding position must explicitly acknowledge that a new generation of Conservative politicians and theorists have been at the forefront of reforming and modernising the party's social policy agenda since the late 1990s, and that this indicates a notable degree of change at a basic level. In doing so they have faced internal political opposition and wider public and media scepticism, but they have persisted in pursuing this socio-political strategy, actively seeking to develop a new image for the party in relation to a range of welfare policy spheres such as education, healthcare and broader public service delivery and reform. In adopting such an approach they have sought to reflect the changing nature of British society, namely by engaging with such new socio-political moods and attitudes as well as embracing new, diverse means of service delivery, challenging the traditional post-war role of the state by emphasising the role of the private, community and charitable sectors separate from centralised government. They have aspired to instil a specific localist and grassroots flavour in such associated policy, ensuring that they are located within an overarching model of governance aligned with the broad theme of a debureaucratised 'leaner' state.[1]

As a practical consequence of this approach, they advocate public services and social policy traditionally provided by central government should be fragmented, outsourced or subcontracted to devolved, potentially more efficient, bodies, offering empowerment to individual citizens and local communities in the process. While this approach has echoes of the New Right's neo-liberal agenda for public service provision during the 1980s, a repeatedly expressed and frequently re-emphasised desire of the post-2010 coalition government has been to reinvigorate a decentralised model of the state that does not entail dismantling institutions on purely ideological grounds, but which focuses on practicality while maintaining a compassionate undercurrent to social policy. Within this context of devising a pro-active, strategic and co-ordinating role for a more limited and reconstituted state structure, it is envisaged that the more durable and flexible components of the state can function effectively and efficiently, albeit within a more streamlined model of service delivery. This approach has in turn sought to encourage the emergence of a resurgent and revitalised civil society, identified as the key mechanism for empowering individuals and communities, which will seek to generate social action emanating from 'civic institutions and forms of collective activity that are not state activity',[2] and which genuinely transcends the post-1945 model of centralised, bureaucratic universalism.

This approach to remoulding governance and related best practices has been expressed and promoted as the 'Big Society', a symbolic policy that reflects a concerted agenda to generate enhanced innovation and 'progressive' new thought in the provision of social policy via a diverse range of providers from across the public, private and third sectors. The ambivalent term 'progressive' reflects an optimistic approach that 'things could get better, problems are not intractable and things weren't just inevitably getting worse',[3] and its aspirations have been succinctly expressed in two key documents produced by the Conservative–Liberal Democrat coalition: the White Paper 'Open Public Services'[4] (July 2011), and the 2011 Localism Act.[5] Both legislative initiatives have focused on individual choice and control, decentralisation, diversity, fairness and accountability; a range of vocabulary that when fused together suggests dynamism in promoting the 'collaboration and diversity in the provision of public services'.[6] In the wider context of rising financial costs in the provision of welfare and social policy, the two documents describe the government's ongoing programme of public service reform for much of its term of office up to 2015, although how successful such 'progressive social conservatism' has actually been in social, economic and political terms has been open to criticism and sceptical review as the coalition government's policy agenda has evolved.[7] In particular, evidence has emerged from the radical reforms to key public services such as the welfare benefits system, the educational system and the NHS attempted since 2010, that efforts to 'debureaucratise' such key areas of social policy have failed to liberate them from the tentacles of state control, and have actually created additional layers of bureaucracy in the process.

The state vs. voluntarism as a vehicle for social justice

Alongside the persistent aspiration towards improved levels of economic efficiency, progressive innovation and streamlined bureaucratic performance in the delivery of key social policies, the need to achieve positive and constructive outcomes such as a fairer society or greater social justice have also been prominent features of the contemporary social policy debate. This has particularly been so in the post-Thatcher era from the early 1990s onwards, given that the divisions between rich and poor grew considerably during this period under governments of both major parties, continuing a socially divisive trend that began during the 1980s. However, the means and methods of achieving such 'socially just' ends have been the subject of intense political debate, with the competing yet overlapping roles of the state, the voluntary sector and the private sector all closely examined, compared and contrasted. Indeed, the need to strike an appropriate balance between the functions and interests of such bodies has been an integral feature to this political dialogue. As discussed in Chapter 3, although such terms and concepts associated with social justice have been broadly associated with the left of the political spectrum, and were exploited by New Labour to its political advantage from the mid-1990s onwards, mainstream British Conservatism has attempted to reinvent and detoxify its image in the early years of the 21st century. Many pragmatic right-of-centre politicians and think-tanks have sought to adapt to and remould the tone of this vocabulary, seeking to develop their own version of social justice by instigating innovative and electorally appealing policy responses in the process.

Despite a historical Conservative acceptance of the reality of socioeconomic inequality, new influences have come to affect the formulation of modern Conservative social policy. On the one hand there has been an acknowledgement of the vigorous ideological influence of the 'New Right' and its more radical critique and proposed reforms of the bureaucratic state, yet there has also been some degree of acceptance of the impact of 13 years of New Labour rule and its steady, yet allegedly inefficient, investment in key public services nestled within local communities. Conservative modernisers have accepted this development and cautiously embraced some functional aspects of existing public policy provision, while also seeking to steadily 'nudge' public opinion in a different, more 'conservative' direction, in an approach that is aligned with gradual 'Burkean' tendencies, seeking to maintain aspects of the existing state and its 'organic' nature, as well as its associated community values where practical and appropriate. The former neo-liberal influence has led some academic commentators to remark on links between the Thatcher agenda of the 1980s and the Cameron programme since 2010 in relation to attitudes towards key public services traditionally provided by the state. This viewpoint suggests that despite their contrasting rhetoric in relation to terms such as 'society' and 'community', both the Thatcher administration and the post-2010 Conservative-led coalition are 'founded on the same neo-liberal antagonism towards the public sector which is seen as crowding out the private sector',[8] and both administrations can be viewed as being ultimately sceptical of 'the state'.

The Burkean tradition could be said to retain some influence over post-2010 social policy direction, accepting the need to maintain and preserve key public institutions and services which have the necessary capacity, utility and flexibility to function in a more limited and peripheral role for the state. This approach retains a key streak of Conservative pragmatism and respect for tradition, adhering to the view that British society and its broader political structure is an evolving, organic entity which seeks to maintain and conserve the best aspects of the existing socio-political order while developing and improving in terms of functionality, efficiency and value for money. This has been evident in recent Conservative attempts to deliver high-quality public services in an innovative and decentralised manner, an approach that symbolises modern Conservatism's desire to emphasise and align with the communitarian and altruistic values that prevail in early 21st century society. In seeking to adapt traditional, viable public institutions, Conservatives have sought to utilise, wherever possible, the energy of charitable activity, the vibrancy of voluntarism alongside the commercial values of private sector providers in preference to monolithic state power/ This has been summarised by a contemporary Cabinet Minister as follows:

> Conservatives believe that voluntarism is a good thing, and sometimes the state can be an obstacle to effective voluntarism, but at other times such voluntary organisations need support from the

state. Your value system has to be that voluntary support comes first.[9]

Recent concerted, spirited attempts to revive voluntarism alongside a range of private agencies as alternative sources of public service provision have therefore been central to attempts to create a 're-imagined' or revised role for the post-war state as part of this devolved approach to social policy. However, it remains a matter of conjecture as to whether social entrepreneurs along with smaller, voluntarist and localised bodies can realistically compete with the financial might of established multinational private bodies and existing public agencies in the supply of public services while maintaining adequate value for money for the taxpayer, as such larger providers will often 'provide the cheapest option... and this may drive out smaller providers who are more local and accountable'.[10] This suggests that what is being proposed in terms of more diverse public service provision does not equate to a 'level playing field', and such practical issues do offer potential obstacles to this policy approach, yet it still appears to be the case that the gut instinct of mainstream British Conservatism is to be sceptical of the role of the state, and sceptical of the likelihood or feasibility of the centralised, interventionist model having the capacity to deliver genuine levels of equality and conventional social justice. This reflects the evolution of Conservative social policymaking, indicating an inherent dilemma of contemporary British Conservatism: how to identify the role for the state's various organs in conjunction with alternative (and arguably more dynamic) components of public service delivery. The party appears to be sceptical of predetermined rationalist outcomes moulded by statist influences, on the premise that an enhanced degree of social autonomy and individual responsibility is preferable to an overbearing, 'meddling' state, which tends to create greater levels of dependency, bureaucracy and state influenced social 'injustice' across society, while being 'highly centralised and paternalistic... intrusive (and) pervasive'.[11]

This position can be linked to the writings of Edmund Burke, who, in analysing the French Revolution from a conservative perspective, praised the value of a multitude of devolved 'little platoons'[12] of social activity, as opposed to the 'monolithic, top-down, repressive society'[13] that he believed the post-revolutionary French state had developed into. Burke's preference for a limited yet paternalistic state can be said to have influenced the Big Society agenda: his theory of such platoons of localised activity providing the 'bottom-up' dynamism to generate desired communitarian activity resembles Cameron's social policy approach. However, more libertarian commentators have argued that the state's role will tend to evolve negatively into a corrosive social influence over time, its centralising tendency 'not only destroys the sense of community spirit and individual initiative, but also destroys the very possibility of their revival'.[14] This political viewpoint views the state as a negative influence that ought to 'retreat to the role of regulator instead of being a direct provider of services'.[15] In many contemporary Western societies shaped by social democratic pressures such a scenario has clearly not happened, much to the chagrin and frustration of many neo-liberal inclined Conservatives. In a rebuttal of such Conservative scepticism towards the state, notable contemporary books such as *The Spirit Level*[16] have challenged the pessimism about the state's effectiveness, developing the alternative argument that a more egalitarian society is both achievable and indeed a more desirable aspiration, even though it can only arise through the efforts of an active and interventionist state that retains a significant centralised co-ordination role. Such a rationalist, determinist outlook continues to be at odds with mainstream Conservative hostility to centralised planning, abstract ideals and artificially imposed outcomes.

Cameron's Social Conservatism: A blend of communitarianism, autonomous localism and fiscal retrenchment

The rhetorical emphasis of David Cameron's leadership since its first appearance at the end of 2005 has represented something a departure from the sharp, explicitly economic edge of Thatcherism; specifically it acknowledges the importance of a communitarian focus alongside a revitalised civil society, the latter concept one which was somewhat neglected by Thatcherism and suffocated by New Labour. This revised Conservative viewpoint accepts the requirement for some element of coordinating, regulatory activity by the state, yet at the same time aspires to a more financially efficient, devolved and localised form of public service delivery. There is evidence of some flexibility and distinctiveness of approach within modern Conservatism relating to its social policy agenda, which distinguishes its approach to the delivery of key social policies from the party's Thatcherite legacy. In attaching the concepts of localism, autonomy and community to modern social Conservatism, this revised version of Conservatism advocates a more streamlined, decentralised model of government. In its rejection of the hegemonic state as core provider of public services (the belief that has prevailed for most of the post-war era), advocates of this 'New

Conservatism' introduce a more compassionate and moralising tone into the social policy debate, while arguing that a fundamental revision of the relationship between citizens and the state is essential to the achievement of greater personal self-fulfilment. Its ultimate goal is a less intrusive state and a more efficient and productive government, allowing for the emergence of a 'connected society, organised horizontally, not vertically, so as to place these intermediate institutions at its heart.[17]

This provides a radical edge to this social policy approach, but, again, it is unclear how, in practical terms, such a decentralised, horizontal, 'connected' society can emerge, particularly given the drive towards austerity and the limited public funds available since 2010. Such practical difficulties have led to discontent in the inner circle of Cameron's Conservatives caused the failure to launch this policy agenda wholeheartedly, with prominent advocates such as Steve Hilton[18] and Baron Wei departing from the political frontline between mid 2011 and mid 2012 due to deep frustration with the various bureaucratic and institutional obstacles that their initiatives encountered. Nevertheless, the desire for a more 'horizontal' structure of society in relation to the state is an interesting one. In philosophical and theoretical terms, at least, this model, espoused by Jesse Norman and Janan Ganesh, represents an attractive socio-political approach that envisages the natural linkage of citizens 'horizontally' alongside each other in social terms, communally bonded by the key institutions of a more voluntarist model of civil society rather than their being obliged to respond to an invasive, interventionist and prescriptive state. This vision demands the creation of semi-independent bodies such as Free Schools and devolved sectors within the NHS, which would be essentially 'autonomous institutions governing themselves but publicly funded, providing their own identity as a hospital or school but not be seen as the arm of a local authority or a district health authority'.[19] The new variant of social Conservatism of the Cameron era argues that such bodies can deliver enhanced value for money and guarantee the necessary financial savings while maintaining adequate public service provision.

There do, however, appear to be some practical dangers in the such a radical reorientation of society's basic structure and the re-alignment of key social policies, namely that if this ambitious experiment in autonomy, localism and a revived civil society fails to overcome existing structures and an austerity agenda, it could result in newly devolved public services such as Free Schools and a revamped NHS failing in their practical implementation. They may then, ironically, end up even more reliant on the centralised state, and, as Birchall warns, this could result in a Conservative-led administration having to 'fall back on the more authoritarian policies of its predecessors',[20] forced to impose less flexible variants of social policy from the centre again, generating further expense in the process. Other academic observers, such as Flinders and Moon, have also identified this negative theme of the inability to escape a mentality where accountability ultimately rests at the level of the central state, due to inherent structural pressures and the failings of often half-hearted and ineffective devolution of powers from central government.[21]

The likelihood of such policy failures has been exacerbated by the austerity agenda and fiscal restraints imposed by the coalition government since 2010, and some former supporters turned critics of the coalition's social policy direction (such as Philip Blond), implied that such failings were already evident by the end of 2012. This viewpoint claims that Cameron's grand social project has met with failure in its social impact. Its adherents accuse the Conservative Leader of baulking at the prospect of genuine social policy reform, instead appearing to endorse a programme fuelled by retrenchment rather than social radicalism, in the process retoxifying the party brand[22] rather than reinvigorating it. In a practical sense, therefore, this new Conservative social policy agenda has been a major political gamble in its attempts to redefine the role of the state and public service provision while at the same time seeking to rebrand the party's formerly tarnished image in this policy area. Cameron's socially oriented focus of seeking to offer innovation by disentangling social policy from tentacles of the centralised state, developed in the crucible of three successive electoral defeats, might lead to apparently fluid and flexible policy, but it is politically risky. However, such an agenda does represent a legitimate attempt to strike a new balance between the state and the individual in modern British society, and in this sense 'develop public policies that recognise, protect and enhance our connected society... enrich(ing) the cultural conversation within it'.[23] While this approach seeks to reject 'big government' and to retain some aspects of the moral and individualistic imperatives of the New Right socio-economic agenda of the 1980s, it does acknowledge the need for a co-ordinating state initiating social policies that impel the nation towards a more individualistic variant of social justice, an improved culture of citizenship and increased social mobility. This civil and cultural emphasis, alongside the promotion of a more diverse, radical and innovative range of public–private methods for policy delivery, suggests a degree of detachment from the more marketised focus of the New Right during the 1980s, although not a complete abandonment of this approach, due to the lingering attachment to the neo-liberal notion of more autonomous, diversified public service provision.

In addressing this contemporary socio-political challenge, the Cameron leadership has appeared to contribute to the development of a further variation within 'the complex ideological configurations within contemporary British conservatism',[24] although whether his specific form of Conservatism is a genuinely new variant is open to debate. In rhetorical terms at least, Cameron appears to have resisted calls from the Conservative right for an explicit move to full-blown neo-liberal economics and deregulation, and in rejecting this position he has sought to transcend a primarily economic agenda, acknowledging and 'rediscovering'[25] the significance of 'society' as an alternative to the state. At times he has adopted a softer and more compassionate political tone, which has led to the notion of a 're-imagined state', a stance that can be linked to the communitarian, socially-focused 'Red Tory' agenda of Phillip Blond. In electoral terms, Cameron and the Conservative 'modernisers' have therefore acknowledged the importance of crossing a political boundary in relation to previously negative images of the party in office, trying to secure for the party a broader 'appeal across the political spectrum'[26] that has led to the determined pursuit of a revived brand of Conservatism associated with a more communitarian and social flavour[27] in conjunction with a distinctly remodelled vision of the state.

However, in practical terms, compassionate and communitarian rhetoric has been coupled with an agenda of fiscal austerity since May 2010, and this has proved to be a major stumbling block in turning aspiration into political reality. This is because it is arguably the case that if the Big Society agenda is to work and function broadly in the way that Cameron and his allies envisage, there have to be sufficient public funds to support and achieve its aims (at least in the short-term), and these have not been forthcoming. Indeed, such has been the scale of retrenchment since 2010 that there is a consensus that the scale of cuts is much greater than even the 1980s, with the post-2010 government presiding over 'the biggest cuts in public expenditure since the 1920s'.[28] Severe austerity, meaning a lack of investment to stimulate the desired grassroots activity, has undermined Cameron's promise of a revised and reinvigorated social Conservatism working in harmony with a diverse, devolved, flexible range of public service providers. Indeed, some alarms from the front line of local government have warned that the culture of financial austerity runs the risk of instigating the collapse of the civil society[29] on which Cameron's leadership has placed so much emphasis

on revitalising. Austerity has created something of a paradox in relation to the original goals of the 'Big Society', with attempts to replace
a creaking centralised state with a buoyant decentralised alternative
subject to significant questioning and scepticism.

The Conservative Party's approach to social policy matters since 1997
has been shaped by a variety of pressures that culminated in a 'debate
between modernisers and traditionalists on social issues (that) has also
become inextricably intertwined with the wider question of how the
party should seek to revive its electoral fortunes'.[30] While the rhetorical
focus and emphasis on social issues has certainly become ascendant, and
appears to have evolved in a more distinctively communitarian manner
since the last period of Conservative government, challenging financial
and electoral realities have often meant that well-meaning sentiments
have been crushed by the rigours of everyday politics and have failed
to deliver in practical policy terms. Practical financial aspects have certainly hindered the promotion of the 'Big Society' agenda since 2010,
and this has meant that aligning fiscal conservatism to the delivery of
enhanced social justice has proved to be a conundrum for Conservative
modernisers. According to one acute observation, it will be a struggle
to deliver socially just outcomes, on the basis that the government is
ideologically driven by a:

> neo-liberal economic agenda which prioritises cuts in public expend-
> iture and, therefore, fails to deliver even the minimum resources
> necessary to transform rhetoric into reality'.[31]

This in turn raises the question as to whether the pivotal factor in
the making of a revamped and rebranded social Conservatism is in
fact a renewed sense of ideological vigour that has been more subtly
promoted to instil a revised clarity and focus on social policy matters,
and which has generated a distinct, original and remarketised style of
political language. Also evident has been the presence of flexible, pragmatic Conservative manoeuvring and measured political calculation
in the reaction to changing socio-economic circumstances since the
2008 recession. Such developments have favoured the party's fiscally
conservative and lingering neo-liberal instincts, and this once again
illustrates the party's atavistic pursuit of political power, policy agenda-
setting and the means of achieving enhanced electoral popularity.
According to Phillip Blond, who since 2010 appears to have lost faith
in Cameron's ability to deliver the 'Big Society' agenda within a more
devolved governmental structure attached to a 'fairer' and 'progressive'

social model, the Cameron leadership is 'surrounded by pragmatists who constantly behave as if short-term electoral advantage is long-term strategic thinking'.[32] This would suggest that there is in fact no real overarching vision of the party's social policy, which in turn hints at a cosmetic and artificial aura to the party's revised 'compassionate' image, undermining its drive to attract a broader range of political support. Difficulties in this sphere became evident in late 2012 when George Osborne recruited to his staff Neil O'Brien of the think tank Policy Exchange, who has 'warned that the party is still seen as the champion of the rich'.[33] Similar contemporary sentiments have been echoed by prominent Conservative donor Lord Ashcroft, offering further indication that the detoxification strategy has not been an absolute success.

The Impact of coalition with the Liberal Democrats on Conservative social policy

As has been suggested previously, the fact that the Conservatives have governed since 2010 at the head of a formal coalition with the Liberal Democrats has been a significant factor in the way in which government policy has evolved. There has been much speculation in media and political circles as to what extent social and economic policy would have differed if the Conservatives had governed alone, and whether the general thrust and direction of the government would have been different if the Conservatives had achieved an absolute majority. Some modernising Conservatives appear to have welcomed the coalition as a means of pursuing a more moderate socio-political course with 'the position of the right wing of the Conservative Party... notably weakened',[34] while others from the party's traditional right-wing factions have become frustrated by the party's blurred identity post-2010. However, a number of commentators and observers have argued that the key reason for the 2010 electoral outcome was that the party had failed to sufficiently modernise and 'detoxify' its policy agenda and image: 'because the modernisation process was stalled when it was – at best – half-complete, the voters were still unsure about the Tories on May 6, 2010'.[35] In this sense, the coalition with the Liberal Democrats can be seen as logical necessary catalyst for the final thrust of attempted modernisation and detoxification of the contemporary Conservative Party, based on the premise (accepted by pragmatic Conservatives) that by 2010 'Mr Cameron may have tried hard to change his party during the previous five years, but it seems that it still left many voters less than impressed'.[36]

It is on this basis that the Conservatives have rhetorically at least, embraced a more 'liberal' and 'progressive' line on various social policy issues, covering both public service and lifestyle, ranging from enhanced and protected investment in the NHS, to support for same-sex marriage and promotion of the pupil premium in educational policy, prompting the Liberal Democrat leadership to accept during coalition negotiations that 'we could agree sensible positions with the Conservatives on most issues'.[37] The coalition agreement could therefore be viewed from one perspective as a natural consequence of the Conservative Party's failure to sufficiently change its image and win both a parliamentary majority and a more convincing proportion of the national vote, despite having emphasised a clearly more 'liberal' and compassionate tone for much of the previous parliament, with David Cameron regularly referring to himself as a 'liberal' Conservative.[38] Such factors will certainly have increased the likelihood of a constructive and viable governmental arrangement emerging with the Liberal Democrats, as would the fact that there were many collaborations between the parties at a local level prior to 2010. Although the Conservatives have undoubtedly been the majority players within the post-2010 coalition and have succeeded in instigating the agenda on many policy fronts, certain aspects of social policy in particular appear to have been modified following interventions from the junior coalition partners. In terms of economic policy, many in the 'Orange Book' Liberal Democrat faction and across the wider party have supported the fundamental policy of tackling the legacy of New Labour's 'big government' and the associated programme of deficit reduction, and as a consequence have also been willing to embrace some aspects of welfare reform since 2010. In this sense there has been clear ideological crossover and affinity in both rhetorical and political terms between the 'modernising' elements of each coalition partner.[39]

However in some key aspects of social policy reform, co-operation and affinity has not been obvious, notably in the dilution of some of the more libertarian aspects of the Free Schools programme[40] and the scale of the reorganisation of the NHS. While both sides appear to share common ground in terms of 'localism' and devolution of services, many from the social democrat tradition of the Liberal Democrats have seemed to prefer to retain a more 'statist' and explicitly regulatory role for the state in core areas of social policy provision, principally for fear of creating a potential 'postcode lottery'. They claim that 'the problem with localism is that the government is applying localist principles to issues in which there are also universal rights',[41] which thus potentially erodes such rights and levels of key public services. This has been a broader criticism of the whole 'Big Society' agenda since 2010. It can therefore be argued that the radicalism of the Conservative social policy agenda has been blunted, which some of the party appear to have welcomed while others have not. Such apparent policy dilution and Liberal Democrat scepticism can be linked to comments made during the coalition negotiations that 'Nick (Clegg) was doubtful about Conservative social policies'.[42] However, as the coalition has survived for just about the full duration of a five year parliament, some grassroots elements of the Liberal Democrat Party have suggested that there do exist aspects of compatibility and dynamic policy connection between the parties in key areas of social policy. This has been evident in comments from party activists such as: 'I don't have a problem if the profit is ploughed back into the school like a social business... (and as) liberals (who) believe in diversity, we ought to be supporting a range of schools'.[43] Whether any further 'fusion' on such social policy matters continues to filter back towards the national party leadership and impacts on coalition policy-making up to May 2015 remains to be seen, but there have been some areas of common socio-political ground that have been established between the coalition partners, notably in relation to a less centralised state that rejects the perceived micro-management of the previous Labour government. In social policy terms this has entailed a combined focus on localism and a 'common shared instinct which is about giving people the chance to not be told every minute of every day what needs to happen'.[44] This shared rejection of a 'one-size-fits all' range of social policies imposed by a bureaucratic and centralised state indicates common ground and would suggest the evolution of a more pragmatic approach to social policy for a Conservative-led government, appearing to transcend the more prescriptive and ideological aspects of the 'strong state' evident during the Thatcher era, and moving towards a more liberal socio-political agenda.

Social policy has therefore taken on a distinct and perhaps more libertarian shape as a result of the post-2010 coalition government. A number of right-wing Conservative politicians[45] and political commentators viewed such a development negatively, with repeated calls for an ending of the coalition and for a minority Conservative administration to be established as an alternative basis for governance, although this would not have guaranteed the passage of 'purer' Conservative policies by any means, given the leadership's post-Thatcher 'modernised' rhetoric. This right-wing analysis stemmed from a belief that it was a specific lack of traditional 'Conservatism' that cost the party the necessary votes to secure a clear parliamentary majority at the 2010 general election, and in turn this led to a growing frustration in some Conservative circles at what they perceived to have been a lack of ideological direction at the heart of government between 2010 and 2015, accompanied by too much policy compromise with the coalition partners and the erosion of their party's identity in the process. It has been acknowledged that the Liberal Democrats have succeeded in steering government policy in directions that many Conservatives have disagreed with,[46] although in some high-profile social policy areas such as tuition fees and welfare benefits reform, it has not been apparent that they have diverted the Conservatives far, if at all, from their original course. How much their influence and presence has shaped, or indeed derailed, the Cameron social policy agenda and 'modernising' outlook is open to debate, but there appears to have been scope for some degree of alignment, given David Cameron's self-proclaimed 'liberal' image on broader social issues. There is, therefore, evidence to suggest that common ground existed between the coalition partners in some notable aspects of social policy, and that this was bolstered by experiences of local government power-sharing. It is on that basis that the Liberal Democrats made some impact on this sphere of policy after 2010. However, the precise extent of this influence is open to conjecture; certainly, it varied from issue to issue and at different phases of the coalition government's time in office. Over the broader context of the five-year parliament, polling evidence suggests that most voters did not believe that the Liberal Democrats had a sufficiently significant influence on policy-making within the coalition.[47]

Overview: New and changed Conservatism?

Given such well-identified problems regarding the Conservative Party's image and socio-political agenda from the mid-1990s onwards, it appears that since returning to national office in 2010 the Conservatives have offered the rhetoric of change regarding social policy, but have struggled to convince the media and public opinion about the precise nature of such change, as indeed they have with their broad political direction, contemporary identity and specific values. In joining a coalition with the Liberal Democrats, the party displayed statecraft to achieve and maintain political office, and also provided some indications of the emergence of its own 'liberal' values through its new rhetorical emphasis – thanks, perhaps, to the nature of its coalition partner. However, whether such liberal influences have genuinely prevailed to shape a fundamental, long-term change in the making of social policy is a matter of conjecture. In the period that followed the coalition's formation, the Conservative-led government appeared to make some more explicitly ideological gestures in economic policy, motivated by a determination to tackle the national budget deficit thus restoring its former reputation for financial prudence and fiscal conservatism, something that was damaged during the 1990s. In the context of addressing the deficit, the austere approach to economics seemed to have the potentially to enhance electoral appeal in the long-term. Whether this alone will be sufficient to secure outright electoral success is questionable, particularly given that the austerity-driven economic approach has antagonised many and provoked heightened opposition among centre-left voters. In social policy terms the Conservative approach has been less focused and more ambivalent in direction, in practical terms at least. It can be described as gradual and hazy, at times seeking to 'nudge' public opinion in a preferred general direction that seeks wider approval for a dynamic and diverse public service delivery, yet without necessarily offering a definite vision and fundamental 'modernisation' of the party's identity and image. The liberal rhetoric and communitarian focus of the Cameron leadership has not always delivered in practical terms, primarily due to the imposition of financial austerity, yet its focus, albeit a vague one, on utopian visions of a much-vaunted 'Big Society' within a teleocratic and determinist outlook, has made its approach to the making of social policy distinct from other modern periods of Conservative governance.

Since 2010, there has certainly been evidence of compromise and retreat from original proposals in some areas of social policy, inflicted by a combination of ideological uncertainty, public and media criticism, and Liberal Democrat scepticism, although some radical tenets were maintained due to the determination of politicians, Michael Gove in particular. His Free Schools agenda offered the dynamism and ethos of a 'permanent revolution' according to some observers, and its radical implications continued to prevail in the run up to the 2015 general election,[48] despite his removal from the education ministry in 2014. The need to revolutionise and restructure social policy has been stressed by the more radical thinkers, reformist groups and commentators in the Conservative camp,[49] and such full-blown modernisation of social and political attitudes is seen as essential by those who seek the outright 'detoxification' of the Conservative Party's formerly negative and regressive image on social policy matters, and aspire to the creation of a new version of 'Popular Conservatism' in the process. The ultimate aim of this tendency is the emergence of a genuinely distinct Conservative vision for the 21st century, approaching policy-making from a compassionate direction while being concerned with more socially 'just' outcomes, enhanced 'fairness', improved social mobility, all contained within a distinct and more 'individualistic' framework of social justice. This socio-political model is to be complemented by a streamlined and efficient state structure infused with a more commercial and competitive ethos, yet with a strengthened communitarian, mutualist and localist values.[50] How much of this approach is about public relations rebranding and how much is about a genuine shift in social policy outlook has been the source of considerable speculation, with David Cameron's background in PR generating cynicism among political commentators and some of his own MPs, who question how genuinely innovative his social policy agenda has been at times, despite his earlier demands for 'fundamental change' in the party's policies and attitudes.[51]

Whether this new 21st-century Conservative social vision is practically deliverable has been the subject of vigorous political debate, with some inherent contradictions in evidence: key Cameron themes such as 'communitarian altruism' having potentially conflicting motives to 'commercial dynamism'. Yet such a fused agenda for policy-making appears to be the basis for a reformulated version of Conservative 'ideology' for the 21st century, and while this may appear to represent change in theory, in practical policy terms it has struggled to come to fruition, appearing to be an extremely ambitious and difficult project to fulfil. Challenges stem from the fact that this new variant of Conservatism seeks to reject the extremes of Thatcherite neo-liberal marketisation, while also detaching itself from the 'big government' of the state that was said to prevail both during the New Labour era and the 'years of consensus' that dominated post-war politics until the mid-1970s. On the basis of the available evidence there has clearly been some remarketised rhetoric and political gestures indicating some degree of 'New Conservatism' in the sphere of social policy, with the Conservatives seeking to reduce the extent of centralised state monopoly in the provision of key public services such as education and health in particular. However, although some specific policy initiatives have made more impact than others, this 'new' approach generally struggled to reach sustained fulfilment in a coherent sense throughout the 2010–15 parliament. Whether it will ever achieve its bold aspirations is a matter of serious doubt due to the adverse political and electoral implications of the austerity regime that now face the Conservative Party.

There has been evidence of practical policy in action in the form of innovations such as Free Schools, significant, radical welfare reforms and the reformist aspirations for a post-bureaucratic NHS, all aligned in the theoretical framework of the 'Big Society', with such measures cumulatively attempting to reposition and remould the party's message on social policy.

None the less, the practical aims and principles of these 'liberating' measures of public service reform have evidently failed to convince much of the British public, the popular perception being that such terms are merely a cloak for spending cuts.[52] This viewpoint has been dismissed by advocates of the 'Big Society', who argue that their distinctly revised approach to governance pre-dated the 2008 economic crisis and its agenda of 'budget cuts and austerity, so it's obviously not purely about justifying cuts'.[53] However, though obviously wishing to continue the time-honoured process of adapting to survive, evolving in classic conservative style while also seeking to promote a revived socio-political image to capture the mood of 21st-century British society, the Conservative Party appears to have been either unwilling or unable to support the full-blown introduction of such policies with the necessary funding or practical support. This resistance to large-scale social policy renewal is possibly due to the party's shift in emphasis from initial policy and image modernisation to the more mundane reality of rigid fiscal responsibility following the economic downturn after 2008. On the basis of the evidence assessed within this book, in addressing the shifting political and social attitudes arising from a prolonged economic recession, the Conservative Party's individualistic, neo-liberal philosophy continues to acknowledge the realities of socio-economic inequality while the party in office offers limited evidence of its ability to close the wealth gap and offer wider opportunities for the poorer members of society. Indeed, the lingering Thatcherite strand in the party continues to be sceptical of the communitarian and state-centred instincts still detectable in significant swathes of the British public, conditioned to an extent by 13 years of New Labour government. On this basis, the modernising, socially 'progressive' faction of the Conservative Party can therefore demand further movements in the party's collective attitude and image in order for it to become better-aligned with mainstream British public opinion, and hence more electable. This has certainly not always been the case since 1997, although attempts to 'nudge' the public mood may hasten such a correlation on more individualistic, right-of-centre terms.

It is, perhaps, finally the case that the practical restraints of coalition government and the intermittent moderating presence of the Liberal Democrats as junior partners since May 2010 has inhibited the re-emergence of a revised Conservative social policy agenda emblazoned with ideological vigour, and this may explain the more adaptable and pragmatic aspects of David Cameron's political acts since coming to power. At the same time, circumstances may have provided Cameron and his inner-circle with the pretext for a more moderate and modernising socio-political agenda, one that they would have preferred to pursue anyhow, one which has a milder flavour than the 1980s variety of Conservatism, in social policy terms at least. How different in an ideological sense, or how more or less vigorous in policy terms, a majority Conservative government would have been post-2010 is not easy to guess; whether the Cameron leadership would want to explicitly align with the party's ideological heritage of the 1980s (in both political and strategic terms) is open to question, as is the effect of such a change on long-term electoral popularity. It can, however, be convenient for some Conservatives to blame the junior coalition partners for what has been viewed as an often stuttering and inconsistent social policy agenda that has at times appeared to lack practical direction, and which has failed to break away from the failed policies and initiatives connected to the orthodoxies of both the Thatcherite and New Labour eras. This may be seen to reinforce the premise that in order to indicate a real, significant change in the Conservative Party's socio-political approach, the focus on social policy needs to be more coherent and radical in nature, rooted in a new 'ideological' consistency. A benefit of this new approach would be the indication of a clear break from the neo-liberal socio-economic consensus established during the 1980s, reflecting the 'modernised' communitarian values that appeared to be neglected during this period, but which have been emphasised and cultivated by various governments since. In the early 21st century, with dynamic social changes detached from the often divisive class-based attitudes of the past, such a new approach might accept yet transcend valued Conservative traditions, potentially leading to a more original and innovative approach to social policy in both theory and practice. Both political opponents and internal party modernisers[54] would argue that this has been not been the case so far.

While the rhetoric has at times been bold, suggesting that real change is a central feature of the party's modern, 'post-bureaucratic' and 'progressive' social policy agenda, practical delivery has often significantly faltered, and in some cases, bureaucracy has actually expanded. Although there is evidence that the political opposition has had to adapt to this reinvigorated Conservative social policy agenda, the party's attempts in office to fundamentally redefine the role of the state in a more 'horizontal' direction and to streamline bureaucracy in the process have met obstacles and ultimately failed to convince significant opinion-formers in the media and across society. Such stuttering developments strike at the heart of the Conservative Party's response to significant socio-political change and highlight the problems it has encountered in trying to take action in line with Burkean gradualism. The apparently refreshed and reformulated social policy agenda has struggled to flourish and deliver convincing change in policy terms, and it only be put to the absolute test in a practical sense by the achievement of the first majority Conservative government for almost 25 years.[55] In order for its revised approach to governance to deliver appropriate policy 'change' to the maximum extent, party strategists and modernisers need a more favourable parliamentary scenario to enable the public to discover the inherent meaning of modern Conservatism, to observe its viability as a coherent political entity and ideology, and to observe the extent to which it really does empathise with 21st-century British social attitudes.

However, there is a challenging paradox in the pursuit of a decisive election result: the Conservative Party's determined drive to tackle the budget deficit has led to the imposition of severe austerity measures, as the government attempts to rebalance what it believes to be an inflated state structure by a greater emphasis on private sector growth. This strategy has appeared to undermine aspects of the party's revived social policy agenda. Insufficient public funding and reduced financial support since 2010 has resulted in social 'compassion' being transformed into a more 'brutal' economic approach once in office, as Iain Duncan Smith, in particular, has highlighted.[56] This in turn threatens to alienate significant numbers of voters, diminishing the likelihood of a majority Conservative administration in the near future.[57] In this sense, economic policy has continued to converge with social policy in moulding the socio-political consensus of the day, and the economic agenda has appeared to take precedence over social policy in terms of urgent political priorities since 2010, with negative implications for the making of social policy. One prominent political commentator has explicitly argued that this relentless focus on austerity has resulted in the neglect of the Conservative Party's formerly innovative 'Big Society' social agenda, and that 'austerity has produced a Pavlovian dog reflex, and it's recreated the Thatcherite dog, and that's a real shame'.[58] This indicates a reversion to the party's fiscally conservative instincts and to economics-driven policy-making. Aligned with divisive and controversial economic policies such as the reduction of the top rate in income tax in 2012 (from 50p to 45p), this has led to a degree of 'retoxification' of the Conservative brand in the eyes of some voters that the party had tried to woo, creating a negative perception that the modern brand of Conservatism has prioritised a small social elite over the wider 'social interest' in a period of national economic sacrifice and austerity. The outcome of the 2015 General Election will therefore indicate whether any economic upturn can outweigh the negative social consequences of the post-2010 austerity agenda.

In this context, parallels can clearly be made with the socio-economic trends and developments that occurred during the early phase of the Thatcher government in the 1980s, which also prioritised fundamental and deep-rooted economic issues on taking office, with social policy also often appearing to be sidelined when it came to the crunch. Since 2010, such major economic challenges have fused with the practical limitations of coalition government, and at the heart of this approach to social policy reform there has appeared to be a clear tension between the Conservative-led government's rediscovered desire for altruistic, civic engagement and competitive, profit-orientated public service provision in a 'reimagined' state. Given the added pressures faced by the Conservatives in seeking to boost their electoral popularity as the 2010–15 parliament has progressed in order to achieve that elusive parliamentary majority at the general election, it has been increasingly open to question as to whether these tendencies can effectively work together. Ultimately, if this revised party image and renewed policy emphasis keeps the appearance of being incoherent, short-term and artificial in nature, while connected to an unpopular period of 'state-craft' and cloaked with an aura of ideological haze and austerity, then there will almost certainly be policy and electoral failure, despite the Conservative leadership's concerted rhetorical emphasis on a 'modern-ised' social agenda. Given that a Conservative-led administration is at the forefront of British government and exposed to the harsh realities of electoral politics and media scrutiny up to 2015 at least, any significant degree of perceived failure to sufficiently 'change' the party's image, ideological direction and social policy attitudes is likely to have signifi-cant implications for its electoral fortunes.

Despite determined attempts to restore the foundations of a bygone Conservative electoral hegemony, contemporary social and demo-graphic trends are unfavourable. The difficulties of 21st-century Conservatism in convincingly rebranding and imposing a consistent, coherent social policy agenda created the climate for dysfunctional statecraft to prevail until 2015, and this may lead to further long-term electoral damage and another sustained exile from national office.[59] The Cameron social agenda has ultimately struggled to deliver in a practical sense, which is ironic given that the Conservative Party has made unprecedentedly energetic attempts to reformulate social policy, to detoxify and to renew itself since the cataclysmic electoral nadir of 1997, and particularly so under Cameron's leadership. A negative electoral outcome in 2015 could potentially trigger future internal disputes over the extent to which British Conservatism has appropriately revised its broader public image and message, and on the precise nature of its policy reforms and pace of modernisation in recent years – specifically as to whether modernisation has been too extensive or insufficient. The 2015 General Election may answer these speculative socio-political questions about the future prospects of the British Conservative Party in a definitive manner.

Notes

Introduction and background

1. The 165 Conservative MPs was the lowest number for the party since 1906; David Butler and Dennis Kavanagh, *The British General Election of 1997*, (Macmillan Press, Basingstoke, 1997), Ch. 13, p. 244
2. Anthony Seldon and Peter Snowdon, 'The barren years: 1997–2005', cited in Stuart Ball and Anthony Seldon (eds.), *Recovering Power: The Conservatives in Opposition Since 1867*, (Palgrave Macmillan, Basingstoke, 2005), Ch. 11, p. 243
3. Ibid., Ch. 11, p. 247
4. See David Butler and Dennis Kavanagh, *The British General Election of 1997*, (Macmillan Press, Basingstoke, 1997), Ch. 13, p. 244
5. Anthony Seldon and Peter Snowdon, 'The barren years: 1997–2005', cited in Stuart Ball and Anthony Seldon (eds.), *Recovering Power: The Conservatives in Opposition Since 1867*, (Palgrave Macmillan, Basingstoke, 2005), Ch. 11, p. 248
6. Andrew Gamble, 'The crisis of Conservatism', *New Left Review*, (No.214, November-December 1995), p. 3 http://newleftreview.org/I/214/andrew-gamble-the-crisis-of-conservatism
7. Peter Snowdon, *Back from the Brink: The Inside Story of the Tory Resurrection*, (Harper Press, London, 2010), Ch. 3, p. 78
8. See Peter Snowdon: 'The Conservatives may have come back from the brink of annihilation – but the party now faces the closest election battle in decades', 8 March 2010, http://conservativehome.blogs.com/platform/2010/03/peter-snowdon-the-conservatives-may-have-come-back-from-the-brink-of-annihilation-but-the-party-now-.html
   See also: Peter Snowdon, *Back from the Brink: The Inside Story of the Tory Resurrection*, (Harper Press, London, 2010)
9. See academics and commentators such as Snowdon (above), Tim Bale, *The Conservative Party: From Thatcher to Cameron*, (Polity Press, London , 2011), Phillip Blond, *Red Tory: How Left and Right Have Broken Britain and How We Can Fix It*, (Faber, London 2010), Francis Elliott and James Hanning, *Cameron: Practically a Conservative*, (Fourth Estate, London, 2012), Richard Hayton *Conservatism? The Conservative Party in Opposition, 1997–2010. New Perspectives on the Right.* (Manchester University Press, Manchester, 2012), Dylan Jones, *Cameron on Cameron: Conversations with Dylan Jones*, (Fourth Estate, London, 2008)
10. See Jim Bulpitt, 'The discipline of the New Democracy: Mrs Thatcher's domestic statecraft', *Political Studies*, (1986)
11. See Phillip Blond, 'David Cameron has lost his chance to redefine the Tories', *Comment is Free*, *The Guardian*, 3 October 2012, http://www.guardian.co.uk/commentisfree/2012/oct/03/cameron-one-nation-u-turn-tory-tragedy

12. 2005 Conservative Party Manifesto, '*Are You Thinking What We're Thinking? It's Time for Action*', http://www.conservatives.com/pdf/manifesto-uk-2005.pdf
13. Peter Snowdon, *Back from the Brink: The Inside Story of the Tory Resurrection,* (Harper Press, London, 2010), Ch. 5, p. 182
14. 2010 Conservative Party manifesto, *Invitation to join the Government of Britain,* http://www.conservatives.com/~/media/Files/Activist%20Centre/Press%20 and%20Policy/Manifestos/Manifesto2010
15. The only other post-war hung parliament of February 1974 had resulted in a minority Labour government rather than a coalition. A further general election in October 1974 produced a Labour government with a small parliamentary majority

1 Ideological influences on Conservative Party social policy

1. Richard Hayton, 'Conservative Party modernisation and David Cameron's politics of the family', *Political Quarterly*, Volume 81, No.4, (October–December 2010), p. 499
2. Peter Snowdon, *Back from the Brink: The Inside Story of the Tory Resurrection,* (Harper Press, London, 2010), Introduction, p. viii
3. See also Richard Hayton, *Conservatism? The Conservative Party in Opposition, 1997–2010.* New Perspectives on the Right. (Manchester University Press, Manchester, 2012)
4. This term was originally cited in Andrew Gamble, *The Conservative Nation,* (Routledge & Kegan Paul, London, 1974)
5. W.H Greenleaf, *The British Political Tradition Volume II: The Ideological Heritage,* (Methuen, London, 1983), Ch. 1, pp. 7–8
6. Ibid., Ch. 1, p. 8
7. See Maurice Cowling, *The Impact of Labour: 1920–1924,* (Cambridge University Press, 1971), Introduction
8. Robert Crowcroft, Review Article, 'Maurice Cowling and the writing of British political history', *Contemporary British History,* (Volume 22, No.2, June 2008), p. 283
9. Ibid., p. 280
10. Anthony Seldon and Peter Snowdon, 'The barren years: 1997–2005', cited in Stuart Ball and Anthony Seldon (eds.), *Recovering Power: The Conservatives in Opposition Since 1867,* (Palgrave Macmillan, Basingstoke, 2005), Ch. 11, p. 255. See also Simon Walters, *Tory Wars: Conservatives in Crisis,* (Politicos, London, 2001)
11. Richard Hayton, 'Conservative Party modernisation and David Cameron's politics of the family', *The Political Quarterly,* Volume 81, (No.4, October–December 2010, p. 492)
12. See T. Heppell, 'The ideological composition of the British Conservative Party (1992–1997)', *British Journal of Politics and International Relations,* 4 (2), (2002), p. 299–324
13. George Osborne, cited by Darren McCaffrey, 'PM faces Tory rebellion over gay marriage', Sky News, 24 November 2012, http://news.sky.com/story/1015789/pm-faces-tory-rebellion-over-gay-marriage

14. Anthony Seldon and Peter Snowdon, 'The barren years: 1997–2005', cited in Stuart Ball and Anthony Seldon (eds.), *Recovering Power: The Conservatives in Opposition Since 1867*, (Palgrave Macmillan, Basingstoke, 2005), Ch. 11, pp. 252–3
15. Hugh Bochel (ed.), *The Conservative Party and Social Policy*, (Policy Press, University of Bristol, 2011), Ch. 1, p. 13
16. Stephen J. Lee, *Aspects of British Political History 1914–1995*, (Routledge, London, 1996), Ch. 15, p. 231
17. Heppell, T. and Hill, M., 'Ideological typologies of contemporary British Conservatism', *Political Studies Review*, Volume 3, p. 335, (2005)
18. Jesse Norman, *The Big Society: The Anatomy of the New Politics*, (University of Buckingham Press, Buckingham, 2010), Ch. 5, p. 90
19. Robert M. Page, 'The Conservative Party and the Welfare State since 1945', Ch. 2, p. 24, cited in Hugh Bochel (ed.), *The Conservative Party and Social Policy*, (Policy Press, University of Bristol, 2011)
20. Paul Goodman, Executive Editor of Conservative Home website, 'It's two years away, but the 2015 election is already lost', *Daily Telegraph*, 29 December 2012, http://www.telegraph.co.uk/news/politics/conserva-tive/9770710/Its-two-years-away-but-the-2015-election-is-already-lost.html
21. Jim Bulpitt, 'The discipline of the New Democracy: Mrs Thatcher's domestic statecraft', *Political Studies*, (1986), p. 21
22. Andrew Gamble, 'The crisis of Conservatism', *New Left Review*, (No.214, November-December 1995), http://newleftreview.org/I/214/andrew-gamble-the-crisis-of-conservatism
23. Jim Bulpitt, 'The discipline of the New Democracy: Mrs Thatcher's domestic statecraft', *Political Studies*, (1986), p. 21
24. Robert Leach, *British Political Ideologies*, (Prentice Hall Europe, Hemel Hempstead, 2nd edn., 1996), Ch. 5, p. 101
25. Philip Norton, 'The lady's not for turning: But what about the rest?, Margaret Thatcher and the Conservative Party (1979–1989)', *Parliamentary Affairs* 43 (1990), p. 58, http://pa.oxfordjournals.org/content/43/1/41.full.pdf
26. David Willetts, *Modern Conservatism*, (Penguin, London, 1992), Ch. 2. p. 3
27. Ted Honderich, *Conservatism*, (Penguin Books, London, 1990), Ch. 2, p. 18
28. See Michael Oakeshott, *Rationalism in Politics and Other Essays*, (Cambridge University Press, Cambridge, 1962)
29. Ian Gilmour, *Dancing With Dogma: Britain Under Thatcherism*, (Simon & Schuster, London, 1992), Ch. 5, p. 118
30. Peter Dorey, *British Conservatism: The Politics and Philosophy of Inequality*, (I.B Tauris, London, 2011), Ch. 1, p. 7
31. W.H Greenleaf, *The British Political Tradition Volume II: The Ideological Heritage*, (Methuen, London, 1983), Ch. 6, p. 189
32. Benjamin Disraeli, *Sybil (or The Two Nations)*, (1845) Book 2, Ch. 5, pp. 65–66
33. In 1848 Disraeli appeared to clearly indicate a class motive to his beliefs, commenting on revolutionary uprisings across Europe that 'The palace is not safe, when the cottage is not happy'.
34. Anthony Seldon and Peter Snowdon, 'The barren years: 1997–2005', cited in Stuart Ball and Anthony Seldon (eds.), *Recovering Power: The Conservatives in Opposition Since 1867*, (Palgrave Macmillan, Basingstoke, 2005), Ch. 11, p. 244

35. Heppell, T. and Hill, M., 'Ideological typologies of contemporary British Conservatism', (2005), *Political Studies Review*, Volume 3, p. 339
36. Ian Gilmour and Mark Garnett, *Whatever Happened To The Tories? The Conservative Party since 1945*, (4th Estate, London, 1997), Ch. 15, p. 383
37. Harold Macmillan, *The Middle Way*, (Macmillan, London, 1938)
38. Norman Barry, 'New Right', cited in Kevin Hickson (ed.*)*, *The Political Thought of the Conservative Party since 1945*, (Palgrave Macmillan, Basingstoke, 2nd edn., 2009), Ch. 2, p. 35
39. Matt Beech, 'Cameron and Conservative ideology', cited in Simon Lee and Matt Beech (eds.), *The Conservatives under David Cameron: Built to Last?*, (Palgrave Macmillan, Basingstoke, 2nd edn., 2009), Ch. 2, p. 21
40. Norman Barry, 'New Right', cited in Kevin Hickson (ed.*)*, *The Political Thought of the Conservative Party since 1945*, (Palgrave Macmillan, Basingstoke, 2nd edn., 2009), Ch. 2, p. 29
41. Heath's position on the Conservative Party spectrum has been the subject of disagreement among academic commentators, with some claiming he adhered to consensus yet with a more 'technocratic' style of government, but others arguing that he was the forerunner of Thatcherism before embarking on some well-publicised policy U-turns in 1971–72. For further analysis of this matter see Mark Garnett, 'Planning for power: 1964–70', cited in Stuart Ball and Anthony Seldon (eds.), *Recovering Power: The Conservatives in Opposition Since 1867*, (Palgrave Macmillan, Basingstoke, 2005), Ch. 9
42. Philip Norton, 'The lady's not for turning: But what about the rest?, Margaret Thatcher and the Conservative Party (1979–1989)', *Parliamentary Affairs* 43 (1990), p. 55, http://pa.oxfordjournals.org/content/43/1/41.full.pdf
43. Andrew Gamble, *The Free Economy and the Strong State: The Politics of Thatcherism*, (Macmillan, Basingstoke, 2nd edn., 1994), Introduction, p. 6
44. Andrew Gamble, 'The crisis of Conservatism', *New Left Review*, (No.214, November-December 1995), p. 8 http://newleftreview.org/I/214/andrew-gamble-the-crisis-of-conservatism
45. David Willetts, *Modern Conservatism*, (Penguin, London, 1992), Ch. 2. p. 4
46. W.H Greenleaf, *The British Political Tradition Volume II: The Ideological Heritage*, (Methuen, London, 1983), Ch. 6, p. 190
47. Robert Leach, *British Political Ideologies*, (Prentice Hall Europe, Hemel Hempstead, 2nd edn., 1996), Ch. 5, p. 102
48. Norman Barry, 'New Right', cited in Kevin Hickson (ed.*)*, *The Political Thought of the Conservative Party since 1945*, (Palgrave Macmillan, Basingstoke, 2nd edn., 2009), Ch. 2, p. 29
49. David Willetts, *Modern Conservatism*, (Penguin, London, 1992), Ch. 3. p. 46
50. F.A. Hayek, *The Road to Serfdom*, (University of Chicago Press, Chicago, 1944)
51. Bulpitt argued that the 'consistency' and 'purpose' of the first term of the Thatcher administration (1979–83) was fuelled '... not in its ideas or ideology, but in the realm of party statecraft'. Cited in Jim Bulpitt, 'The discipline of the New Democracy: Mrs Thatcher's domestic statecraft', *Political Studies*, (1986), p. 39
52. Jonathan Aitken, Conservative MP, Interview with Hugo Young, 1 February 1988, cited in *The Hugo Young Papers: A Journalist's Notes from the Heart of Politics*, Ion Trewin (ed.), (Penguin, London, 2009), p. 271

53. Ian Gilmour, *Dancing With Dogma: Britain Under Thatcherism*, (Simon & Schuster, London, 1992), Ch. 1, p. 8
54. Ibid., p. 1
55. Philip Norton, 'The lady's not for turning: But what about the rest?, Margaret Thatcher and the Conservative Party (1979–1989)', *Parliamentary Affairs* 43 (1990), p. 42, http://pa.oxfordjournals.org/content/43/1/41.full.pdf
56. Cited in Ian Gilmour, *Dancing With Dogma: Britain Under Thatcherism*, (Simon & Schuster, London, 1992), Ch. 1, p. 4
57. Heppell, T. and Hill, M., 'Ideological typologies of contemporary British Conservatism', *Political Studies Review*, Volume 3, p. 335, (2005).
58. Shirley Robin Letwin, *The Anatomy of Thatcherism*, (Fontana, London, 1992), Ch. 2, p. 27
59. Heppell, T. and Hill, M., 'Ideological typologies of contemporary British Conservatism', *Political Studies Review*, Volume 3, p. 335, (2005).
60. See analysis of Gamble's theory by Heppell, T. and Hill, M., 'Ideological typologies of contemporary British Conservatism', (2005), *Political Studies Review*, Volume 3, p. 340
61. See Andrew Gamble, 'The crisis of Conservatism', *New Left Review*, (No.214, November-December 1995), http://newleftreview.org/I/214/andrew-gamble-the-crisis-of-conservatism

2   The 'New Right' and its impact on Conservative social policy

1. See Philip Norton, 'The lady's not for turning: But what about the rest?, Margaret Thatcher and the Conservative Party (1979–1989)', *Parliamentary Affairs* 43 (1990), http://pa.oxfordjournals.org/content/43/1/41.full.pdf
2. See Raymond Plant, *The Neo-Liberal State*, (Oxford University Press, Oxford, 2009)
3. Peter Dorey, *British Conservatism: The Politics and Philosophy of Inequality*, (I.B Tauris, London, 2011), Ch. 1, pp. 45–6
4. Milton Friedman, *Capitalism and Freedom* (1962), (University of Chicago Press, Chicago, 1962), Ch. 12, p. 195
5. Milton Friedman (1912–2006), US economist, associated with the 'Chicago School' of economics and in the development of the concept of monetarism. His key works were *Capitalism and Freedom* (1962), and *Free to Choose*, (1980, and co-authored with his wife), which advocated the importance of economic capitalism as the most appropriate solution to problems that arise within modern post-war societies. Friedrich Hayek (1899–1992), author of *The Road to Serfdom* (1944) which warned of the dangers to individualism of excessive state power, and associated with the 'Austrian School' of political economy.
6. See David C. Green, *The New Right: The Counter-Revolution in Political, Economic and Social Thought*, (Wheatsheaf Books, Brighton, 1987), Ch. 3
7. Ibid., Ch. 5
8. The economic theories of the English economist John Maynard Keynes (1883–1946), who in the 1930s and 40s in particular emphasised the notion of a government spending beyond its budget during a recession in order to stimulate business investment and overall economic growth

9. David C. Green, *The New Right: The Counter-Revolution in Political, Economic and Social Thought,* (Wheatsheaf Books, Brighton, 1987), Ch. 3, p. 74
10. Shirley Robin Letwin, *The Anatomy of Thatcherism,* (Fontana, London, 1992), Ch. 3, p. 74
11. Ibid., Ch. 3, p. 74
12. Robert M. Page, 'The Conservative Party and the Welfare State since 1945', cited in Hugh Bochel (ed.), *The Conservative Party and Social Policy,* (Policy Press, University of Bristol, 2011), Ch. 2, p. 31
13. Extract from Excerpt from Daniel Yergin and Joseph Stanislaw, (ed.), *The Commanding Heights,* pp. 92–105 (Simon & Schuster, New York, 1998), http://www-tc.pbs.org/wgbh/commandingheights/shared/pdf/prof_keithjoseph.pdf. See also Keith Joseph and Jonathan Sumption, *Equality,* (W & J MacKay, Chatham, 1979)
14. Robert M. Page, 'The Conservative Party and the Welfare State since 1945', cited in Hugh Bochel (ed.), *The Conservative Party and Social Policy,* (Policy Press, University of Bristol, 2011), Ch. 2, p. 31
15. Alan Sked and Chris Cook, *Post War Britain: A Political History* (Penguin, London, 4th edn., 1993), Ch. 12, p. 328
16. Norman Barry, 'New Right', cited in Kevin Hickson (ed*.*), *The Political Thought of the Conservative Party since 1945,* (Palgrave Macmillan, Basingstoke, 2nd edn., 2009), Ch. 2, p. 34
17. See Margaret Thatcher, *The Downing Street Years,* (Harper-Collins, London, 1993), Introduction, p. 7
18. Harold Wilson, *Final Term: The Labour Government 1974–1976,* (Michael Joseph, London, 1979), Epilogue, p. 241
19. The swing of 5.2% from Labour to the Conservatives was the biggest change in public opinion between elections since 1945, suggesting a notable shift in public support away from the post-war consensus
20. Shirley Robin Letwin, *The Anatomy of Thatcherism,* (Fontana, London, 1992), Ch. 3, p. 49
21. C. Collette and K. Laybourn, *Modern Britain Since 1979,* (I.B. Tauris, London, 2003), Ch. 1, p. 8
22. Stephen J. Lee, *Aspects of British Political History 1914–1995* (Routledge, Oxford, 1996), Ch. 15, p. 229
23. In 1980 Margaret Thatcher made the following comments about 'consensus' politics which appeared to typify her views on this matter: 'To me consensus appears to be: the process of abandoning all beliefs, principles, values and policies in search of something in which no-one believes.' Speech at Monash University (6 October, 1981 Sir Robert Menzies Lecture, Melbourne, Australia), cited in Margaret Thatcher, *The Downing Street Years,* (Harper-Collins, London, 1993), Ch. 6, p. 167, see also: Margaret Thatcher Foundation: http://www.margaretthatcher.org/document/104712
24. Shirley Robin Letwin, *The Anatomy of Thatcherism,* (Fontana, London, 1992), Ch. 1, p. 23
25. Ibid., Ch. 2, p. 29
26. Source: http://www.ukpublicspending.co.uk/
27. At the 1976 Labour Party Conference, Prime Minister James Callaghan said: 'We used to think that you could spend your way out of recession by cutting taxes and increasing government spending. I tell you in all candour that this

option no longer exists', 28 September 1976, cited in Kevin Hickson, *The IMF crisis of 1976 and British Politics*, (I.B Tauris, London, 2005) p. 103

28. Shirley Robin Letwin, *The Anatomy of Thatcherism*, (Fontana, London, 1992), Ch. 5, p. 125
29. See Kevin Hickson, *The IMF crisis of 1976 and British Politics*, (I.B Tauris, London, 2005)
30. See Eric J. Hobsbawm, *The Age of Extremes: The Short Twentieth Century, 1914–1991*, (Michael Joseph, London, 1994)
31. See Milton Friedman, *Capitalism and Freedom*, (University of Chicago Press, Chicago, 1962)
32. Nick Ellison, 'The Conservative Party and public expenditure', Ch. 3, p. 48, cited in Hugh Bochel (ed.), *The Conservative Party and Social Policy*, (Policy Press, University of Bristol, 2011)
33. Shirley Robin Letwin. *The Anatomy of Thatcherism*, (Fontana, London, 1992), Ch. 1, p. 20
34. 'Milton Friedman: An Enduring Legacy', *The Economist*, November 17 2006, http://www.economist.com/node/8190872?story_id=8190872
35. Peter Dorey, *British Conservatism: The Politics and Philosophy of Inequality*, (I.B Tauris, London, 2011), Ch. 3, p. 134
36. See Andrew Gamble, *The Free Economy and The Strong State: The Politics of Thatcherism*, (Macmillan, Basingstoke, 1st edn., 1988), cited in Shirley Robin Letwin. *The Anatomy of Thatcherism*, (Fontana, London, 1992), Ch. 1, p. 20
37. Norman Barry, 'New Right', cited in Kevin Hickson (ed.), *The Political Thought of the Conservative Party since 1945*, (Palgrave Macmillan, Basingstoke, 2nd edn., 2009), Ch. 2, p. 28
38. See Andrew Gamble, *The Free Economy and The Strong State: The Politics of Thatcherism*, (Macmillan, Basingstoke, 1st edn., 1988)
39. Andrew Gamble, 'The Free Economy and the Strong State: The Politics of Thatcherism', (Macmillan, Basingstoke, 2nd edn., 1994), Ch. 2, p. 40
40. Ibid., Ch. 2, p. 44
41. Ian Gilmour, *Dancing With Dogma: Britain Under Thatcherism*, (Simon & Schuster, London, 1992), Ch. 2, p. 14
42. Robert M. Page, 'The Conservative Party and the Welfare State since 1945', cited in Hugh Bochel (ed.), *The Conservative Party and Social Policy*, (Policy Press, University of Bristol, 2011), Ch. 2, p. 38
43. Hugo Young, *One of Us*, (Pan Macmillan, London, 1989), Ch. 12, p. 239
44. Ian Gilmour, *Dancing With Dogma: Britain Under Thatcherism*, (Simon & Schuster, London, 1992), Ch. 3, p. 48
45. Larry Elliott, 'Budget 2010: George Osborne's austerity package haunted by spectre of 1981', *The Guardian*, 22 June 2010, http://www.guardian.co.uk/uk/2010/jun/22/budget-budget-deficit
46. Norman Tebbit, Speech to the Annual Conservative Party Conference, Blackpool (15 October, 1981)
47. David Willetts, *Modern Conservatism*, (Penguin, London, 1992), Ch. 4. p. 55
48. C. Collette and K. Laybourn, *Modern Britain Since 1979*, (I.B Tauris, London, 2003), Ch. 1, p. 9
49. Margaret Thatcher, interview with *Woman's Own* Magazine, published 31 October 1987. Source – Margaret Thatcher Foundation: http://www.margaretthatcher.org/document/106689

50. David Willetts MP, interview with author, 10 September 2012
51. Richard Hayton, 'Conservative Party modernisation and David Cameron's politics of the family', *Political Quarterly*, Volume 81, No.4, (October–December 2010), pp. 494–5
52. Stephen Driver, '"Fixing our broken society": David Cameron's Post-Thatcherite social policy', cited in Simon Lee and Matt Beech (eds.), *The Conservatives under David Cameron: Built to Last?*, (Palgrave Macmillan, Basingstoke, 2009), Ch. 6, p. 82
53. Carl Cross, Chairman of Merseyside Conservative Party (2009–12), E-mail questionnaire to author, 4 March 2011
54. The Housing Act of 1980 allowed council tenants to buy their council properties at much reduced discount rates ('right to buy'). It became established as one of the most popular and distinct 'Thatcherite' policies. See: http://www.legislation.gov.uk/ukpga/1980/51
55. Chris Patten, Interview with Hugo Young, 18 April 1991, cited in *The Hugo Young Papers: A Journalist's Notes from the Heart of Politics*, Ion Trewin (ed.), (Penguin, London, 2009), p. 325
56. Howard Glennerster, 'Health and social policy', cited in Dennis Kavanagh and Anthony Seldon (eds.), *The Major Effect*, (Macmillan, London, 1994), Ch. 18. p. 320
57. Ibid., Ch. 18. p. 330
58. See also the Coalition Government's 2010 Comprehensive Spending Review (CSR) proposals, outlining £83 billion of public spending cuts: http://www.hm-treasury.gov.uk/spend_index.htm   http://www.telegraph.co.uk/news/newstopics/spending-review/
59. Larry Elliott, 'Budget 2010: George Osborne's austerity package haunted by spectre of 1981', *The Guardian*, 22 June 2010, http://www.guardian.co.uk/uk/2010/jun/22/budget-budget-deficit
60. In February 2009, David Cameron drew parallels with the economic challenges that he was likely to face as Prime Minister with those faced by Margaret Thatcher in 1979:
    'I think we are at a time particularly with the economy where it is clear that difficult decisions are going to have to be taken. I think that influence, that character she (Thatcher) had, that conviction she had, I think that will be very important. Some of the things she said about the importance of living within your means, of not spending money you don't have, about cutting your cloth was wise then and it is wise now. Perhaps we need to listen to that again.' Cited from Rosa Prince, 'David Cameron praises Baroness Thatcher and vows to emulate her as PM', *Daily Telegraph*, 18 February 2009. http://www.telegraph.co.uk/news/newstopics/politics/conservative/4691260/David-Cameron-praises-Baroness-Thatcher-and-vows-to-emulate-her-as-PM.html
61. Robert M. Page, 'The Conservative Party and the Welfare State since 1945', cited in Hugh Bochel (ed.), *The Conservative Party and Social Policy*, (Policy Press, University of Bristol, 2011), Ch. 2, p. 35
62. 'Labour's private polls reported that before and during the election around 70 per cent of voters expected to pay more taxes under a Labour government'. Cited in David Butler and Dennis Kavanagh, *The British General Election of 1992*, (Macmillan Press, Basingstoke, 1992), Ch. 12, p. 268

63. John Major, *The Autobiography*, (Harper-Collins, London, 1999), Ch. 14, p. 312

64. John Major noted that in relation to Black Wednesday: 'On that day, a fifth consecutive Conservative election victory... became remote, if not impossible', cited in Ibid., Ch. 14, p. 312

65. Alex Singleton, 'Is David Cameron reinventing himself as a Thatcherite?', *Daily Telegraph*, February 21 2011, http://blogs.telegraph.co.uk/news/alexsingleton/100076991/is-david-cameron-reinventing-himself-as-a-thatcherite/

66. The Cornerstone group consists of approximately 40 Conservative MPs after the 2010 General Election (13% of the parliamentary party), see: http://cornerstone-group.org.uk/

67. David Curry, Conservative MP, Interview with Hugo Young, 3 September 2000, cited in *The Hugo Young Papers: A Journalist's Notes from the Heart of Politics*, Ion Trewin (ed.), (Penguin, London, 2009), p. 667

68. Simon Lee, 'Convergence, critique and divergence: The development of economic policy under David Cameron', cited in Simon Lee and Matt Beech (eds.), *The Conservatives under David Cameron: Built to Last?*, (Palgrave Macmillan, Basingstoke, 2nd edn., 2009), Ch. 5, p. 78, adapted from Dylan Jones, *Cameron on Cameron: Conversations with Dylan Jones*, (Fourth Estate, London, 2008), p. 288

69. Michael Portillo, Interview with Hugo Young, 24 September 1988, cited in *The Hugo Young Papers: A Journalist's Notes from the Heart of Politics*, (Penguin, 2009), p. 573

70. William Hague, Interview with Hugo Young, Centre for Policy Studies Dinner, 19 January 1999, cited in Ibid., p. 584

71. David Willetts, *Modern Conservatism*, (Penguin, London, 1992), Ch. 4. p. 51

72. Dennis Kavanagh and Philip Cowley, *The British General Election of 2010*, (Palgrave Macmillan, Basingstoke, 2010), Ch. 16, p. 351

73. Michael Ashcroft, *Smell the Coffee: A Wakeup Call for the Conservative Party*, (Politicos, London, 2005)

74. Dennis Kavanagh and Philip Cowley, *The British General Election of 2010*, (Palgrave Macmillan, Basingstoke, 2010), Ch. 4, p. 70

75. Theresa May, speech to Conservative Party Conference in Bournemouth, cited in *The Guardian*, 7 October 2002, http://www.guardian.co.uk/politics/2002/oct/07/conservatives2002.conservatives1

76. Andrew Rawnsley, *The End of the Party: The Rise and Fall of New Labour*, (Penguin, London, 2010), Ch. 26, p. 451

77. Rob Baggott, 'Conservative health policy', cited in Hugh Bochel (ed.), *The Conservative Party and Social Policy*, (Policy Press, University of Bristol, 2011), Ch. 5, p. 89

78. Patrick Hennessy, 'Not the nasty party: the Conservatives have changed significantly, says Theresa May', *Daily Telegraph*, 1 October 2011, http://www.telegraph.co.uk/news/politics/conservative/8801264/Not-the-nasty-party-the-Conservatives-have-changed-significantly-says-Theresa-May.html

79. Kevin Hickson, 'The New Tories may be a puzzle but the pieces do make up a new kind of Britain', *Parliamentary Brief Online*, 30 March 2010, p. 1, http://www.parliamentarybrief.com/2010/03/the-new-tories-may-be-a-puzzle-but-the-pieces

80. Simon Griffiths, 'Cameron's Conservatives and the public services', cited in Simon Lee and Matt Beech (eds.), *The Conservatives under David Cameron: Built to Last?*, (Palgrave Macmillan, Basingstoke, 2nd edn., 2009), Ch. 7, p. 98 See also Matthew Taylor, 'Likeability to electability', Comment is Free, *The Guardian*, 17 July 2008: 'Deliberately, boldly and often in the face of sotto voce carping from his own side, Cameron has decontaminated the Tory brand'. http://www.guardian.co.uk/commentisfree/2008/jul/17/davidcameron.conservatives

81. Matt Beech, 'Cameron and Conservative ideology', cited in Simon Lee and Matt Beech (eds.), *The Conservatives under David Cameron: Built to Last?*, (Palgrave Macmillan, Basingstoke, 2nd edn., 2009), Ch. 2, p. 21

82. See Anthony Seldon and Peter Snowdon, 'The barren years: 1997–2005', cited in Stuart Ball and Anthony Seldon (eds.), *Recovering Power: The Conservatives in Opposition Since 1867*, (Palgrave Macmillan, Basingstoke, 2005), Ch. 11

83. Ibid., p. 255

84 Andrew Rawnsley, 'Two-tribe politics is over. But the likes of John Prescott can't see it', *The Observer*, 28 November 2010, http://www.guardian.co.uk/commentisfree/2010/nov/28/andrew-rawnsley-electoral-reform

85. See: http://www.hm-treasury.gov.uk/d/junebudget_complete.pdf

86. Nick Ellison, 'The Conservative Party and public expenditure', cited in Hugh Bochel (ed.), *The Conservative Party and Social Policy*, (Policy Press, University of Bristol, 2011), Ch. 2, p. 59

87. Andrew Rawnsley, *The End of the Party: The Rise and Fall of New Labour*, (Penguin, London, 2010), Ch. 35, p. 603

88. Stephen Driver, '"Fixing our broken society": David Cameron's Post-Thatcherite Social Policy', cited in Simon Lee and Matt Beech (eds.), *The Conservatives under David Cameron: Built to Last?*, (Palgrave Macmillan, Basingstoke, 2nd edn., 2009), Ch. 6, p. 95

89. Paul Pierson, *Dismantling the Welfare State: Reagan, Thatcher and the Politics of Retrenchment*, (Cambridge University Press, 1994), Introduction, page 1

90. Andrew Gamble, *The Free Economy and the Strong State: The Politics of Thatcherism*, (Macmillan, Basingstoke, 2nd edn., 1994), Ch. 1, p. 21

91. Ibid., Ch. 1, p. 22

92. Evidence of this can be seen in Kavanagh and Cowley's analysis of Cameron's new approach to policy after 2005: 'Several internal party studies had demonstrated that many voters still viewed new Conservative policies and statements through the prism of the party's unattractive brand... (and) that Thatcherism had concentrated too much on economy and wealth creation'. Dennis Kavanagh and Philip Cowley, *The British General Election of 2010*, (Palgrave Macmillan, Basingstoke, 2010), Ch. 4, p. 66–67

93. Nick Ellison, 'The Conservative Party and public expenditure', cited in Hugh Bochel (ed.), *The Conservative Party and Social Policy*, (Policy Press, University of Bristol, 2011), Ch. 2, p. 58

94. Ibid., p. 65

95. For further information on public opinion on this issue as expressed in British Social Attitudes surveys, see Defty (2011) who cites that 'public support for spending restraint, and especially cuts, is limited to particular groups, and there remains a high level of public support for state provision, which may call into question the level of support for a more widespread

rolling back of the state'. Ibid., cited in Hugh Bochel (ed.), *The Conservative Party and Social Policy,* (The Policy Press, University of Bristol, 2011), Ch. 4, pp. 66–7

96. Nick Ellison, cited in Hugh Bochel (ed.), *The Conservative Party and Social Policy,* (The Policy Press, University of Bristol, 2011), p. 59

97. John Hills, *'Thatcherism, New Labour and the Welfare State',* Centre for Analysis of Social Exclusion, London School of Economics, (August 1998), http://eprints.lse.ac.uk/5553/1/Thatcherism_New_Labour_and_the_Welfare_State.pdf

3   Conservatism and social justice in theory

1. Andrew Defty, 'The Conservatives, social policy and public opinion', cited in Hugh Bochel (ed.), *The Conservative Party and Social Policy,* (Policy Press, University of Bristol, 2011), Ch. 4, p. 73

2. See Ipsos-Mori Survey, 'Private Provision of Public Services', (19 June 2008), which indicated that the number of respondents in 'strong agreement' with the following statement 'In principle, public services should be run by the government or local authorities, rather than by private companies', had risen from 27% to 50% between 2000 and 2008. The number of those agreeing with the statement had risen from an already high 66% to 79% in the same time period: http://www.ipsos-mori.com/researchpublications/researcharchive/2428/Private-Provision-of-Public-Services.aspx?view=wide

3. David Willetts, *Modern Conservatism,* (Penguin, London, 1992), Ch. 8. p. 112

4. Keith Joseph and Jonathan Sumption, *Equality,* (W & J MacKay, Chatham, 1979), Ch. 1, p. 1

5. Ibid.

6. Peter Dorey, *British Conservatism: The Politics and Philosophy of Inequality*, (I.B Tauris, London, 2011), Ch. 1, p. 19

7. David Willetts, *Modern Conservatism,* (Penguin, London, 1992), Ch. 8. p. 112

8. Peter Dorey, *British Conservatism: The Politics and Philosophy of Inequality*, (I.B Tauris, London, 2011), Ch. 1, p. 5. This author argues that 'all Conservatives are emphatic that inequality per se is both desirable and necessary', Ch. 1, p. 5

9. David Willetts, *Modern Conservatism,* (Penguin, London, 1992), Ch. 8. p. 112

10. See Peter Dorey, *British Conservatism: The Politics and Philosophy of Inequality*, (I.B Tauris, London, 2011), Ch. 1, p. 18–22

11. Peter Dorey, *British Conservatism: The Politics and Philosophy of Inequality*, (I.B Tauris, London, 2011), Ch. 1, p. 5

12. Thomas Hobbes, *Leviathan*, (1651)

13. See Andrew Gamble, *The Free Economy and the Strong State: The Politics of Thatcherism,* (Macmillan, Basingstoke, 2nd edn., 1994), for a more contemporary analysis of this viewpoint

14. Peter Dorey, *British Conservatism: The Politics and Philosophy of Inequality*, (I.B Tauris, London, 2011), Ch. 1, p. 7

15. See Adam Smith, *Wealth of Nations,* (1776)

16. Peter Dorey, *British Conservatism: The Politics and Philosophy of Inequality*, (I.B Tauris, London, 2011), Ch. 1, p. 7

17. Peter Dorey, *British Conservatism: The Politics and Philosophy of Inequality*, (I.B Tauris, London, 2011), Ch. 1, p. 8
18. See Ian Gilmour, *Inside Right; A Study of Conservatism*, (Quartet, London, 1978)
19. See Roy Hattersley and Kevin Hickson, 'In praise of social democracy', *Political Quarterly*, Volume 83, Issue 1, (January-March 2012), p. 7 http://onlinelibrary.wiley.com/doi/10.1111/j.1467-923X.2011.02259.x/pdf
20. See Hugo Young, *One of Us*, (Pan Macmillan, London, 1989), p. 607: 'The Thatcher years saw the largest redistribution of income in favour of the well-off in modern economic history'.
21. Report of the National Equality Panel, *An Anatomy of Economic Inequality in the UK*, (January 2010), http://news.bbc.co.uk/1/shared/bsp/hi/pdfs/27_01_10_inequalityfull..pdf
22. Rachel Sylvester, 'Letwin: We will redistribute wealth', *Daily Telegraph*, 23 December 2005, http://www.telegraph.co.uk/news/uknews/1506160/Letwin-We-will-redistribute-wealth.html
23. David Willetts, *Modern Conservatism*, (Penguin, London, 1992), Ch. 8. p. 112
24 See 1987 Conservative Party Manifesto, *The Next Moves Forward*, p. 59 http://www.conservativemanifesto.com/1987/1987-conservative-manifesto.shtml
25. Michael Freeden, *Ideologies and Political Theory: A Conceptual Approach*, (Clarendon Press, Oxford, 1996), Ch. 10, p. 390
26. Ian Gilmour, *Dancing With Dogma: Britain Under Thatcherism*, (Simon & Schuster, London, 1992), Ch. 6, p. 131
27. Michael Young, *The Rise of the Meritocracy*, (Transaction Publishers, Chicago, 1958)
28. See the hierarchical class-based social order evident in novels such as Benjamin Disraeli's *Sybil (or The Two Nations)*, (1845)
29. Peter Dorey, *British Conservatism: The Politics and Philosophy of Inequality*, (I.B Tauris, London, 2011), Ch. 1, p. 47
30. David Willetts, *Modern Conservatism*, (Penguin, London, 1992), Ch. 8. p. 118
31. Peter Dorey, *British Conservatism: The Politics and Philosophy of Inequality*, (I.B Tauris, London, 2011), Ch. 1, p. 16
32. At Crystal Palace, London, 24 June 1872 Benjamin Disraeli, the founding father of One Nation Conservatism, stated that: 'The palace is unsafe if the cottage is unhappy', emphasising the perceived need for the established governing classes to ensure that the lower classes were reasonably content.
33. See Peter Dorey, *British Conservatism: The Politics and Philosophy of Inequality*, (I.B Tauris, London, 2011), Ch. 1, p. 10
34. See John Rawls, *A Theory of Justice*, (Harvard University Press, Cambridge, MA, 1971)
35. Keith Joseph and Jonathan Sumption, *Equality*, (W & J MacKay, Chatham, 1979), Ch. 5, p. 89
36. David Willetts, *Modern Conservatism*, (Penguin, London, 1992), Ch. 8. p. 112
37. Michael Freeden, *Ideologies and Political Theory: A Conceptual Approach*, (Clarendon Press, Oxford, 1996), Ch. 10, p. 389
38. See Friedrich von Hayek, *Law, Legislation and Liberty*, Volume 2: '*The Mirage of Social Justice*, (Routledge & Kegan Paul, London, 1973)
39. Paul Kelly, 'The Big Society in the New Conservatism', cited in Jason Edwards (ed). *Retrieving the Big Society*, (Wiley-Blackwell, Chichester, 2012), p. 32

40. See Thomas Hobbes, *Leviathan*, (1651)
41. Kevin Hickson, 'Thatcherism, poverty and social justice', *Journal of Poverty and Social Justice*, (Volume 18, Number 2, June 2010), p. 137
42. David Willetts MP, interview with author, 10 September 2012
43. F.A. Hayek, *The Road to Serfdom*, (University of Chicago Press, Chicago, 1944)
44. Andrew Gamble, *The Free Economy and the Strong State: The Politics of Thatcherism*, (Macmillan, Basingstoke, 2nd edn., 1994), Ch. 2, p. 58
45. See Robert Nozick, *Anarchy, State and Utopia*, (Basic Books, New York, 1974)
46. Andrew Gamble, *The Free Economy and the Strong State: The Politics of Thatcherism*, (Macmillan, Basingstoke, 2nd edn., 1994), Ch. 2, p. 57
47. Ibid
48. Ted Honderich, *Conservatism*, (Penguin Books, London, 1990), Ch. 2, p. 20
49. For a full and more modern analysis and critique of this Hayekian model of society, see Raymond Plant, *The Neo-Liberal State*, (Oxford University Press, Oxford, 2009)
50. John Gray, 'Book Review: *The Neoliberal State* by Raymond Plant', *New Statesman*, 7 January 2010, http://www.newstatesman.com/non-fiction/2010/01/neoliberal-state-market-social
51. See Andrew Gamble, *The Free Economy and the Strong State: The Politics of Thatcherism*, (Macmillan, Basingstoke, 1st edn., 1988)
52. John Gray, 'Book Review: *The Neoliberal State* by Raymond Plant', *New Statesman*, 7 January 2010, http://www.newstatesman.com/non-fiction/2010/01/neoliberal-state-market-social
53. Raymond Plant, *The Neo-Liberal State*, (Oxford University Press, Oxford, 2009), Ch. 7, p. 153
54. Friedrich von Hayek, *Law, Legislation and Liberty*, Volume 2: '*The Mirage of Social Justice*, (Routledge & Kegan Paul, London, 1973), Ch. 8. p. 33
55. Kevin Hickson, 'Thatcherism, poverty and social justice', *Journal of Poverty and Social Justice*, (Volume 18, Number 2, June 2010) p. 136
56. Michael Freeden, *Ideologies and Political Theory: A Conceptual Approach*, (Clarendon Press, Oxford, 1996), Ch. 10, p. 390
57. Kevin Hickson, 'Thatcherism, poverty and social justice', *Journal of Poverty and Social Justice*, (Volume 18, Number 2, June 2010), p. 135
58. William Waldegrave, (Chief Secretary to the Treasury), Interview with Hugo Young, 15 July 1996, cited in *The Hugo Young Papers: A Journalist's Notes from the Heart of Politics*, Ion Trewin (ed.), (Penguin, London, 2009), p. 490
59. Kevin Hickson, 'Thatcherism, poverty and social justice', *Journal of Poverty and Social Justice*, (Volume 18, Number 2, June 2010), p. 142
60. Ibid
61. Heppell, T. and Hill, M., 'Ideological typologies of contemporary British Conservatism', (2005), *Political Studies Review*, Volume 3, p. 353
62. Milton Friedman. Introduction to the 50th anniversary edition of *The Road to Serfdom* (1994), p. xi
63. David Willetts, *Civic Conservatism*, (Social Market Foundation, London, 1994)
64. Paddy Ashdown (Liberal Democrat Leader 1988–1999), Interview with Hugo Young, 13 September 1994, cited in *The Hugo Young Papers: A Journalist's Notes from the Heart of Politics*, Ion Trewin (ed.), (Penguin, London, 2009), p. 433

65. Matthew D'Ancona, 'Ditching their modernisation campaign was the Tories' worst strategic error since the poll tax', *Daily Telegraph*. 30 December 2012, http://www.telegraph.co.uk/comment/columnists/matthewd_ancona/9770645/Ditching-their-modernisation-campaign-was-the-Tories-worst-strategic-error-since-the-poll-tax.html
    An edited version of Matthew D'Ancona's chapter in Ryan Shorthouse (ed.), *Tory modernisation 2.0: the future of the Conservative Party*, (Bright Blue, London, 2013), e-book: http://brightblue.org.uk/bbtory20.pdf
66. Nick Ellison, 'The Conservative Party and public expenditure', cited in Hugh Bochel (ed.), *The Conservative Party and Social Policy*, (Policy Press, University of Bristol, 2011), Ch. 2, p. 58
67. William Waldegrave, (Minister of Agriculture), Interview with Hugo Young, 6 October 1994, cited in *The Hugo Young Papers: A Journalist's Notes from the Heart of Politics*, (Penguin, 2009), p. 436
68. Hugh Bochel, 'Cameron's Conservatism: influences, interpretations and implications', University of Lincoln (2010), p. 1 http://www.social-policy.org.uk/lincoln/Bochel_H.pdf
69. Hugh Bochel, 'Conservative approaches to social policy since 1997', cited in Hugh Bochel (ed.), *The Conservative Party and Social Policy*, (Policy Press, University of Bristol, 2011), Ch. 1, p. 13
70. Michael Gove, Shadow Secretary of State for Children, Schools and Families, cited in James Kirkup, 'Michael Gove says Cameron's Conservatives are the heirs to New Labour', *Daily Telegraph*, March 16 2010, http://blogs.telegraph.co.uk/news/jameskirkup/100030201/michael-gove-says-camerons-conservatives-are-the-heirs-to-new-labour/
71. David Cameron, speech to Policy Exchange think tank, 29 June 2005, cited in Dennis Kavanagh and Philip Cowley, *The British General Election of 2010'*, (Palgrave Macmillan, Basingstoke, 2010), Ch. 4, p. 72
72. Peter Snowdon, *Back from the Brink: The Inside Story of the Tory Resurrection*, (Harper Press, London, 2010), Ch. 6, p. 214
73. Jesse Norman, *The Big Society: The Anatomy of the New Politics*, (University of Buckingham Press, Buckingham, 2010), Ch. 3, p. 43
74. Rob Baggott, 'Conservative health policy', cited in Hugh Bochel (ed.), *'The Conservative Party and Social Policy'*, (Policy Press, University of Bristol, 2011), Ch. 5, p. 89
75. Andrew Pierce, 'Horror as Cameron brandishes the B word', *The Times*, 25 October 2005, http://www.timesonline.co.uk/tol/news/politics/article574814.ece
76. Robert M. Page, 'The Conservative Party and the Welfare State since 1945', cited in Hugh Bochel (ed.), *The Conservative Party and Social Policy*, (Policy Press, University of Bristol, 2011), Ch. 2, p. 36
77. Matthew West, 'Comment: Cameron's Thatcherite manifesto', Politics.co.uk, 13 April 2010, http://www.politics.co.uk/comment-analysis/2010/04/13/comment-cameron-s-thatcherite-manifesto
78. Michael Freeden, *Ideologies and Political Theory: A Conceptual Approach*, (Clarendon Press, Oxford, 1996), Ch. 10, p. 394
79. Michael Freeden, *Ideologies and Political Theory: A Conceptual Approach*, (Clarendon Press, Oxford, 1996), Ch. 10, p. 394

80. David Cameron, 'Speech to Centre for Social Justice Kids' symposium', cited in *The Guardian*, 10 July 2006, http://www.guardian.co.uk/politics/2006/jul/10/conservatives.law

4   Social policy case study 1: Modern Conservatism, practical social justice and welfare reform

1. Philip Blond, 'David Cameron has lost his chance to redefine the Tories', Comment is Free, *The Guardian*, 3 October 2012, http://www.guardian.co.uk/commentisfree/2012/oct/03/cameron-one-nation-u-turn-tory-tragedy
2. Full text: David Cameron's speech to the Conservative conference 2005, *The Guardian*, 4 October 2005, http://www.theguardian.com/politics/2005/oct/04/conservatives2005.conservatives3
3. See David Cameron, 'Let's mend our broken society', 27 April 2010, http://www.conservatives.com/News/Speeches/2010/04/David_Cameron_Lets_mend_our_broken_society.aspx
4. Simon Lee, 'David Cameron's political challenges', cited in Simon Lee and Matt Beech (eds.), *The Conservatives under David Cameron: Built to Last?*, (Palgrave Macmillan, Basingstoke, 2nd edn., 2009), Ch. 1, p. 13
5. Simon Lee, 'Convergence, critique and divergence: The development of economic policy under David Cameron', cited in Simon Lee and Matt Beech (eds.), *The Conservatives under David Cameron: Built to Last?*, (Palgrave Macmillan, Basingstoke, 2nd edn., 2009), Ch. 5, p. 78
6. Peter Snowdon, *Back from the Brink: The Inside Story of the Tory Resurrection*, (Harper Press, London, 2010), Ch. 4, p. 154
7. David Willetts MP, interview with author, 10 September 2012
8. Anthony Seldon and Peter Snowdon, 'The barren years: 1997–2005', cited in Stuart Ball and Anthony Seldon (eds.), *Recovering Power: The Conservatives in Opposition Since 1867*, (Palgrave Macmillan, Basingstoke, 2005), Ch. 11, p. 260
9. See Peter Snowdon, *Back from the Brink: The Inside Story of the Tory Resurrection*, (Harper Press, London, 2010), Ch. 6, p. 221
10. See *'Breakdown Britain: Interim Report on the State of the Nation'*, The Centre for Social Justice (2006), http://www.centreforsocialjustice.org.uk/default.asp?pageRef=180
    'Breakthrough Britain: Ending the Costs of Social Breakdown" – Policy Recommendations to the Conservative Party', The Centre for Social Justice (2007), http://www.centreforsocialjustice.org.uk/client/downloads/family%20breakdown.pdf
11. Ibid., Iain Duncan Smith, Chairman's Overview, page 6 http://www.centreforsocialjustice.org.uk/client/downloads/overview.pdf
12. Stephen Driver, '"Fixing our broken society": David Cameron's post-Thatcherite social policy', cited in Simon Lee and Matt Beech (eds.), *The Conservatives under David Cameron: Built to Last?*, (Palgrave Macmillan, Basingstoke, 2nd edn., 2009), Ch. 6, p. 80
13. Dennis Kavanagh and Philip Cowley, *The British General Election of 2010*, (Palgrave Macmillan, Basingstoke, 2010), Ch. 4, p. 75
14. See Lawrence M. Mead, *Beyond Entitlement: the Social Obligations of Citizenship*, (Free Press, New York, 1986)

15. See: Charles Murray, 'Charles Murray and the Underclass: The Developing Debate', The IEA Health and Welfare Unit in Association with The Sunday Times (London, November 1996), http://www.sociology.org.uk/as4p6a.pdf

16. David Hencke, Patrick Wintour and Hélène Mulholland, 'Cameron launches Tory "broken society byelection" campaign', The Guardian, 7 July 2008, http://www.guardian.co.uk/politics/2008/jul/07/davidcameron.conservatives
Cameron's speech at this event stated: 'But our mission is to repair our broken society – to heal the wounds of poverty, crime, social disorder and deprivation that are steadily making this country a grim and joyless place to live for far too many people. Because while our society is broken today, it is not broken forever. We can and will repair it. We can and will bring hope and aspiration to places where there is resignation and despair.'
Source: http://conservativehome.blogs.com/torydiary/files/fixing_our_broken_society.pdf

17. In the Glasgow East by-election of July 2008, the Conservatives received only 6.3% of the vote.

18. Peter Snowdon, Back from the Brink: The Inside Story of the Tory Resurrection, (Harper Press, London, 2010), Ch. 6, p. 222

19. Jonathan Aitken, 'Yes, prisons are full of people who shouldn't be there. But where would Ken Clarke put them?', Mail on Sunday, 25 July 2010, http://www.dailymail.co.uk/debate/article-1297445/JONATHAN-AITKEN-Yes-prisons-people-shouldn-t-But-Ken-Clarke-them.html

20. Robert M. Page, University of Birmingham, 'Clear Blue Water? The Conservative Party's Approach to Social Policy Since 1945', Paper presented at the Social Policy Association's Annual Conference, University of Lincoln (5–7 July 2010), p. 11 http://www.social-policy.org.uk/lincoln/Page.pdf

21. See Andrew Gamble, The Free Economy and the Strong State , (Macmillan, Basingstoke, 1st edn., 1988)

22. David Willetts MP, interview with author, 10 September 2012

23. Robert M. Page, University of Birmingham, 'Clear Blue Water? The Conservative Party's Approach to Social Policy Since 1945', Paper presented at the Social Policy Association's Annual Conference, University of Lincoln (5–7 July 2010), p. 14 http://www.social-policy.org.uk/lincoln/Page.pdf

24. See Demos website: 'The progressive Conservatism Project: Conservative means can serve progressive ends', http://www.demos.co.uk/projects/progressiveconservatism/

25. Jesse Norman, The Big Society: The Anatomy of the New Politics, (University of Buckingham Press, Buckingham, 2010), Ch. 2, p. 37

26. Hugh Bochel (ed.), 'Conservative approaches to social policy since 1997', cited in Hugh Bochel (ed.), The Conservative Party and Social Policy, (Policy Press, University of Bristol, 2011), Ch. 1, p. 1

27. Nick Ellison, 'The Conservative Party and public expenditure', cited in Hugh Bochel (ed.), The Conservative Party and Social Policy, (Policy Press, University of Bristol, 2011), Ch. 2, p. 58

28. Louise Bamfield, 'Beginning the Big Society in the early years', cited in Jason Edwards (ed). Retrieving the Big Society, (Wiley-Blackwell, Chichester, 2012), p. 173

29. Iain Duncan Smith: 'Labour has left the poor even more dependent on the state', The Independent, 16 September 2003, http://www.independent.co.uk/

opinion/commentators/iain-duncan-smith-labour-has-left-the-poor-even-more-dependent-on-the-state-580062.html

Duncan Smith said after leaving Easterhouse in 2003: 'When I left Easterhouse, I committed the Conservative Party to a new mission with these words: "A nation that leaves its vulnerable behind, diminishes its own future."'

30. Andrew Gamble, *The Free Economy and the Strong State: The Politics of Thatcherism*, (Macmillan, Basingstoke, 2nd edn., 1994), Ch. 1, p. 28

31. David Willetts MP, interview with author, 10 September 2012

32. Andrew Rawnsley, *The End of the Party: The Rise and Fall of New Labour*, Ch. 40, p. 740, (Penguin, London, 2010)

33. Jesse Norman, *The Big Society: The Anatomy of the New Politics*, (University of Buckingham Press, Buckingham, 2010), Ch. 2, p. 43

34. Jason Edwards, 'Freedom, free institutions and the Big Society', cited in Jason Edwards (ed). *Retrieving the Big Society*, (Wiley-Blackwell, Chichester, 2012), p. 100

35. 'Labour failed on welfare reform – Ed Miliband', BBC News website, 25 November 2010, http://www.bbc.co.uk/news/uk-politics-11842711
   See also: Institute for Fiscal Studies, *Public Spending under Labour* (2010), 2010 Election Briefing Note No.5, (Robert Chote, Rowena Crawford, Carl Emmerson, Gemma Tetlow), p. 10 http://www.ifs.org.uk/bns/bn92.pdf

36. 'Is welfare spending ever under control?', BBC News website, 1 October 2010, http://www.bbc.co.uk/news/magazine-11443372

37. Iain Duncan Smith, 'Iain Duncan Smith: we've brought back fairness to welfare', *Daily Telegraph*, 30 December 2012, http://www.telegraph.co.uk/news/politics/9772131/Iain-Duncan-Smith-weve-brought-back-fairness-to-welfare.html

38. Jesse Norman, *The Big Society: The Anatomy of the New Politics*, (University of Buckingham Press, Buckingham, 2010), Ch. 5, p. 78

39. Nick Ellison, 'The Conservative Party and public expenditure', cited in Hugh Bochel (ed.), *The Conservative Party and Social Policy*, (Policy Press, University of Bristol, 2011), Ch. 2, pp. 57–8

40. Phillip Blond is particularly critical of the practical outcome of the Conservative Party's social policy agenda after 2010, stating: 'The greatest disaster is austerity, because austerity empowered (George) Osborne … (to) produce what we've produced, which is nothing, and it is a terrible shame... Cameron hasn't been able to marshal his intuition into concepts that triumph over other concepts, and we've had a mix and the old Toryism has won out'.
   Phillip Blond, Respublica think-tank, interview with author in Liverpool, 19 February 2013

41. Lord Michael Ashcroft, '"Suspicious Strivers" hold the key to Tory election prospects', Lord Ashcroft Polls, 5 October 2012, http://lordashcroftpolls.com/2012/10/suspicious-strivers-hold-the-key-to-tory-election-prospects/

42. See HM Government, *Social Justice: transforming lives*, Presented to Parliament by the Secretary of State for Work and Pensions by Command of Her Majesty (March 2012), http://www.dwp.gov.uk/docs/social-justice-transforming-lives.pdf

43. Ibid., Introduction, page 4

44. Charlotte Pickles, Policy Director, The Centre for Social Justice, E-mail to author, 4 May 2010
45. Samira Shackle, 'Philippa Stroud given special adviser role', *New Statesman*, 24 May 2010, http://www.newstatesman.com/blogs/the-staggers/2010/05/duncan-smith-win-seat-sutton
46. Charlotte Pickles, Policy Director, The Centre for Social Justice, E-mail to author, 4 May 2010
47. Iain Duncan Smith: 'Labour has left the poor even more dependent on the state', *The Independent*, 16 September 2003, http://www.independent.co.uk/opinion/commentators/iain-duncan-smith-labour-has-left-the-poor-even-more-dependent-on-the-state-580062.html
48. See The Conservative Party, 'Get Britain Working' (October 2009), http://www.conservatives.com/News/News_stories/2009/10/Radical_welfare_reform_to_Get_Britain_Working.aspx
49. Iain Duncan Smith, 'Benefits system overhaul "to make work pay"', cited in BBC News website, 11 November 2010, http://www.bbc.co.uk/news/uk-politics-11728546
50. See Policy Network, *A Discussion Paper: In the black Labour: Why fiscal conservatism and social justice go hand-in-hand*, 2 December 2011, http://www.policy-network.net/publications/4101/-In-the-black-Labour
51. See Bruce Anderson and Robin Harris, 'Is Cameron a Thatcherite?', *Standpoint* magazine, October 2008, http://standpointmag.co.uk/is-david-cameron-a-thatcherite-october+?page=0%2C0%2C0%2C0%2C0%2C0%2C0%2C0%2C0%2C0%2C0
52. Ian Gilmour, *Dancing With Dogma: Britain Under Thatcherism*, (Simon & Schuster, London, 1992), Ch. 6, p. 163
53. Eric J. Evans, *Thatcher and Thatcherism*, (Routledge, London, 2nd edn., 2004), Ch. 6, p. 65
54. Robert M. Page, 'The Conservative Party and the Welfare State since 1945', cited in Hugh Bochel (ed.), *The Conservative Party and Social Policy*, (Policy Press, University of Bristol, 2011), Ch. 2, p. 31
55. Unemployment was approximately 1 million in1979, while it was approximately 2.5 million in 1990. See 'The Thatcher years in statistics', BBC News website, 22 November 2005 http://news.bbc.co.uk/1/hi/in_depth/4447082.stm
56. See Paul Marshall and David Laws (ed.), *The Orange Book: Reclaiming Liberalism*, (Profile Books, London, 2004)
57. The Coalition Agreement of May 2010, http://www.cabinetoffice.gov.uk/news/coalition-documents
58. Hugh Bochel (ed.), 'Conservative approaches to social policy since 1997', cited in Hugh Bochel (ed.), *The Conservative Party and Social Policy*, (Policy Press, University of Bristol, 2011), Ch. 1, p. 20
59. Allister Hayman, 'Clegg's battle for "real localism"', *Local Government Chronicle*, 20 January 2011, http://www.lgcplus.com/review/agenda/politics/cleggs-battle-for-real-localism/5024321.blog
60. Hugh Bochel , 'Cameron's Conservatism: influences, interpretations and implications', University of Lincoln (2010), p. 1 http://www.social-policy.org.uk/lincoln/Bochel_H.pdf

61. See Universal Credit: welfare that works: http://www.dwp.gov.uk/docs/ universal-credit-full-document.pdf
62. Universal Credits, which round up a number of different benefits into one single benefits payment, comes into force in April 2013. See DWP website: http://www.dwp.gov.uk/policy/welfare-reform/universal-credit/
63. Frank Field, 'The universal credit programme is on course for disaster', Comment is Free, *The Guardian*, 10 September 2012, http://www.guardian. co.uk/commentisfree/2012/sep/10/universal-credit-benefits-disaster
64. 'Now George Osborne and Iain Duncan-Smith clash over child benefit cuts', *Daily Mail*, 31 October 2010, http://www.dailymail.co.uk/news/arti-cle-1325292/Now-George-Osborne-Iain-Duncan-Smith-clash-child-benefit-cuts.html

5 Social policy case study 2: The 'Big Society' Policy Framework

1. See Conservative Party 2010 Manifesto, 'Big Society': http://www.conserva-tives.com/Policy/Where_we_stand/Big_Society.aspx
2. Patrick Winter and Julian Glover, 'General election 2010: David Cameron eyes the prize', *The Guardian*, 6 May 2010, http:// www.guardian.co.uk/politics/2010/may/05/general-election-2010-david-cameron
3. Nigel Morris, 'Tory manifesto: The case for the big society', *The Independent*, 14 April 2010, http://www.independent.co.uk/news/uk/politics/tory-mani-festo-the-case-for-the-big-society-1944058.html
4. Jane Merrick, 'The Big Society in crisis: Are the wheels coming off the PM's Big Idea?', *The Independent on Sunday*, 15 May 2011, http://www.independ-ent.co.uk/news/uk/politics/the-big-society-in-crisis-are-the-wheels-coming-off-the-pms-big-idea-2284251.html
5. Jesse Norman, MP for Hereford and South Herefordshire, interview with author, 16 March 2012.
6. Dennis Kavanagh and Philip Cowley, *The British General Election of 2010*, (Palgrave Macmillan, Basingstoke, 2010), Ch. 4, p. 89. See also: Speech, Rt Hon David Cameron: 'The Big Society, Hugo Young Memorial Lecture', 10 November 10 2009, http://www.conservatives.com/News/Speeches/2009/11/ David_Cameron_The_Big_Society.aspx
7. Rt. Hon David Cameron: 'The Big Society, Hugo Young Memorial Lecture', 10 November 2009, cited in Jesse Norman, *The Big Society: The Anatomy of the New Politics*, (University of Buckingham Press, Buckingham, 2010), Introduction, p. 1
8. Jesse Norman, MP for Hereford and South Herefordshire, interview with author, 16 March 2012
9. David Willetts MP, interview with author, 10 September 2012
10. Stephen Driver, '"Fixing our broken society": David Cameron's post-Thatcherite social policy', cited in Simon Lee and Matt Beech (eds.), *The Conservatives under David Cameron: Built to Last?*, (Palgrave Macmillan, Basingstoke, 2nd edn., 2009), Ch. 6, p. 88

11. Hannah Fearn, 'True Blue?', *Charity Times*, Jan–Feb. 2007, http://www.chari-tytimes.com/pages/ct_features/jan-feb07/text_features/ct_jan-feb07_feature6_true_blue.htm
12. David Willetts MP, interview with author, 10 September 2012
13. The 'Third Sector' broadly incorporates the charity, voluntary and fundraising sectors within society
14. Phillip Blond, Respublica think-tank, interview with author, 19 February 2013
15. Andrew Defty, 'The Conservatives, social policy and public opinion', cited in Hugh Bochel (ed.), *The Conservative Party and Social Policy*, (Policy Press, University of Bristol, 2011), Ch. 4, p. 76
16. See James Langdale, 'Election 2010: Assessing the campaign as end approaches', BBC News website, 5 May 2010: '(His) vision of a "big society" that would transform public services in this country... was perhaps sprung on the electorate too late with many voters still struggling to understand what it might mean for them'. http://news.bbc.co.uk/1/hi/uk_politics/election_2010/8662442.stm
17. Catherine Bennett, 'The "Big Society" is collapsing under its inherent absurdity', *The Observer*, 6 February 2011, http://www.guardian.co.uk/commentisfree/2011/feb/06/david-cameron-big-society-coalition
18. Brian Wheeler, 'Big society: More than a soundbite?', BBC News website, 14 February 2011 http://www.bbc.co.uk/news/uk-politics-12163624
19. See Simon Heffer, 'That he can't connect with his party is worrying. That he can't connect with the public may be fatal', *Daily Mail*, 21 November 2011, http://www.dailymail.co.uk/debate/article-2063387/That-connect-party-worrying-That-connect-public-fatal.html
20. 'Election 2010: First hung parliament in UK for decades', BBC News website, 7 May 2010, http://news.bbc.co.uk/1/hi/8667071.stm
21. 'Cameron and Clegg set out "Big Society" policy ideas', BBC News website, 18 May 2010, http://news.bbc.co.uk/1/hi/uk_politics/8688860.stm
22. See 'Building the Big Society', Cabinet Office document, 18 May 2010: http://www.cabinetoffice.gov.uk/sites/default/files/resources/building-big-society_0.pdf
23. Peter Oborne, 'Big Society RIP?', *Daily Telegraph*, 4 February 2011, http://www.telegraph.co.uk/news/politics/david-cameron/8303188/Big-Society-RIP.html
24. Steve Hilton, 'Our positive alternative to Labour's big government is the big society' – Extracts from 'The Steve Hilton Strategy Bulletins', 5 January 2010, http://blogs.ft.com/westminster/2010/01/the-steve-hilton-strategy-bulletins/ Steve Hilton was David Cameron's Director of Strategy between 2006 and 2012.
25. See: http://www.respublica.org.uk/
26. See Phillip Blond, *Red Tory: How Left and Right Have Broken Britain and How We Can Fix It*, (Faber, London 2010)
27. Phillip Blond, 'David Cameron has lost his chance to redefine the Tories', Comment is Free, *The Guardian*, 3 October 2012, http://www.guardian.co.uk/commentisfree/2012/oct/03/cameron-one-nation-u-turn-tory-tragedy
28. See Kevin Hickson, 'The New Tories may be a puzzle but the pieces do make up a new kind of Britain', *Parliamentary Brief Online*, 30 March

2010, http://www.parliamentarybrief.com/2010/03/the-new-tories-may-be-a-puzzle-but-the-pieces

29. Blond describes 'mutualism' as: 'Mutualism represents perhaps the most flexible and beneficial way of transforming our public services... based on principles of reciprocity, equity and fairness. It is a system that allows for equity (what you put in and therefore can take out), be that in terms of finance or services, to be realised in any number of ways. To achieve the positive transformation of our public services, we need to find new models of mutualism fit for the 21st century... creating innovative ways of bringing together public and private capital, enabling private companies to make a fair return from their capital investments, while at the same time giving all those involved a stake or return of some sort'. Cited in Philip Blond and Jane Dudman, 'Common Purpose', *Ethos Journal*, (October 2011), http://www.ethosjournal.com/home/item/265-common-purpose

30. Phillip Blond, 'Rise of the red Tories', *Prospect* magazine, 28 February 2009, http://www.prospectmagazine.co.uk/2009/02/riseoftheredtories/

31. Phillip Blond, Respublica think-tank, interview with author in Liverpool, 19 February 2013

32. Ibid.

33. Ibid.

34. Dermot Murnaghan debates the Big Society with Phillip Blond (former Cameron advisor), Rev Peter Smith Archbishop of Southwark and Sir Stephen Bubb, ACEVO, Sky News, 13 February 2011, http://skynewstranscripts.co.uk/transcript.asp?id=946

35. David Cameron, speech in Liverpool, 19 July 2010, cited on BBC News website, 19 July 2010, 'David Cameron launches Tories' "Big Society" plan', http://www.bbc.co.uk/news/uk-10680062

36. Jesse Norman, *The Big Society: The Anatomy of the New Politics*, (University of Buckingham Press, Buckingham, 2010), Introduction, p. 3

37. See Hugo Young, *One of Us*, (Pan Macmillan, London, 1989), p. 607: '(During the Thatcher government) the average rise of anyone in the top 10 per cent of earners was 47 percent (1979–90); for a man in the lowest 10 per cent it was 2.9 per cent'.

38. Nick Ellison, 'The Conservative Party and public expenditure', cited in Hugh Bochel (ed.), *The Conservative Party and Social Policy*, (Policy Press, University of Bristol, 2011), Ch. 2, p. 41

39. Phillip Blond, Extract from *Red Tory: How Left and Right Have Broken Britain and How We Can Fix it*, (Faber, London, 2010), cited in Conservative Home website, 28 March 2010, http://conservativehome.blogs.com/thinktank-central/2010/03/thatcher-failed-says-selfstyled-red-tory-phillip-blond-as-he-launches-twenty-policy-ideas.html

40. Dermot Murnaghan debates the Big Society with Phillip Blond (former Cameron advisor), Rev Peter Smith Archbishop of Southwark and Sir Stephen Bubb, ACEVO, Sky News, 13 February 2011, http://skynewstranscripts.co.uk/transcript.asp?id=946

41. Carl Cross, Chairman of Merseyside Conservative Party (2009–12), E-mail questionnaire to author, 4 March 2011

42. Jane Merrick, 'The Big Society in crisis: Are the wheels coming off the PM's Big Idea?', *The Independent on Sunday*, 15 May 2011 http://www.independent.

co.uk/news/uk/politics/the-big-society-in-crisis-are-the-wheels-coming-off-the-pms-big-idea-2284251.html
In the ComRes poll of 15 May 2011, '40% of respondents did not know what it meant', a 10% increase since February 2011, see: http://www.comres.co.uk/page1902473831.aspx

43. Andrew Defty, 'The Conservatives, social policy and public opinion', cited in Hugh Bochel (ed.), *The Conservative Party and Social Policy,* (Policy Press, University of Bristol, 2011), Ch. 4, pp. 67–8. Defty's research also suggests that: 'Data from Ipsos MORI suggests that under Labour more than two-thirds of the public believed that public services should be run by the government or local authorities rather than private companies, and that there has been a slight increase in support for state provision since 2000'.
A 2004 British Social Attitudes Survey found that while 55% of those asked thought that private companies could run public services more cost effectively, 73% believed the government would be better to deliver such services to those that needed them most, A. Defty cited in H. Bochel (ed.), (2011), Ch. 4, p. 68

44. David Willetts MP, interview with author, 10 September 2012

45. Nick Ellison, 'The Conservative Party and public expenditure', cited in Hugh Bochel (ed.), *The Conservative Party and Social Policy,* (Policy Press, University of Bristol, 2011), Ch. 2, p. 58

46. See *Powerful People, Responsible Society,* The report of the Commission on Big Society (16 May 2011), http://www.acevo.org.uk/page.aspx?pid=191&nccsm=21&_nccscid=28&_nccsct=Free+Downloads&_nccspID=1077
A YouGov poll carried out for the Commission found that 78% of the public believed that the government had failed to effectively articulate what 'The Big Society' meant

47. Polly Curtis, 'Government urged to take stronger lead on "Big society"', *The Guardian,* 16 May 2011, http://www.guardian.co.uk/society/2011/may/16/government-urged-stronger-lead-big-society

48. BBC News website, 'David Cameron aims to boost Big Society', 23 May 2011, http://www.bbc.co.uk/news/uk-politics-13496397

49. 'David Cameron: deficit reduction is my duty, Big Society my passion', *Daily Telegraph,* 14 February 2011, http://www.telegraph.co.uk/news/politics/david-cameron/8322788/David-Cameron-deficit-reduction-is-my-duty-Big-Society-my-passion.html

50. 'Big Society doomed unless civil servants change – MPs', BBC News website, 22 September 2011, http://www.bbc.co.uk/news/uk-politics-15019689

51. Bernard Jenkin MP cited in 'Big Society is being hampered by lack of clarity – MPs', BBC News website, 14 December 2011, http://www.bbc.co.uk/news/uk-politics-16168695

52. Dermot Murnaghan debates the Big Society with Phillip Blond (former Cameron advisor), Rev Peter Smith Archbishop of Southwark and Sir Stephen Bubb, ACEVO, Sky News, 13 February 2011, http://skynewstran-scripts.co.uk/transcript.asp?id=946

53. Toby Helm, 'David Cameron's guru attacks the failings of the "Big Society"', *The Guardian,* 18 June 2011, http://www.guardian.co.uk/society/2011/jun/18/david-cameron-guru-big-society

See also: Phillip Blond, 'David Cameron has lost his chance to redefine the Tories', Comment is Free, *The Guardian*, 3 October 2012, http://www.guardian.co.uk/commentisfree/2012/oct/03/cameron-one-nation-u-turn-tory-tragedy

54. Patrick Butler, 'Cameron's "big society" undermined by cuts and distrust, says study', *The Guardian*, 7 May 2012, http://www.guardian.co.uk/society/2012/may/07/david-cameron-big-society-cuts-distrust
   See also: Civil Exchange, 'The Big Society Audit 2012' (May 2012), http://www.civilexchange.org.uk/wp-content/uploads/2012/09/THE-BIG-SOCIETY-AUDIT-2012finalwebversion.pdf

55. Sarah Neville and Jonathan Moules, '"Big society bank" to start providing capital', *Financial Times*, 4 April 2012, http://www.ft.com/cms/s/0/51466676-7d8f-11e1-bfa5-00144feab49a.html#axzz1rANxkGjJ

56. 'Cuts "destroying 'big society' concept", says CSV head', BBC News website, 7 February 2011, http://www.bbc.co.uk/news/uk-politics-12378974

57. Steve Corbett and Alan Walker, 'The Big Society: Back to the future', *Political Quarterly*, Volume 3, Issue 3, (July–September 2012), p. 490

58. '"It's all talk and no action": David Cameron's Big Society plans blasted after 7,000 charities were forced to close last year', *Daily Mail*, 17 August 2012, http://www.dailymail.co.uk/news/article-2189666/David-Camerons-Big-Society-plans-blasted-7-000-charities-forced-close-year.html#ixzz258mL6Jcj

59. Emma Barnett, Digital Media Editor, 'How will the "Big Society" work if no one has time to volunteer?', *Daily Telegraph*, 19 May 2011, http://www.mydaily.co.uk/2011/05/19/how-will-the-big-society-work-if-no-one-has-time-to-volunteer

60. Patrick Butler's Cuts Blog, 'The Work Programme's "Big Society" logic: Get charities to do it for free', *The Guardian*, 10 November 2011, http://www.guardian.co.uk/society/patrick-butler-cuts-blog/2011/nov/10/work-programme-charities-working-for-free

61. David Willetts MP, interview with author, 10 September 2012

62. Baroness Sayeeda Warsi, House of Lords (Hansard), 9 February 2011, Column 221, http://www.publications.parliament.uk/pa/ld201011/ldhansrd/text/110209-0001.htm#11020963000771

63. Patrick Hennessy, 'No place for Big Society at Conservative conference', *Daily Telegraph*, 10 September 2011, http://www.telegraph.co.uk/news/politics/conservative/8754793/No-place-for-Big-Society-at-Conservative-conference.html

64. *The Independent*, 'Conservative Party Conference 2012 in Birmingham: Full transcript of David Cameron's speech', 10 October 2012, http://www.independent.co.uk/news/uk/politics/conservative-party-conference-2012-in-birmingham-full-transcript-of-david-camerons-speech-8205536.html

65. Stephen Bates, 'New Year honours list reflects my aims for "Big Society"', says David Cameron', *The Guardian*, 31 December 2011 http://www.guardian.co.uk/uk/2011/dec/31/new-year-honours-david-cameron

66. Anthony Seldon, 'The big society must be grounded in goodness', Guardian Comment Network, 3 January 2012, http://www.guardian.co.uk/commentisfree/2012/jan/03/big-society-goodness-government-morality

See also Anthony Seldon, 'The Politics of Optimism', Policy Exchange research note, January 2012, http://www.policyexchange.org.uk/images/publications/pdfs/The_Politics_of_Optimism_-_Jan__12.pdf

67. Ed Miliband, Labour Leader from 2010, described the approach of the 'Big Society' as 'a return to Victorian philanthropy', cited in: Nicholas Watt, 'David Cameron reveals "Big Society" vision – and denies it is just cost cutting', *The Guardian*, 19 July 2010, http://www.guardian.co.uk/politics/2010/jul/19/david-cameron-big-society-launch

68. See Roy Hattersley and Kevin Hickson, 'In praise of social democracy', *Political Quarterly*, Volume 83, Issue 1, (January–March 2012). The authors defend the role of the state and refer to 'The Big Society' agenda as the coalition government's "ideological narrative..... (and) a justification for a determination to reduce the role of government and cut public expenditure"'. (p. 3) http://onlinelibrary.wiley.com/doi/10.1111/j.1467-923X.2011.02259.x/pdf

69. Polly Toynbee, 'David Cameron's men go where Margaret Thatcher never dared', Comment is Free, *The Guardian*, 17 September 2012, http://www.guardian.co.uk/commentisfree/2012/sep/17/cameron-goes-where-thatcher-never-dared
See also: Polly Toynbee and David Walker, *Dogma and Disarray: Cameron at Half-Time*, (Granta Books, London, 2012), e-book

70. See Jon Cruddas and Andrea Nahles, *'Building the Good Society: the project of the democratic left'*, (Compass Think tank, 2009): http://www.compassonline.org.uk/publications/item.asp?d=985

71. Helen Grady, BBC Radio 4, 21st March 2011, 'Blue Labour: Party's radical answer to the Big Society?', http://www.bbc.co.uk/news/uk-12759902

72. See Robert Philpot (ed.), *The Purple Book: A Progressive Future for Labour*, Progress, (Biteback , London, 2011)

73. Allegra Stratton, 'Ed Miliband rehearses "good society" guru's lines in conference speech', *The Guardian*, 28 September 2010, http://www.guardian.co.uk/politics/2010/sep/28/ed-miliband-speech-maurice-glasman

74. Anthony Crosland, *The Future of Socialism*, (Jonathan Cape, London, 1956)

75. Lord Maurice Glasman, a Labour peer and an academic at London Metropolitan University, has been credited with framing Labour's response to the 'Big Society' agenda, coining terms such as 'Blue Labour' and the 'Good Society' in the process.

76. Jesse Norman, Conservative MP for Hereford and South Herefordshire, 'Stealing the Big Society', Comment is Free, *The Guardian*, 8 February 2011, http://www.guardian.co.uk/commentisfree/2011/feb/08/stealing-big-society-ed-miliband

77. Respublica sources speaking to author at Labour Party Conference, Liverpool, September 2011. See also: Oliver Wright, 'Labour to embrace David Cameron's "big society"', *The Independent*, 1 October 2012, http://www.independent.co.uk/news/uk/politics/labour-to-embrace-david-camerons-big-society-8192956.html
See also, Phillip Blond, Respublica think-tank, interview with author, 19 February 2013, who claimed that it is 'perfectly possible for the Labour Party to go back to genuine formative first principles and have a different relationship to The Big Society'.

78. Jon Cruddas, IPPR fringe event, Labour Party Conference (October 2012), Manchester, cited in Kayte Rath, 'Jon Cruddas backs Labour version of Big Society', BBC News website, 1 October 2012, http://www.bbc.co.uk/news/uk-politics-19779457

79. Oliver Wright, 'Labour to embrace David Cameron's "Big Society"', *The Independent*, 1 October 2012, http://www.independent.co.uk/news/uk/politics/labour-to-embrace-david-camerons-big-society-8192956.html

80. Jesse Norman, Conservative MP for Hereford and South Herefordshire, 'Hands off our big society', Comment is Free, *The Guardian*, 30 September 2011, http://www.guardian.co.uk/commentisfree/2011/sep/30/ed-miliband-speech-conservatives-business

81. Jesse Norman, *The Big Society: The Anatomy of the New Politics*, (University of Buckingham Press, Buckingham, 2010), Introduction, p. 7

82. David Willetts MP, interview with author, 10 September 2012

83. Jason Beattie, 'Tory MPs turn on Big Society architect Steve Hilton', *Daily Mirror*, 25 January 2011, http://www.mirror.co.uk/news/politics/2011/01/25/tory-mps-turn-on-big-society-architect-steve-hilton-115875-22873820/#ixzz1gKUxZfxp

84. Jo Johnson, Conservative MP for Orpington, cited in: 'Tory MPs turn on Big Society architect Steve Hilton', *Daily Mirror*, 25 January 2011

85. Tim Montgomerie, Editor of Conservative Home website, 'David Cameron may be error-strewn. But there's no alternative ... yet', Comment is Free, *The Guardian*, 12 April 2012, http://www.guardian.co.uk/commentisfree/2012/apr/12/david-cameron-no-alternative-yet

86. F.A Hayek. 'Material Conditions And Ideal Ends', cited in *The Road to Serfdom* (1944), Ch. 14, p. 235

87. Phillip Blond, 'Rise of the red Tories', *Prospect* magazine, 28 February 2009, http://www.prospectmagazine.co.uk/2009/02/riseoftheredtories/

88. Dennis Kavanagh and Philip Cowley, *The British General Election of 2010*, (Palgrave Macmillan, Basingstoke, 2010), Ch. 4, p. 89

89. See Matthew Taylor, 'Why the old ways won't work for Labour', 22 January 2009, which highlights how Cameron's Conservatives 'have been pretty successful at detoxifying their brand'. http://www.matthewtaylorsblog.com/politics/why-the-old-ways-wont-work-for-labour/

90. David Cameron, August 2008, cited in Philip Blond, 'Rise of the red Tories', *Prospect* magazine, 28 February 2009, http://www.prospectmagazine.co.uk/2009/02/riseoftheredtories/

91. See Matthew Taylor, 'The post-bureaucratic state', June 18 2008, which describes the 'post-bureaucratic state' as a concept that 'combines social ambition with scepticism about the state'. http://www.matthewtaylorsblog.com/politics/the-post-bureaucratic-state/

92. Andrew Gamble, *The Free Economy and the Strong State: The Politics of Thatcherism*, (Macmillan, Basingstoke, 2nd edn., 1994), Ch. 2, p. 44

93. Stephen Driver, '"Fixing our broken society": David Cameron's post-Thatcherite social policy', cited in Simon Lee and Matt Beech (eds.), *The Conservatives under David Cameron: Built to Last?*, (Palgrave Macmillan, Basingstoke, 2nd edn., 2009), Ch. 6, p. 95

94. Archbishop of Canterbury Rowan Williams, cited in 'Williams attacks Big Society idea', Press Association, *The Observer*, 24 June 2012, http://www.guardian.co.uk/uk/feedarticle/10304929

95. See Andrew Rawnsley, 'David Cameron's ambivalent relationship with the lady in blue', *The Observer*, 10 October 2010, http://www.guardian.co.uk/commentisfree/2010/oct/10/cameron-thatcher-spending-cuts

96. In 1981, Conservative Cabinet Minister Norman Tebbit demanded that the unemployed 'get on their bikes' and look for jobs, comments that were criticised as being unsympathetic to those living in areas with a high volume of unemployment

97. Ben Kisby, 'The Big Society: Power to the people?', *Political Quarterly*, Volume 81, No. 4, (October–December 2010), p. 490

98. Jesse Norman, *The Big Society: The Anatomy of the New Politics*, (University of Buckingham Press, Buckingham, 2010), Ch. 1, p. 25

99. Boris Johnson, 'What on earth has come over our aimless, feckless, hopeless youth?', cited in the *Daily Telegraph*, 19 August 2008, http://www.telegraph.co.uk/comment/columnists/borisjohnson/3561544/What-on-earth-has-come-over-our-aimless-feckless-hopeless-youth.html

100. Stephen Driver, '"Fixing our broken society": David Cameron's Post-Thatcherite social policy', cited in Simon Lee and Matt Beech (eds.), *The Conservatives under David Cameron: Built to Last?*, (Palgrave Macmillan, Basingstoke, 2nd edn., 2009), Ch. 6, p. 90

6 Social policy case study 3: The Free Schools policy

1. 2010 Conservative Party manifesto, *Invitation to join the Government of Britain*, 'Raise Standards in Schools', pp. 51–53, http://www.conservatives.com/~/media/Files/Activist%20Centre/Press%20and%20Policy/Manifestos/Manifesto2010

2. See *The Coalition: our programme for government* (May 2010), pp. 28–29, https://www.gov.uk/government/publications/the-coalition-documentation

3. Jesse Norman, MP for Hereford and South Herefordshire, interview with author, 16 March 2012

4. Sonia Exley and Stephen J. Ball, 'Something old, something new: understanding Conservative education policy', cited in Hugh Bochel (ed.), *The Conservative Party and Social Policy*, (Policy Press, University of Bristol, 2011), Ch. 6, p. 97

5. Adam Leeder and Deborah Mabbett, 'Free Schools: Big Society or small interests?', cited in Jason Edwards (ed). *Retrieving the Big Society*, (Wiley-Blackwell, Chichester, 2012), p. 133

6. David Laws, *22 Days in May: The Birth of the Lib Dem–Conservative Coalition*, (Biteback, London, 2010), Diary extract 10 May 2010, p. 139

7. Jesse Norman, MP for Hereford and South Herefordshire, interview with author, 16 March 2012. See also David Laws, Diary extract 7 May 2010, p. 69: 'George (Osborne) replied that the Conservatives supported the policy (pupil premium) and that he was happy to work with us to look how it could be funded'

8. Institute for Fiscal Studies, *'Public Spending under Labour'* (2010), 2010 Election Briefing Note No.5, (Robert Chote, Rowena Crawford, Carl Emmerson, Gemma Tetlow), p. 9 http://www.ifs.org.uk/bns/bn92.pdf

9. See *School Standards and Framework Act (1988)*, that diluted Conservative introduced Grant-Maintained Schools and replaced them with 'Foundation Schools', which retained some, if less, autonomy: http://www.legislation.gov.uk/ukpga/1998/31/contents

10. Sonia Exley and Stephen J. Ball, 'Something old, something new: understanding Conservative education policy', cited in Hugh Bochel (ed.), *The Conservative Party and Social Policy*, (Policy Press, University of Bristol, 2011), Ch. 6, p. 110

11. Clyde Chitty, *Education Policy in Britain*, (Palgrave Macmillan, Basingstoke, 2004), Ch. 3, p. 33

12. PFI (Private Finance Initiatives) – A model of funding public services, e.g. schools or hospitals, first used in the UK in the early 1990s. The bulk of investment is provided by a private company, and the state then pays back the amount involved (with interest) over a period of years.

13. An example of this could be seen in the abolition of the assisted places scheme that subsidised low-income families to send their children to independent or private schools, see *Education (Schools) Act (1997)*: http://www.educationengland.org.uk/documents/pdfs/1997-education-(schools)-act.pdf

14. Maurice Glasman and Jesse Norman, 'The Big Society in question', cited in Jason Edwards (ed). *Retrieving the Big Society*, (Wiley-Blackwell, Chichester, 2012), p. 11

15. Matthew d'Ancona, 'Ditching their modernisation campaign was the Tories' worst strategic error since the poll tax', *Daily Telegraph*. 30 December 2012, http://www.telegraph.co.uk/comment/columnists/matthewd_ancona/9770645/Ditching-their-modernisation-campaign-was-the-Tories-worst-strategic-error-since-the-poll-tax.html
    An edited version of Matthew d'Ancona's chapter in Ryan Shorthouse (ed.), *Tory modernisation 2.0: the future of the Conservative Party*, (Bright Blue, London, 2013)

16. Susanne Wiborg, 'Swedish Free Schools: Do They Work?', *LLAKES Research Paper 18*, (Institute of Education, University of London, 2010), p. 8: http://www.llakes.org/wp-content/uploads/2010/09/Wiborg-online.pdf

17. Sonia Exley and Stephen J. Ball, 'Something old, something new: understanding Conservative education policy', cited in Hugh Bochel (ed.), *The Conservative Party and Social Policy*, (Policy Press, University of Bristol, 2011), Ch. 6, p. 101

18. Susanne Wiborg, 'Swedish Free Schools: Do They Work?', *LLAKES Research Paper 18*, (Institute of Education, University of London, 2010), p. 11: http://www.llakes.org/wp-content/uploads/2010/09/Wiborg-online.pdf

19. Sonia Exley and Stephen J. Ball, 'Something old, something new: understanding Conservative education policy', cited in Hugh Bochel (ed.), *The Conservative Party and Social Policy*, (Policy Press, University of Bristol, 2011), Ch. 6, p. 112

20. See Michael Gove, 'A failed generation: Educational inequality under Labour' (2008), http://educar.files.wordpress.com/2008/08/a_failed_generation.pdf
    Also cited in Sonia Exley and Stephen J. Ball, 'Something old, something new: understanding Conservative education policy', cited in Hugh Bochel (ed.), *The Conservative Party and Social Policy*, (Policy Press, University of Bristol, 2011), Ch. 6, p. 101

21. Michael Gove, 'We need a Swedish education system', *The Independent*, 3 October 2008, http://www.independent.co.uk/opinion/commentators/michael-gove-we-need-a-swedish-education-system-1048755.html
22. See Anders Böhlmark and Mikael Lindahl, IZA (Institute for the Study of Labour, Bonn, Germany), Discussion Paper Series No.2786, 'The impact of school choice on pupil achievement, segregation and costs: Swedish evidence', (May 2007), ftp://repec.iza.org/RePEc/Discussionpaper/dp2786.pdf
23. See Michael Oakeshott, *On Human Conduct*, (Clarendon Press, London, 1975)
24. Jesse Norman, *The Big Society: The Anatomy of the New Politics* (University of Buckingham Press, Buckingham, 2010), Ch. 6, p. 97
25. Robert M. Page, University of Birmingham, 'Clear blue water? The Conservative Party's approach to social policy since 1945', Paper presented at the Social Policy Association's Annual Conference, University of Lincoln (5–7 July 2010), p. 11 http://www.social-policy.org.uk/lincoln/Page.pdf
26. See Anders Böhlmark and Mikael Lindahl, IZA (Institute for the Study of Labour, Bonn, Germany), Discussion Paper Series No.2786, 'The impact of school choice on pupil achievement, segregation and costs: Swedish evidence', (May 2007), ftp://repec.iza.org/RePEc/Discussionpaper/dp2786.pdf
27. Robert M. Page, University of Birmingham, 'Clear blue water? The Conservative Party's approach to social policy since 1945', Paper presented at the Social Policy Association's Annual Conference, University of Lincoln (5–7 July 2010), p. 13 http://www.social-policy.org.uk/lincoln/Page.pdf
28. Jesse Norman, MP for Hereford and South Herefordshire, interview with author, 16 March 2012
29. West London Free School: http://www.westlondonfreeschool.co.uk/
30. Toby Young, 'Swedish-style free schools will raise standards – and, more importantly, they will increase choice', *Daily Telegraph*, 19 February 2010, http://blogs.telegraph.co.uk/news/tobyyoung/100026654/swedish-style-free-schools-will-raise-standards-but-more-importantly-they-will-increase-choice/
31. Department for Education, 'Free Schools opening in 2012 and beyond', http://education.gov.uk/schools/leadership/typesofschools/freeschools/b00197715/free-schools-2012
32. BBC News website, 'Free school numbers to rise by 55, government reveals', 3 September 2012, http://www.bbc.co.uk/news/education-19460927
33. Ben Turner, 'Everton FC's new free school opens', *Liverpool Echo*, 2 October 2012, http://www.liverpoolecho.co.uk/liverpool-news/local-news/2012/10/02/everton-fc-s-new-free-school-opens-100252-31944651/
    See also Everton Free School website: http://community.evertonfc.com/education/everton-free-school/
34. Jessica Shepherd, 'Free-school applications reopen with ex-soldiers and evangelicals in running', *The Guardian*, 13 February 2012, http://www.guardian.co.uk/education/2012/feb/13/free-school-applications-soldiers-evangelicals
35. Andrew Woodcock, '102 new free schools win approval', *The Independent*, 13 July 2012, http://www.independent.co.uk/news/education/education-news/102-new-free-schools-win-approval-7941333.html
    See also: Department of Education, Free Schools, http://www.education.gov.uk/schools/leadership/typesofschools/freeschools/a00211685/2013

36. Jeevan Vasagar, 'Third of new free schools are religious', *The Guardian*, 13 July 2012, http://www.guardian.co.uk/education/2012/jul/13/third-new-free-schools-religious

37. Anna David, 'London poised for new wave of free schools', *London Evening Standard*, 2 July 2012, http://www.standard.co.uk/news/education/london-poised-for-new-wave-of-free-schools-7903632.html

38. Toby Young, The Commentator website, 'The free schools revolution', 11 October 2012, http://www.thecommentator.com/article/1788/the_free_schools_revolution

39. Toby Young, E-mail interview with author, 28 March 2012

40. Toby Young, The Commentator website, 'The free schools revolution', 11 October 2012, http://www.thecommentator.com/article/1788/the_free_schools_revolution

41. Graeme Paton, Education Editor, 'Anger as Coalition halts free school project', *Daily Telegraph*, 27 August 2012, http://www.telegraph.co.uk/education/educationnews/9502200/Anger-as-Coalition-halts-free-school-project.html

42. Local Government Association (LGA), 'Schools duck "moral duty" to dish up healthy meals', 13 January 2013, http://www.local.gov.uk/web/guest/media-releases/-/journal_content/56/10171/3839479/NEWS-TEMPLATE

43. Richard Garner, '70 per cent of free schools not filled two years after opening, Labour claims', *The Independent*, 24 April 2014 http://www.independent.co.uk/news/education/schools/70-per-cent-of-free-schools-not-filled-two-years-after-opening-labour-claims-9278569.html

44. Stephen Twigg MP, Shadow Secretary of State for Education (2010–13), E-mail questionnaire response, 24 January 2012

45. Seamus Milne, 'Crony capitalism feeds the corporate plan for schools', *The Guardian*, 14 February 2012, http://www.guardian.co.uk/commentisfree/2012/feb/14/crony-capitalism-corporate-schools?newsfeed=true

46. Roy Hattersley and Kevin Hickson, 'In praise of social democracy', *Political Quarterly*, Volume 83, Issue 1, (January–March 2012), p. 7 http://onlinelibrary.wiley.com/doi/10.1111/j.1467-923X.2011.02259.x/pdf

47. Andrew Adonis, 'Labour should support free schools — it invented them', *New Statesman*, 15 March 2012, http://www.newstatesman.com/education/2012/03/free-schools-labour-academies
See also Andrew Adonis, *Education, Education, Education: Reforming England's Schools*, (Biteback, London, 2012)

48. See S.Wiborg, *Education and Social Integration: Comprehensive Schooling in Europe*, (Palgrave Macmillan, Basingstoke, 2009)

49. See Anders Böhlmark and Mikael Lindahl, IZA (Institute for the Study of Labour, Bonn, Germany), Discussion Paper Series No.2786, 'The impact of school choice on pupil achievement, segregation and costs: Swedish evidence', (May 2007), ftp://repec.iza.org/RePEc/Discussionpaper/dp2786.pdf

50. Richard Garner, 'Government's flagship free schools accused of allowing 'stealth selection' as they fail to admit poorest kids', *The Independent*, 7 August 2014, http://www.independent.co.uk/news/education/educationnews/governments-flagship-free-schools-accused-of-allowing-stealth-selection-as-they-fail-to-admit-poorest-kids-9652592.html

51. Lord Hill, 'Free Schools are a grassroots revolution', *Politics Home*, 12 February 2012, http://politicshome.com/uk/article/46063/lord_hill_free_schools_are_a_grass_roots_revolution_.html
52. Department for Education, 'Free Schools Policy': http://www.education.gov.uk/schools/leadership/typesofschools/freeschools
53. Department for Education: 'Academies', http://www.education.gov.uk/schools/leadership/typesofschools/academies
54. Jesse Norman, *The Big Society: The Anatomy of the New Politics*, (University of Buckingham Press, Buckingham, 2010), Introduction, Ch. 4, p. 74
55. Toby Young, E-mail interview with author, 28 March 2012.
56. Michael Gove, 'We need a Swedish education system', *The Independent*, 3 October 2008, http://www.independent.co.uk/opinion/commentators/michael-gove-we-need-a-swedish-education-system-1048755.html
57. Toby Young, E-mail interview with author, 28 March 2012
58. Jesse Norman, MP for Hereford and South Herefordshire, interview with author, 16 March 2012
59. Toby Blume, 'Free schools: why applying was "utterly horrendous"', *The Guardian*, 16 July 2012, http://www.guardian.co.uk/education/2012/jul/16/free-school-community-involvement
60. Ibid.
61. Sonia Exley and Stephen J. Ball, 'Something old, something new: understanding Conservative education policy', cited in Hugh Bochel (ed.), *The Conservative Party and Social Policy*, (Policy Press, University of Bristol, 2011), Ch. 6, p. 101
62. See Gabriel H. Sahlgren, 'Swedish education and the role of the profit motive', IEA Discussion paper No.33 (2010), http://www.iea.org.uk/sites/default/files/publications/files/Schooling%20for%20money%20-%20web%20version_0.pdf
63. See an example of a Free schools admissions policy: http://www.westlondon-freeschool.co.uk/overview/admissions.html
64. Toby Young, E-mail interview with author, 28 March 2012
65. Jessica Shepherd, 'Most free schools take fewer deprived pupils than local average, figures show', *The Guardian*, 23 April 2012, http://www.guardian.co.uk/education/2012/apr/23/free-schools-deprived-pupils-average
66. See: Sutton Trust Research Report, 'Ensuring less privileged pupils benefit from the Government's school reforms', 2 September 2010, http://www.suttontrust.com/research/ensuring-less-privileged-pupils-benefit/
67. Ibid. pp. 3 and 6
68. Jesse Norman, *The Big Society: The Anatomy of the New Politics*, (University of Buckingham Press, Buckingham, 2010), Ch. 2, p. 27
69. Sonia Exley and Stephen J. Ball, 'Something old, something new: understanding Conservative education policy', cited in Hugh Bochel (ed.), *The Conservative Party and Social Policy*, (Policy Press, University of Bristol, 2011), Ch. 6, p. 109
70. Hilary Wilce, 'Time for change: How a young woman plans to shake up the school system', *The Independent*, 12 November 2009, http://www.independent.co.uk/news/education/schools/time-for-change-how-a-young-woman-plans-to-shake-up-the-school-system-1818636.html

71. Jesse Norman, *The Big Society: The Anatomy of the New Politics,* (University of Buckingham Press, Buckingham, 2010), Ch. 2, p. 27
72. Clyde Chitty, *Education Policy in Britain,* (Palgrave Macmillan, Basingstoke, 2004), Ch. 3, p. 47
73. Ibid.
74. See Andrew Gamble, *The Free Economy and The Strong State: The Politics of Thatcherism,* (Macmillan, Basingstoke, 1st edn., 1988),
75. 1988 Education Reform Act: http://www.legislation.gov.uk/ukpga/1988/40/contents
76. See the National School Curriculum: http://www.education.gov.uk/schools/teachingandlearning/curriculum
77. Clyde Chitty, *Education Policy in Britain,* (Palgrave Macmillan, Basingstoke, 2004), Ch. 3, p. 51
78. Department for Education, 'National Curriculum review launched', 20 January 2011 (updated 26 April 2012), http://www.education.gov.uk/inthenews/inthenews/a0073149/national-curriculum-review-launched
79. Lord Hill, 'Free Schools are a grassroots revolution', *Politics Home,* 12 February 2012, http://politicshome.com/uk/article/46063/lord_hill_free_schools_are_a_grass_roots_revolution_.html
80. Fraser Nelson, 'Politics: Michael Gove's free schools are a triumph – but can they keep up with the baby boom?', *The Spectator,* 3 September 2011, http://www.spectator.co.uk/politics/all/7204973/politics-michael-goves-free-schools-are-a-triumph-but-can-they-keep-up-with-the-baby-boom.thtml
81. See Department for Education, Free Schools Model Funding Agreement: http://www.education.gov.uk/schools/leadership/typesofschools/freeschools/guidance/a0074737/funding-agreement
82. Simon Jenkins, 'Gove's claim to be "freeing" schools is a cloak for more control from the centre', Comment is Free, *The Guardian,* 27 May 2010, http://www.guardian.co.uk/commentisfree/2010/may/27/michael-gove-free-schools-admissions-policy
83. Stephen Twigg MP, Shadow Secretary of State for Education (2010–13), 'Evidence, not dogma', Progress Online, 2 February 2012, http://www.progressonline.org.uk/2012/02/02/evidence-not-dogma/
84. Simon Jenkins, 'Michael Gove's centralism is not so much socialist as Soviet', Comment is Free, *The Guardian,* 11 October 2012, http://www.guardian.co.uk/commentisfree/2012/oct/11/michael-gove-more-soviet-than-socialist
85. Ibid.
86. Toby Young, E-mail interview with author, 28 March 2012
87. Jessica Shepherd, 'Barclays puts up £1.25m for parents starting free schools', *The Guardian,* 18 January 2012, http://www.guardian.co.uk/education/2012/jan/18/free-schools-barclays-money-parents
88. Jesse Norman, MP for Hereford and South Herefordshire, interview with author, 16 March 2012
89. Jesse Norman, *The Big Society: The Anatomy of the New Politics,* (University of Buckingham Press, Buckingham, 2010), Ch. 7, p. 140
90. See Max Weber, *Economy and Society,* (1922)

91. Clyde Chitty, *Education Policy in Britain*, (Palgrave Macmillan, Basingstoke, 2004), Ch. 3, p. 33
92. Sonia Exley and Stephen J. Ball, 'Something old, something new: understanding Conservative education policy', cited in Hugh Bochel (ed.), *The Conservative Party and Social Policy*, (Policy Press, University of Bristol, 2011), Ch. 6, p. 101
93. Jesse Norman, *The Big Society: The Anatomy of the New Politics*, (University of Buckingham Press, Buckingham, 2010), Ch. 2, p. 26
94. Ben Kisby, 'The Big Society: Power to the people?', *Political Quarterly*, Volume 81, No. 4, (October-December 2010), p. 490
95. Ibid., p. 488. Kisby argues that such schools 'work in favour of middle-class, advantaged communities with high levels of trust and strong networks or "social capital"'
96. Jessica Shepherd, 'Academies and free schools get right to reserve places for poorer pupils', *The Guardian*, May 27 2011, http://www.guardian.co.uk/education/2011/may/27/academies-free-schools-poorer-pupils
97. Michael Oakeshott, *On Human Conduct*, (Clarendon Press, Oxford, 1975)
98. Jesse Norman, *The Big Society: The Anatomy of the New Politics*, (University of Buckingham Press, Buckingham, 2010), Ch. 6, p. 101
99. NASUWT, 'Free schools: Why does NASUWT oppose free schools?', http://www.nasuwt.org.uk/Whatsnew/Campaigns/VoteforEducation/FreeSchools/
100. Jesse Norman, MP for Hereford and South Herefordshire, interview with author, 16 March 2012
101. Jesse Norman, *The Big Society: The Anatomy of the New Politics*, (University of Buckingham Press, Buckingham, 2010), Ch. 7, p. 141
102. Adam Leeder and Deborah Mabbett, 'Free Schools: Big Society or small interests?', cited in Jason Edwards (ed). *Retrieving the Big Society*, (Wiley-Blackwell, Chichester, 2012), p. 134
103. Toby Young, E-mail interview with author, 28 March 2012
104. Adam Leeder and Deborah Mabbett, 'Free Schools: Big Society or small interests?', cited in Jason Edwards (ed). *Retrieving the Big Society*, (Wiley-Blackwell, Chichester, 2012), p. 143

7 Social policy case study 4: Reform of the NHS

1. Brian Salter, *The Politics of Change in the Health Service*. (Macmillan, Basingstoke, 1998), Introduction, p. 1
2. The NHS employs 1.7 million people according to figures from 2011: 'Only the Chinese People's Liberation Army, the Wal-Mart supermarket chain and the Indian Railways directly employ more people'
Source: 'About the NHS': http://www.nhs.uk/NHSEngland/thenhs/about/Pages/overview.aspx
3. Jesse Norman, *The Big Society: The Anatomy of the New Politics*, (University of Buckingham Press, Buckingham, 2010), Ch. 9, p. 173
4. Jesse Norman, MP for Hereford and South Herefordshire, interview with author, 16 March 2012

5. Brian Salter, *The Politics of Change in the Health Service,* (Macmillan, Basingstoke, 1998), Ch. 1, p. 4
6. Ibid., p. 15
7. Ken Hesketh, Chief Executive Medway NHS Trust, Foreword p. ix, cited in Salter, (1998)
8. Rob Baggott, 'Conservative health policy: change, continuity and policy influence', in Hugh Bochel (ed.), *The Conservative Party and Social Policy,* (Policy Press, University of Bristol, 2011), Ch. 5, p. 77
9. Brian Salter, *The Politics of Change in the Health Service,* (Macmillan, Basingstoke, 1998), Introduction, Ch. 1, p. 5
10. Rob Baggott, 'Conservative health policy: change, continuity and policy influence', cited in Hugh Bochel (ed.), *The Conservative Party and Social Policy,* (Policy Press, University of Bristol, 2011), Ch. 5, p. 77
11. Ibid., p. 89
12. UK Polling Report, 'What causes poll movements', 21 February 2012, http://ukpollingreport.co.uk/blog/archives/category/nhs
13. Daniel Hannan MEP, Interview with Fox News, 4 April 2009, http://www.youtube.com/watch?v=FiSPRkq28iU
14. Institute for Fiscal Studies, *'Public Spending under Labour'* (2010), 2010 Election Briefing Note No.5, (Robert Chote, Rowena Crawford, Carl Emmerson, Gemma Tetlow), p. 5 http://www.ifs.org.uk/bns/bn92.pdf
15. Ibid., p. 9
16. Rob Baggott, 'Conservative health policy: change, continuity and policy influence', in Hugh Bochel (ed.), *The Conservative Party and Social Policy,* (Policy Press, University of Bristol, 2011), Ch. 5, p. 79
17. Ibid., p. 77
18. Conservative Home website, 'Labour claim victory after Cameron abandons Patient's Passport', 4 January 2006, http://conservativehome.blogs.com/torydiary/2006/01/labour_claim_vi.html
19. David Cameron, Speech to Conservative Party Conference, 4 October 2006, Bournemouth, cited in: BBC News website, 'NHS safe in my hands says Cameron', 4 October 2006, http://news.bbc.co.uk/1/hi/uk_politics/5403798.stm
20. David Cameron's son Ivan was born with severe epilepsy and cerebral palsy in 2002 and died in 2009. Cameron's experiences of the NHS treatment of his son were said to have shaped his support for enhanced investment and specific funding commitments in this service
21. See BBC News website, 'David Cameron says NHS at heart of Tory manifesto', 4 January 2010, http://news.bbc.co.uk/1/hi/8438965.stm
22. Cited in Patrick Wintour, 'Cameron claims role of NHS protector', *The Guardian,* 4 October 2006, http://www.guardian.co.uk/society/2006/oct/04/publicservices.politics
23. Rob Baggott, 'Conservative health policy: change, continuity and policy influence', in Hugh Bochel (ed.), *The Conservative Party and Social Policy,* (Policy Press, University of Bristol, 2011), Ch. 5, p. 79
24. See Conservative Party 2010 Manifesto, *Invitation to join the Government of Britain,* 'Back the NHS', p. 45: http://www.conservatives.com/~/media/Files/Activist%20Centre/Press%20and%20Policy/Manifestos/Manifesto2010

25. See *The Coalition: our programme for government* (May 2010), pp. 24–26 http://www.cabinetoffice.gov.uk/sites/default/files/resources/coalition_ programme_for_government.pdf

26. See Conservative Party 2010 Manifesto, *Invitation to join the Government of Britain*, 'Change the Economy, pp. 6–7: http://www.conservatives. com/~/media/Files/Activist%20Centre/Press%20and%20Policy/Manifestos/ Manifesto2010,

27. Rob Baggott, 'Conservative health policy: change, continuity and policy influence', in Hugh Bochel (ed.), *The Conservative Party and Social Policy*, (Policy Press, University of Bristol, 2011), Ch. 5, p. 83

28. David Cameron, Speech: 'Protecting the NHS for Tomorrow', 7 June 2011, http://www.conservatives.com/News/Speeches/2011/06/David_Cameron_ Protecting_the_NHS_for_tomorrow.aspx

29. Ibid

30. Rosa Prince, 'David Cameron accused of breaking pledge as NHS spending falls again', *Daily Telegraph*, 6 July 2012, http://www.telegraph.co.uk/ health/9381598/David-Cameron-accused-of-breaking-pledge-as-NHS-spending-falls-again.html

31. Steve Corbett and Alan Walker, 'The Big Society: Back to the future', *Political Quarterly*, Volume 3, Issue 3, (July–September 2012), p. 490

32. Andrew Lansley, The Andrew Marr Show, BBC TV, 7 November 2010, cited in Conservative Home website, http://conservativehome.blogs.com/think-tankcentral/2010/07/civitas-warns-against-lansleys-nhs-reorganisation-plans.html

33. David Cameron, Speech: 'Protecting the NHS for Tomorrow', 7 June 2011, http://www.conservatives.com/News/Speeches/2011/06/David_Cameron_ Protecting_the_NHS_for_tomorrow.aspx

34. 'In his statement of 7 May (2010), David Cameron said "No Government will be in the national interest unless it deals with the biggest threat to our national interest – and that is the deficit"', cited in David Laws, *22 Days in May: The Birth of the Lib Dem–Conservative Coalition*, (Biteback, London, 2010), Appendix 1, p. 287.

35. Jesse Norman, *The Big Society: The Anatomy of the New Politics*, (University of Buckingham Press, Buckingham, 2010), Ch. 12, p. 216

36. 21st Century Challenges website, 'Britain's Ageing Population', http://www.21stcenturychallenges.org/60-seconds/britains-ageing-population/ See also Office for National Statistics (2008): http://www.statistics.gov.uk/ hub/index.html

37. 21st Century Challenges website, 'Britain's Ageing Population', http:// www.21stcenturychallenges.org/60-seconds/britains-ageing-population/

38. Brian Salter, *The Politics of Change in the Health Service*, (Macmillan, Basingstoke, 1998), Introduction, Ch. 1, p. 14

39. Laura Donnelly, 'Spending on NHS bureaucracy up 50 per cent', *Daily Telegraph*, 26 December 2009, http://www.telegraph.co.uk/health/healthnews/ 6890335/Spending-on-NHS-bureaucracy-up-50-per-cent.html

40. David Cameron, Speech: 'Protecting the NHS for Tomorrow', 7 June 2011, http://www.conservatives.com/News/Speeches/2011/06/David_Cameron_ Protecting_the_NHS_for_tomorrow.aspx

41. Cristina Odone, 'Why should fat people take precedence over the elderly in the NHS?', *Daily Telegraph*, 26 March 2012, http://blogs.telegraph.co.uk/news/cristinaodone/100146838/why-should -fat-people-take-precedence-over-the-elderly-in-the-nhs/
See also Jason Groves, 'People who eat doughnuts for breakfast should be charged for prescriptions, says Tory MP', *Daily Mail*, 26 November 2012, http://www.dailymail.co.uk/news/article-2238780/People-eat-doughnuts-breakfast-charged-prescriptions-says-Tory-MP.html

42. A group specifically highlighted by Owen Jones in his book, *The Establishment: And How They Get Away With It* (Penguin, London, 2014)

43. Stephen McKay and Karen Rowlingson, 'Social security and welfare reform', cited in Hugh Bochel (ed.), *The Conservative Party and Social Policy"*, (Policy Press, University of Bristol, 2011), Ch. 8, p. 145

44. Jesse Norman, *The Big Society: The Anatomy of the New Politics*, (University of Buckingham Press, Buckingham, 2010), Ch. 10, p. 193

45. Francis Elliott and James Hanning, *Cameron: Practically a Conservative*, (Fourth Estate, London, 2012)

46. Owen Bowcott, 'Cameron is trying to set out a clear ideological path on the NHS', Joe Public Blog, *The Guardian*, 5 January 2010, http://www.guardian.co.uk/society/joepublic/2010/jan/05/conservative-nhs-draft-manifesto
See also Des Spence, 'Flawed ideology drives the NHS reforms', *British Medical Journal*, 18 May 2011, http://www.bmj.com/content/342/bmj.d3076

47. White Paper on the NHS (2010): *Equity and Excellence: Liberating the NHS*, 12 July 2010, http://www.dh.gov.uk/en/Publicationsandstatistics/Publications/PublicationsPolicyAndGuidance/DH_117353

48. Phillip Blond, Respublica think-tank, interview with author, 19 February 2013. See also *The Francis Report – the Public Inquiry into the Mid-Staffordshire Foundation Trust*, 6 February 2013. This report was established by then Health Secretary Andrew Lansley in June 2010 in response to the volume of complaints regarding alleged sustained failures of care within this specific NHS trust. The Francis Report reached some damning conclusions about how this part of the NHS was run, and made 290 suggested improvements: http://www.midstaffspublicinquiry.com/report

49. Jesse Norman, *The Big Society: The Anatomy of the New Politics*, (University of Buckingham Press, Buckingham, 2010), Ch. 11, p. 198

50. Helene Mulholland and Patrick Wintour, 'Pressure mounts on Cameron over NHS summit', *The Guardian*, 20 February 2012, http://www.guardian.co.uk/politics/2012/feb/20/pressure-mounts-cameron-nhs-summit

51. Helen Briggs, Health editor, '"Planned 49% limit" for NHS private patients in England', BBC News website, 27 December 2011, http://www.bbc.co.uk/news/health-16337904

52. Jesse Norman, MP for Hereford and South Herefordshire, interview with author, 16 March 2012

53. Denis Campbell and Daniel Boffey, 'Tories fear row over health bill may "retoxify" party on NHS', *The Observer*, 12 February 2012, http://www.guardian.co.uk/politics/2012/feb/12/nhs-bill-toxic-conservatives-lansley?CMP=twt_gu

54. See *The Coalition: our programme for government* (May 2010), p. 24 http://www.cabinetoffice.gov.uk/sites/default/files/resources/coalition_programme_for_government.pdf

55. James Ball and Patrick Sawer, 'NHS chief tells trusts to make £20bn savings', *Daily Telegraph*, 13 June 2009, http://www.telegraph.co.uk/health/health-news/5524693/NHS-chief-tells-trusts-to-make-20bn-savings.html#

56. See House of Commons Health Committee, Public Expenditure, Thirteenth Report of Session 2010–12, Volume 2, Additional Written Evidence, 17 January 2012, p. 35 http://www.publications.parliament.uk/pa/cm201012/cmselect/cmhealth/1499/1499vw.pdf

57. BBC News website, 'The riddle of the NHS budget', 8 November 2010, http://www.bbc.co.uk/news/magazine-11686396

58. Nick Triggle, Health Reporter, BBC News, 'Why the NHS must face up to the new world', BBC News website, 25 February 2011, http://www.bbc.co.uk/news/health-12566719

59. Sir David Nicholson, NHS Chief Executive, cited in BBC News, 'Why the NHS must face up to the new world', BBC News website, 25 February 2011, http://www.bbc.co.uk/news/health-12566719

60. Health and Social Care Act (2012), http://www.legislation.gov.uk/ukpga/2012/7/contents/enacted

61. Andrew Lansley MP, House of Commons (Hansard), 4 April 2011, Column 767, http://www.publications.parliament.uk/pa/cm201011/cmhansrd/cm110404/debtext/110404-0002.htm

62. 'Andrew Lansley, 'Competition is critical for NHS reform', *Health Service Journal*, 13 February 2012, http://www.hsj.co.uk/opinion/columnists/andrew-lansley-competition-is-critical-for-nhs-reform/5041288.article

63. Nick Clegg, speech to Liberal Democrat Spring Conference, Gateshead, 10 March 2012, cited in BBC News website, 'Lib Dems: Party activists reject holding NHS protest vote', 10 March 2012, http://www.bbc.co.uk/news/uk-politics-17323504

64. See Baroness Shirley Williams, 'Our NHS bill amendments represent a major concession by the government', Comment is Free, *The Guardian*, 3 February 2012, http://www.guardian.co.uk/commentisfree/2012/feb/03/nhs-bill-amendments-major-concession

65. Andrew Lansley MP, House of Commons (Hansard), 4 April 2011, Column 767, http://www.publications.parliament.uk/pa/cm201011/cmhansrd/cm110404/debtext/110404-0002.htm

66. The Cabinet Office, *Open Public Service White Paper*, (2011–12), p. 6 http://www.openpublicservices.cabinetoffice.gov.uk/

67. Polly Toynbee, 'The NHS Bill could finish the Health Service – and David Cameron', Comment is Free, *The Guardian*, 6 February 2012, http://www.guardian.co.uk/commentisfree/2012/feb/06/nhs-bill-finish-cameron-ideology

68. Max Pemberton, 'I wanted Andrew Lansley to face up to the mess he's made', *Daily Telegraph*, 10 September 2012, http://www.telegraph.co.uk/health/9530389/I-wanted-Andrew-Lansley-to-face-up-to-the-mess-hes-made.html

69. Nick Bostock, 'How NHS reforms are increasing bureaucracy', GP Online, 5 August 2011, http://www.gponline.com/News/article/1083701/NHS-reforms-increasing-bureaucracy/

70. See Matthew Finders and David Moon, 'The problem of letting go: The "Big Society", accountable governance and "the curse of the decentralizing minister"', *Local Economy*, November 2011, http://lec.sagepub.com/content/26/8/652.full.pdf+html

71. David Cameron, Speech: 'Protecting the NHS for tomorrow', 7 June 2011, http://www.conservatives.com/News/Speeches/2011/06/David_Cameron_Protecting_the_NHS_for_tomorrow.aspx

72. James Gubb, Director of the Health Unit, Civitas, cited in Conservative Home website, 7 November 2010, 'Civitas warns against Lansley's NHS reorganisation plans', http://conservativehome.blogs.com/thinktankcentral/2010/07/civitas-warns-against-lansleys-nhs-reorganisation-plans.html see also: Civitas Data Briefing, Re Government Plans to transfer Commissioning Responsibility From PCTs to GPs, 10 July 2010, http://www.civitas.org.uk/nhs/download/civitas_data_briefing_gpcommissioning.pdf

73. See Max Weber, *Economy and Society,* (1922)

74. Alan Ware, 'The Big Society and Conservative politics', cited in Jason Edwards (ed). *Retrieving the Big Society,* (Wiley-Blackwell, Chichester, 2012), p. 87

75. Brian Salter, *The Politics of Change in the Health Service,* (Macmillan, Basingstoke, 1998), Introduction, Ch. 1, p. 11

76. The Kings Fund, 'Public satisfaction with the NHS and its services',6 June 2012, http://www.kingsfund.org.uk/current_projects/bsa_survey_results_2011/index.html

77. David Cameron, speech to Conservative Party Spring Forum, London, 3 March 2012, cited in *The Guardian*, 'David Cameron "prepared to take hit" on the NHS', 3 March 2012, http://www.guardian.co.uk/politics/2012/mar/03/david-cameron-nhs-reforms

78. Marina Soteriu, 'Health Bill receives royal assent and becomes law', GP Online, 27 March 2012, http://www.gponline.com/News/article/1124347/Health-Bill-receives-royal-assent-becomes-law/

79. Stephen Dorrell MP, cited in Alex Hunt, 'Political Lives: Stephen Dorrell', BBC News website, 18 June 2012, http://www.bbc.co.uk/news/uk-politics-18352453

80. Cited in Rob Baggott, 'Conservative health policy: change, continuity and policy influence', in Hugh Bochel (ed.), *The Conservative Party and Social Policy,* (Policy Press, University of Bristol, 2011), Ch. 5, p. 94
See also Holly Watt and Rose Prince, 'Andrew Lansley bankrolled by private healthcare provider', *Daily Telegraph*, 14 January 2010, http://www.telegraph.co.uk/news/newstopics/mps-expenses/6989408/Andrew-Lansley-bankrolled-by-private-healthcare-provider.html

81. See Richard H.Thaler and Cass R.Sunstein, *Nudge: Improving Decisions About Health, Wealth and Happiness,* (Yale University Press, New Haven, CT, 2008)

82. Ibid., 'Following the Herd', Ch. 3, p. 68

83. BBC News website, 'Nudge theory trials "are working" say officials', 8 February 2012, http://www.bbc.co.uk/news/uk-politics-16943729

84. Richard H.Thaler and Cass R.Sunstein, *Nudge: Improving Decisions About Health, Wealth and Happiness,* (Yale University Press, New Haven, CT, 2008), Introduction, p. 4

85. See Cabinet Office, 'Behavourial Insights Team' (from July 2010), http://www.cabinetoffice.gov.uk/behavioural-insights-team

86. See Edmund Burke, *Reflections on the Revolution in France* (1790), also Thaler and Sunstein (2008), Ch. 17, p. 238

87. David Willetts MP, interview with author, 10 September 2012

88. Jason Edwards, 'Freedom, free institutions and the Big Society', cited in Jason Edwards (ed). *Retrieving the Big Society*, (Wiley-Blackwell, Chichester, 2012), p. 100

89. Richard H.Thaler and Cass R.Sunstein, *Nudge: Improving Decisions About Health, Wealth and Happiness*, (Yale University Press, New Haven, CT, 2008), Introduction, p. 5

90. House of Lords Science and Technology Sub-Committee, 19 July 2011, http://www.parliament.uk/business/committees/committees-a-z/lords-select/science-and-technology-committee/inquiries/behaviour/

91. Richard H.Thaler and Cass R.Sunstein, *Nudge: Improving Decisions About Health, Wealth and Happiness*, (Yale University Press, New Haven, CT, 2008), Introduction, p. 13

Bibliography

Interviews

Phillip Blond, ResPublica think-tank, interview with author in Liverpool, 19 February 2013

Carl Cross, Chairman of Merseyside Conservative Party (2009–12), E-mail questionnaire to author, 4 March 2011

Paula Keaveney, former leader of Liberal Democrat Group (Liverpool City Council) and Liberal Democrat parliamentary candidate in 2010 general election, interview with author in Liverpool, 11 January 2013

Jesse Norman, MP for Hereford and South Herefordshire, interview with author in Hereford, 16 March 2012

Charlotte Pickles, Policy Director, The Centre for Social Justice, E-mail response to author, 4 May 2010

Stephen Twigg MP, Shadow Secretary of State for Education, E-mail response to author, 24 January 2012

David Willetts MP, Secretary of State for Universities and Science, interview with author at the Houses of Parliament, 10 September 2012

Toby Young, Journalist, author and founder of West London Free School, E-mail interview with author, 28 March 2012

Books

Andrew Adonis, *Education, Education, Education: Reforming England's Schools* (Biteback, London, 2012)

Michael Ashcroft, *Smell the Coffee: A Wakeup Call for the Conservative Party* (Politicos, London, 2005)

Tim Bale, *The Conservative Party: From Thatcher to Cameron* (Polity Press, London, 2011)

Stuart Ball and Anthony Seldon (eds.), *Recovering Power: The Conservatives in Opposition Since 1867* (Palgrave Macmillan, Basingstoke, 2005)

Phillip Blond, *Red Tory: How Left and Right Have Broken Britain and How We Can Fix It* (Faber, London 2010)

Hugh Bochel (ed.), *The Conservative Party and Social Policy* (Policy Press, University of Bristol, 2011)

Tom Bower, *Gordon Brown* (Harper-Collins, London, 2004)

Edmund Burke, *Reflections on the Revolution in France* (1790)

David Butler and Dennis Kavanagh, *The British General Election of 1992* (Macmillan Press, Basingstoke, 1992)

David Butler and Dennis Kavanagh, *The British General Election of 1997* (Macmillan Press, Basingstoke, 1997)

Clyde Chitty, *Education Policy in Britain* (Palgrave-Macmillan, Basingstoke, 2004)

Christine Collette and Keith Laybourn, *Modern Britain Since 1979* (I.B. Tauris, London, 2003)

Maurice Cowling, *The Impact of Labour: 1920–1924* (Cambridge University Press, 1971)

Anthony Crosland, *The Future of Socialism* (Jonathan Cape, London, 1956)

Benjamin Disraeli, *Sybil (or The Two Nations)* (1845)

Peter Dorey, *British Conservatism: The Politics and Philosophy Of Inequality* (I.B. Tauris, London, 2011)

Jason Edwards (ed.), *Retrieving the Big Society* (Wiley-Blackwell, Chichester, 2012)

Francis Elliott and James Hanning, *Cameron: Practically a Conservative* (Fourth Estate, London, 2012)

Eric J. Evans, *Thatcher and Thatcherism* (Routledge, London, 2nd edn., 2004)

Michael Freeden, *Ideologies and Political Theory: A Conceptual Approach* (Clarendon Press, Oxford, 1996)

Milton Friedman, *Capitalism and Freedom* (The University of Chicago Press, Chicago, 1962)

Andrew Gamble, *The Conservative Nation* (Routledge & Kegan Paul, London, 1974)

Andrew Gamble, *The Free Economy and the Strong State: The Politics of Thatcherism* (Macmillan, Basingstoke, 2nd edn., 1994)

Ian Gilmour, *Inside Right; A Study of Conservatism* (Quartet, London, 1978)

Ian Gilmour, *Dancing With Dogma: Britain Under Thatcherism* (Simon & Schuster, London, 1992)

Ian Gilmour and Mark Garnett, *Whatever Happened To The Tories? The Conservative Party since 1945* (4th Estate, London, 1997)

David C. Green, *The New Right: The Counter-Revolution in Political, Economic and Social Thought* (Wheatsheaf Books, Brighton, 1987)

William H Greenleaf, *The British Political Tradition Volume II: The Ideological Heritage* (Methuen, London, 1983)

F.A. Hayek, *The Road to Serfdom* (University of Chicago Press, Chicago, 1944)

Friedrich von Hayek, *Law, Legislation and Liberty, Volume 2: 'The Mirage of Social Justice* (Routledge & Kegan Paul, London, 1973)

Richard Hayton, Conservatism? The Conservative Party in Opposition, 1997–2010. *New Perspectives on the Right.* (Manchester University Press, Manchester, 2012)

Timothy Heppell and David Seawright (eds.), *Cameron and the Conservatives: The Transition to Coalition Government* (Palgrave-Macmillan, Basingstoke, 2012)

Andrew Heywood, *Politics* (Palgrave Macmillan, Basingstoke, 2nd edn., 2002)

Kevin Hickson, *The IMF crisis of 1976 and British Politics* (I.B. Tauris, London, 2005)

Kevin Hickson (ed.), *The Political Thought of the Conservative Party since 1945* (Palgrave Macmillan, Basingstoke, 2nd edn., 2009)

Thomas Hobbes, *Leviathan* (1651)

Eric J. Hobsbawm, *The Age of Extremes: The Short Twentieth Century, 1914–1991* (Michael Joseph, London, 1994)

Ted Honderich, *Conservatism* (Penguin Books, London, 1990)

Dylan Jones, *Cameron on Cameron: Conversations with Dylan Jones* (Fourth Estate, London, 2008)

Keith Joseph and Jonathan Sumption, *Equality* (W & J MacKay, Chatham, 1979)

Dennis Kavanagh and Philip Cowley, *The British General Election of 2010* (Palgrave Macmillan, Basingstoke, 2010)

Dennis Kavanagh and Anthony Seldon (eds.), *The Major Effect* (Macmillan, London, 1994)

Robert Leach, *British Political Ideologies* (Prentice Hall Europe, Hemel Hempstead, 2nd edn., 1996)

Simon Lee and Matt Beech (eds.), *The Conservatives under David Cameron: Built to Last?* (Palgrave Macmillan, Basingstoke, 2nd edn., 2009

Stephen J. Lee, *Aspects of British Political History 1914–1995* (Routledge, London, 1996)

Shirley Robin Letwin, *The Anatomy of Thatcherism* (Fontana, London, 1992)

Harold Macmillan, *The Middle Way* (Macmillan, London, 1938)

David Marsh and Gerry Stoker (eds.), *Theory and Methods in Political Science* (Palgrave-Macmillan, Basingstoke, 3rd edn., 2010)

Paul Marshall and David Laws (eds.), *The Orange Book: Reclaiming Liberalism* (Profile Books, London, 2004)

Lawrence M. Mead, *Beyond Entitlement: The Social Obligations of Citizenship* (Free Press, New York, 1986)

Jesse Norman, *The Big Society: The Anatomy of the New Politics* (University of Buckingham Press, Buckingham, 2010)

Robert Nozick, *Anarchy, State and Utopia* (Basic Books, New York, 1974)

Michael Oakeshott, *Rationalism in Politics and Other Essays* (Cambridge University Press, Cambridge, 1962)

Michael Oakeshott, *On Human Conduct* (Clarendon Press, London, 1975)

Paul Pierson, *Dismantling the Welfare State: Reagan, Thatcher and the Politics of Retrenchment* (Cambridge University Press, 1994)

Robert Philpot (ed.), *The Purple Book: A Progressive Future for Labour* (Biteback , London, 2011)

Raymond Plant, *The Neo-Liberal State* (Oxford University Press, Oxford, 2009)

John Rawls, *A Theory of Justice* (Harvard University Press, Massachusetts, 1971)

Andrew Rawnsley, *The End of the Party: The Rise and Fall of New Labour* (Penguin, London, 2010)

Brian Salter, *The Politics of Change in the Health Service* (Macmillan, Basingstoke, 1998)

Ryan Shorthouse (ed.), *Tory Modernisation 2.0: The future of the Conservative Party* (Bright Blue, London, 2013), e-book: http://brightblue.org.uk/bbtory20.pdf (accessed 9 January 2015)

Adam Smith, *Wealth of Nations* (1776)

Peter Snowdon, *Back from the Brink: The Inside Story of the Tory Resurrection* (Harper Press, London, 2010)

Alan Sked and Chris Cook, *Post War Britain: A Political History* (Penguin, London, 4th edn., 1993)

Richard H.Thaler and Cass R.Sunstein, *Nudge: Improving Decisions About Health, Wealth and Happiness* (Yale University Press, New Haven, CT, 2008)

Polly Toynbee and David Walker, *Dogma and Disarray: Cameron at Half-Time* (Granta Books, London, 2012), e-book

Ion Trewin (ed.), *The Hugo Young Papers: A Journalist's Notes from the Heart of Politics* (Penguin, London, 2009)

Simon Walters, *Tory Wars: Conservatives in Crisis* (Politicos, London, 2001)

Max Weber, *Economy and Society* (Germany, 1922)

Susanne Wiborg, *Education and Social Integration: Comprehensive Schooling in Europe* (Palgrave Macmillan, New York, 2009)

Richard Wilkinson and Kate Pickett, *The Spirit Level: Why More Equal Societies Almost Always Do Better* (Allen Lane, London, 2009)

David Willetts, *Modern Conservatism* (Penguin, London, 1992)

David Willetts, *Civic Conservatism* (The Social Market Foundation, London, 1994)

Daniel Yergin and Joseph Stanislaw (ed.), *The Commanding Heights* (Simon & Schuster, New York, 1998)

Hugo Young, *One of Us* (Pan Macmillan, London, 1989)

Michael Young, *The Rise of the Meritocracy* (Transaction, Chicago, 1958)

Political Memoirs and Biographies

David Laws, *22 Days in May: The Birth of the Lib Dem–Conservative Coalition* (Biteback, London, 2010)

John Major, *The Autobiography* (Harper-Collins, London, 1999)

Margaret Thatcher, *The Downing Street Years* (Harper-Collins, London, 1993)

Harold Wilson, *Final Term: The Labour Government 1974–1976* (Michael Joseph, London, 1979)

Journal Articles and Academic Papers

Philip Blond and Jane Dudman, 'Common Purpose', *Ethos Journal*, (September 2011), http://www.ethosjournal.com/home/item/265-common-purpose (accessed 9 January 2015)

Hugh Bochel, 'Cameron's Conservativism: influences, interpretations and implications', University of Lincoln (2010), p.1 http://www.social-policy.org.uk/lincoln/Bochel_H.pdf (accessed 9 January 2015)

Anders Böhlmark and Mikael Lindahl, IZA (Institute for the Study of Labour, Bonn, Germany), Discussion Paper Series No.2786, 'The Impact of School Choice on Pupil Achievement, Segregation and Costs: Swedish Evidence', (May 2007), ftp://repec.iza.org/RePEc/Discussionpaper/dp2786.pdf (accessed 9 January 2015)

Jim Bulpitt, 'The Discipline of the New Democracy: Mrs Thatcher's Domestic Statecraft', *Political Studies*, (Volume 34, Issue 1, pp. 19–39, 1986)

Steve Corbett and Alan Walker, 'The Big Society: Back to the Future', *Political Quarterly*, (Volume 3, Issue 3, pp. 487–493, July–September 2012)

Andrew Crines, 'The Rhetoric of the Coalition: Governing in the National Interest' (2013), summarised in *Democratic Audit*, 15 October 2013 http://www.democraticaudit.com/?p=1567 (accessed 9 January 2015)

Robert Crowcroft, Review Article, 'Maurice Cowling and the Writing of British Political History', *Contemporary British History*, (Volume 22, No.2, pp. 279–286, June 2008)

Matthew Finders and David Moon, 'The problem of letting go: The "Big Society", accountable governance and "the curse of the decentralizing minister"', *Local Economy*, (Volume 26, No. 8, pp. 652–662, December 2011), (accessed 9 January 2015) http://lec.sagepub.com/content/26/8/652.full.pdf+html

Andrew Gamble, 'The Crisis of Conservatism', *New Left Review*, (No.214, November- December 1995), http://newleftreview.org/I/214/andrew-gamble-the-crisis-of-conservatism (accessed 9 January 2015)

Maurice Glasman, 'Society not state: the challenge of the Big Society', *Public Policy Research* (Volume 17, Issue 2, pp. 59–63, June–August 2010)

Roy Hattersley and Kevin Hickson, 'In Praise of Social Democracy', *The Political Quarterly*, (Volume 83, Issue 1, pp. 5–12, January–March 2012), http://onlinelibrary.wiley.com/doi/10.1111/j.1467-923X.2011.02259.x/pdf (accessed 9 January 2015)

Richard Hayton, 'Conservative Party Modernisation and David Cameron's Politics of the Family', *The Political Quarterly*, (Volume 81, No.4, pp. 492–500, October-December 2010) (accessed 9 January 2015)

Tim Heppell, 'The Ideological Composition of the British Conservative Party (1992–1997)', *British Journal of Politics and International Relations*, (Volume 4, No. 2, pp. 299–324, 2002)

Tim Heppell and Michael Hill, 'Ideological Typologies of Contemporary British Conservatism', *Political Studies Review*, Volume 3, 3, pp. 335–355, 2005)

Kevin Hickson, 'The New Tories may be a puzzle but the pieces do make up a new kind of Britain', *Parliamentary Brief Online*, (30 March 2010),

Kevin Hickson, 'Thatcherism, Poverty and Social Justice', *Journal of Poverty and Social Justice*, (Volume 18, 2, pp. 135–145, June 2010)

Rob Higham, 'Free Schools in the Big Society: Aims, Governance and Inclusion', Institute of Education, University of London, (July 2011), http://www.ioe.ac.uk/newsEvents/53603.html (accessed 9 January 2015)

John Hills, 'Thatcherism, New Labour and the Welfare State', Centre for Analysis of Social Exclusion, London School of Economics, (August 1998), http://eprints.lse.ac.uk/5553/1/Thatcherism_New_Labour_and_the_Welfare_State.pdf (accessed 9 January 2015)

Ben Kisby, 'The Big Society: Power to the People?', *Political Quarterly*, (Volume 81, 4, pp. 484–491, October-December 2010)

Andrew Lansley, 'Competition is critical for NHS reform', *Health Service Journal*, 13 February 2012, http://www.hsj.co.uk/opinion/columnists/andrew-lansley-competition-is-critical-for-nhs-reform/5041288.article (accessed 9 January 2015)

Charles Murray, 'Charles Murray and the Underclass: The Developing Debate', The IEA Health and Welfare Unit in Association with the *Sunday Times* (London, November 1996), http://www.sociology.org.uk/as4p6a.pdf (accessed 9 January 2015)

Philip Norton, 'The Lady's Not For Turning: But What About The Rest? Margaret Thatcher And The Conservative Party (1979–1989)', *Parliamentary Affairs* (Volume 43, pp. 41–58, 1990), http://pa.oxfordjournals.org/content/43/1/41.full.pdf (accessed 9 January 2015)

Robert M. Page, University of Birmingham, 'Clear Blue Water? The Conservative Party's Approach to Social Policy Since 1945', Paper presented at the Social Policy Association's Annual Conference, University of Lincoln (5–7 July 2010), http://www.social-policy.org.uk/lincoln/Page.pdf (accessed 9 January 2015)

Gabriel H. Sahlgren, 'Swedish Education and the Role of the Profit motive', IEA (Institute of Economic Affairs) Discussion paper No.33 (2010), http://www.iea.org.uk/sites/default/files/publications/files/Schooling%20for%20money%20-%20web%20version_0.pdf (accessed 9 January 2015)

Des Spence, 'Flawed ideology drives the NHS reforms', *British Medical Journal*, 18 May 2011, http://www.bmj.com/content/342/bmj.d3076 (accessed 9 January 2015)

Susanne Wiborg, 'Swedish Free Schools: Do They Work?', LLAKES Research Paper 18, (Institute of Education, University of London, 2010), http://www.lla-kes.org/wp-content/uploads/2010/09/Wiborg-online.pdf (accessed 9 January 2015)

Speeches

Theresa May, speech to Conservative Party Conference in Bournemouth, cited in *The Guardian*, Monday 7 October 2002, http://www.guardian.co.uk/politics/2002/oct/07/conservatives2002.conservatives1 (accessed 9 January 2015)

Full text: David Cameron's speech to the Conservative conference 2005, *The Guardian*, 4 October 2005, http://www.theguardian.com/politics/2005/oct/04/conservatives2005.conservatives3 (accessed 9 January 2015)

David Cameron, 'Speech to Centre for Social Justice Kids' Symposium', cited in *The Guardian*, 10 July 2006, http://www.guardian.co.uk/politics/2006/jul/10/conservatives.law (accessed 9 January 2015)

David Cameron, Speech to Conservative Party Conference, 4 October 2006, Bournemouth, cited in: BBC News website, 'NHS safe in my hands says Cameron', 4 October 2006, http://news.bbc.co.uk/1/hi/uk_politics/5403798.stm (accessed 9 January 2015)

David Cameron's speech at the Glasgow East by-election campaign launch, cited in *The Guardian*, 7 July 2008, http://www.guardian.co.uk/politics/2008/jul/07/davidcameron.conservatives (accessed 9 January 2015) Source: http://conservativehome.blogs.com/torydiary/files/fixing_our_broken_society.pdf (accessed 9 January 2015)

David Cameron: 'The Big Society', Hugo Young Memorial Lecture, Tuesday, November 10 2009, http://www.conservatives.com/News/Speeches/2009/11/David_Cameron_The_Big_Society.aspx (accessed 9 January 2015)

David Cameron, 'Let's mend our broken society', 27 April 2010, http://www.conservatives.com/News/Speeches/2010/04/David_Cameron_Lets_mend_our_broken_society.aspx (accessed 9 January 2015)

David Cameron, speech in Liverpool, 19 July 2010, cited on BBC News website, 19 July 2010, 'David Cameron launches Tories' 'big society' plan', http://www.bbc.co.uk/news/uk-10680062 (accessed 9 January 2015)

Iain Duncan Smith cited in BBC News website, 'Benefits system overhaul "to make work pay"', 11 November 2010, http://www.bbc.co.uk/news/uk-politics-11728546 (accessed 9 January 2015)

David Cameron, 'David Cameron: deficit reduction is my duty, Big Society my passion', Speech reported in the *Daily Telegraph*, 14 February 2011, http://www.telegraph.co.uk/news/politics/david-cameron/8322788/David-Cameron-deficit-reduction-is-my-duty-Big-Society-my-passion.html (accessed 9 January 2015)

David Cameron, Speech: 'Protecting the NHS for tomorrow', Tuesday 7 June 2011, http://www.conservatives.com/News/Speeches/2011/06/David_Cameron_Protecting_the_NHS_for_tomorrow.aspx (accessed 9 January 2015)

Nick Clegg, speech in London on Free Schools, reported on BBC News website, 'Nick Clegg rules out running free schools for profit', 5 September 2011, http://www.bbc.co.uk/news/education-14781392 (accessed 9 January 2015)

David Cameron, speech to Conservative Party Spring Forum, London, Saturday 3 March 2012, cited in *The Guardian*, 'David Cameron "prepared to take hit" on the NHS', Saturday 3 March 2012, (accessed 9 January 2015) http://www.guardian.co.uk/politics/2012/mar/03/david-cameron-nhs-reforms

Nick Clegg, speech to Liberal Democrat Spring Conference, Gateshead, 10 March 2012, cited in BBC News website, 'Lib Dems: Party activists reject holding NHS protest vote', 10 March 2012, http://www.bbc.co.uk/news/uk-politics-17323504 (accessed 9 January 2015)

David Cameron, 'Conservative Party Conference 2012 in Birmingham: Full transcript of David Cameron's speech', The Independent, 10 October 2012: http://www.independent.co.uk/news/uk/politics/conservative-party-conference-2012-in-birmingham-full-transcript-of-david-camerons-speech-8205536.html (accessed 9 January 2015)

Parliamentary debates and reports (chronological order)

Health Minister Mike O'Brien MP in response to Peter Bone MP about NHS expenditure in England, 9 September 2009, House of Commons (*Hansard*), Column 1989–1990W, http://www.publications.parliament.uk/pa/cm200809/cmhansrd/cm090909/text/90909w0021.htm (accessed 9 January 2015)

Baroness Sayeeda Warsi, House of Lords (*Hansard*), 9 February 2011, Column 221, http://www.publications.parliament.uk/pa/ld201011/ldhansrd/text/110209-0001.htm#11020963000771 (accessed 9 January 2015)

Andrew Lansley MP, House of Commons (*Hansard*), 4 April 2011, Column 767, http://www.publications.parliament.uk/pa/cm201011/cmhansrd/cm110404/debtext/110404-0002.htm (accessed 9 January 2015)

House of Lords Science and Technology Sub-Committee, 19 July 2011, http://www.parliament.uk/business/committees/committees-a-z/lords-select/science-and-technology-committee/inquiries/behaviour/ (accessed 9 January 2015)

House of Commons Health Committee, Public Expenditure, Thirteenth Report of Session 2010–12, Volume 2, Additional Written Evidence, 17 January 2012, http://www.publications.parliament.uk/pa/cm201012/cmselect/cmhealth/1499/1499vw.pdf (accessed 9 January 2015)

Websites

All accessed 9 January 2015
21st Century Challenges website, http://www.21stcenturychallenges.org/
Big Society Capital: http://www.bigsocietycapital.com/
The Big Society Network: http://www.thebigsociety.co.uk/ Defunct as at 9 January 2015
Bright Blue, think-tank for Progressive Conservatism: http://brightblueonline.com/
Centre for Policy Studies (CPS): http://www.cps.org.uk/
Centre for Social Justice: http://www.centreforsocialjustice.org.uk/

Conservative Home: http://conservativehome.blogs.com/

The Conservative Party: http://www.conservatives.com

Cornerstone Group of MPs: http://cornerstone-group.org.uk/

Demos: 'The progressive Conservatism Project: Conservative means can serve progressive ends', http://www.demos.co.uk/projects/progressiveconservatism/

Everton Free School website: http://community.evertonfc.com/education/everton-free-school/

HM Treasury: http://www.hm-treasury.gov.uk/

Institute of Economic Affairs (IEA): http://www.iea.org.uk/

Margaret Thatcher Foundation: http://www.margaretthatcher.org/

NASUWT: http://www.nasuwt.org.uk/

National Health Service: http://www.nhs.uk/NHSEngland/thenhs/about/Pages/overview.aspx

New Schools Network: http://newschoolsnetwork.org/

Office for National Statistics: http://www.statistics.gov.uk/

Ofsted: http://www.ofsted.gov.uk/

Policy Exchange: http://www.policyexchange.org.uk/

Respublica: http://www.respublica.org.uk/

Socialist Health Association website: http://www.sochealth.co.uk/national-health-service/

Social Market Foundation: http://www.smf.co.uk/

Strong and Compassionate Conservatism: http://www.strongandcompassionate.com/

Sutton Trust: http://www.suttontrust.com/home/

Tax Credits website: http://www.direct.gov.uk/en/MoneyTaxAndBenefits/TaxCredits/index.htm

21st Century Challenges website, http://www.21stcenturychallenges.org/

UK Public Spending: http://www.ukpublicspending.co.uk/

Universal Credit: welfare that works: http://www.dwp.gov.uk/docs/universal-credit-full-document.pdf

Volunteering England: http://www.volunteering.org.uk/

West London Free School: http://www.westlondonfreeschool.co.uk/

Press Releases

Local Government Association (LGA), 'Schools duck "moral duty" to dish up healthy meals', 13 January 2013, http://www.local.gov.uk/web/guest/media-releases/-/journal_content/56/10171/3839479/NEWS-TEMPLATE (accessed 9 January 2015)

Television and radio

Daniel Hannan MEP, Interview with Fox News, 4 April 2009, http://www.youtube.com/watch?v=FiSPRkq28iU (accessed 9 January 2015)

David Cameron, interview with Andrew Marr (BBC), 'David Cameron: I am "Liberal Conservative"', BBC News website, 16 May 2010, http://news.bbc.co.uk/1/hi/uk_politics/8685185.stm (accessed 9 January 2015)

Andrew Lansley, The Andrew Marr Show, BBC TV, 7 November 2010, cited in Conservative Home website, http://conservativehome.blogs.com/thinktank-central/2010/07/civitas-warns-against-lansleys-nhs-reorganisation-plans.html (accessed 9 January 2015)

Dermot Murnaghan debates the Big Society with Phillip Blond (former Cameron advisor), Rev Peter Smith Archbishop of Southwark and Sir Stephen Bubb, ACEVO, Sky News, 13 February 2011, http://skynewstranscripts.co.uk/transcript.asp?id=946 unavailable as at 9 January 2015

Helen Grady, BBC Radio 4, 21 March 2011, 'Blue Labour: Party's radical answer to the Big Society?', http://www.bbc.co.uk/news/uk-12759902 (accessed 9 January 2015)

Opinion Polls (chronological order)

British Social Attitudes surveys, http://www.britsocat.com/Home

Ipsos-Mori Survey, 'Private Provision of Public Services', (19 June 2008), https://www.ipsos-mori.com/researchpublications/researcharchive/2428/Private-Provision-of-Public-Services.aspx?view=wide (accessed 9 January 2015)

ComRes poll on the Big Society (15 May 2011): http://www.comres.co.uk/page1902473831.aspx unavailable as at 9 January 2015

UK Polling Report, 'What causes poll movements', 21 February 2012, http://ukpollingreport.co.uk/blog/archives/category/nhs (accessed 9 January 2015)

Lord Michael Ashcroft, '"Suspicious Strivers" hold the key to Tory election prospects', Lord Ashcroft Polls, 5 October 2012, http://lordashcroftpolls.com/2012/10/suspicious-strivers-hold-the-key-to-tory-election-prospects/ (accessed 9 January 2015)

The Ashcroft National Poll (12 May 2014), http://www.conservativehome.com/wp-content/uploads/2014/05/National-poll-summary-140512.pdf (accessed 9 January 2015)

Government policy documents and information (chronological order)

All accessed 9 January 2015

'The Coalition Agreement of May 2010': https://www.gov.uk/government/publications/the-coalition-documentation

'The Coalition: our programme for government', (May 2010): http://www.cabinetoffice.gov.uk/sites/default/files/resources/coalition_programme_for_government.pdf

'Building the Big Society', Cabinet Office document, 18 May 2010, http://www.cabinetoffice.gov.uk/sites/default/files/resources/building-big-society_0.pdf

Cabinet Office, 'Behavoural Insights Team' (From July 2010), http://www.cabinetoffice.gov.uk/behavioural-insights-team

Department for Education, 'Free Schools Policy' (2010 onwards): hhttps://www.gov.uk/government/collections/opening-a-free-school

Department for Education, 'Free Schools Model Funding Agreement': https://www.gov.uk/government/publications/academy-and-free-school-single-model-funding-agreement

Department for Education. 'Free Schools FAQs Workforce': https://www.gov.uk/government/publications/free-school-staffing-issues

Department for Education: 'Academies': https://www.gov.uk/government/collections/academy-conversion-process

White Paper on the NHS (2010): *Equity and Excellence: Liberating the NHS*, 12 July 2010, http://www.dh.gov.uk/en/Publicationsandstatistics/Publications/PublicationsPolicyAndGuidance/DH_117353

The Cabinet Office, 'Open Public Service White Paper', (2011–12): http://www.openpublicservices.cabinetoffice.gov.uk/

Cabinet Office, 'Lord Wei stands down', 25 May 2011, http://www.cabinetoffice.gov.uk/news/lord-wei-stands-down

The Cabinet Office, 'Open Public Service White Paper', (2011–12), http://www.openpublicservices.cabinetoffice.gov.uk/

Department for Education, 'Building Schools for the Future', https://www.education.gov.uk/consultations/downloadableDocs/211_2.pdf (accessed 9 January 2015)

HM Government, 'Social Justice: transforming lives', Presented to Parliament by the Secretary of State for Work and Pensions by Command of Her Majesty (March 2012), http://www.dwp.gov.uk/docs/social-justice-transforming-lives.pdf

Department for Education, 'Free Schools opening in 2012 and beyond', http://education.gov.uk/schools/leadership/typesofschools/freeschools/b00197715/free-schools-2012 unavailable as at 9 January 2015

Department for Education, 'National Curriculum review launched',20 January 2011 (updated 26 April 2012), http://www.education.gov.uk/inthenews/inthenews/a0073149/national-curriculum-review-launched

Non-government policy documents, reports and party manifestos (chronological order)

All accessed 9 January 2015

1987 Conservative Party Manifesto, The Next Moves Forward, http://www.conservativemanifesto.com/1987/1987-conservative-manifesto.shtml

2005 Conservative Party Manifesto, Are You Thinking What We're Thinking?: It's Time for Action, http://www.conservatives.com/pdf/manifesto-uk-2005.pdf unavailable as at 9 January 2015

Breakdown Britain: Interim Report on the State of the Nation, The Centre for Social Justice (2006), http://www.centreforsocialjustice.org.uk/UserStorage/pdf/Pdf%20Exec%20summaries/Breakdown%20Britain.pdf (accessed 9 January 2015)

Jesse Norman and Janan Ganesh, *Compassionate Conservatism: What it is, why we need it*, Policy Exchange (2006), http://www.policyexchange.org.uk/images/publications/compassionate%20conservatism%20-%20june%2006.pdf

'Breakthrough Britain: Ending the Costs of Social Breakdown - Policy Recommendations to the Conservative Party', The Centre for Social Justice (2007), http://www.centreforsocialjustice.org.uk/UserStorage/pdf/Pdf%20reports/BBChairmansOverview.pdf

Civitas: Institute for the study of Civil Society, 'Commercial Free Schools benefit teachers and disadvantaged pupils', 17 December 2010, http://www.civitas.org.uk/wordpress/2010/12/17/commercial-free-schools-benefit-teachers-and-disadvantaged-pupils/ unavailable as at 9 January 2015

'Civitas Data Briefing, Re Government Plans to transfer Commissioning Responsibility From PCTs to GPs', 10 July 2010, http://www.civitas.org.uk/nhs/download/civitas_data_briefing_gpcommissioning.pdf

'Control Shift: Returning Power to Local Communities', Policy Green Paper No.9, Tuesday 17 February 2009, see: http://www.conservatives.com/News/News_stories/2009/02/Its_time_to_transfer_power_from_the_central_state_to_local_people.aspx

The Conservative Party, *Get Britain Working*, (October 2009), http://www.conservatives.com/News/News_stories/2009/10/Radical_welfare_reform_to_Get_Britain_Working.aspx

Jon Cruddas and Andrea Nahles, 'Building the Good Society: the project of the democratic left', (Compass Think-tank, 2009): http://www.feslondon.org.uk/cms/files/fes/pdf/goodsocietyenglish.pdf

Michael Gove, 'A Failed Generation: Educational Inequality under Labour' (2008), http://educar.files.wordpress.com/2008/08/a_failed_generation.pdf

Institute for Fiscal Studies, 'Public Spending under Labour' (2010), 2010 Election Briefing Note No.5, (Robert Chote, Rowena Crawford, Carl Emmerson, Gemma Tetlow), http://www.ifs.org.uk/bns/bn92.pdf

2010 Conservative Party manifesto, Invitation to join the Government of Britain, http://www.conservatives.com/~/media/Files/Activist%20Centre/Press%20and%20Policy/Manifestos/Manifesto2010

Conservative Party 2010 Manifesto, Big Society: http://www.conservatives.com/Policy/Where_we_stand/Big_Society.aspx

Report of the National Equality Panel, *An Anatomy of Economic Inequality in the UK*, (January 2010), http://news.bbc.co.uk/1/shared/bsp/hi/pdfs/27_01_10_inequalityfull..pdf

Sutton Trust Research Report, 'Ensuring less privileged pupils benefit from the Government's school reforms', 2nd September 2010, http://www.suttontrust.com/research/ensuring-less-privileged-pupils-benefit/

Conservative Party website, 'Pickles unveils Localism Bill', Monday 13 December 2010, http://www.conservatives.com/News/News_stories/2010/12/Pickles_unveils_Localism_Bill.aspx

Powerful People, Responsible Society, The report of the Commission on Big Society (16 May 2011), http://www.acevo.org.uk/page.aspx?pid=191&nccsm=21&_nccscid=28&_nccsct=Free+Downloads&_nccspID=1077

Policy Network, 'A Discussion Paper: In the black Labour: Why fiscal conservatism and social justice go hand-in-hand', 2 December 2011, http://www.policy-network.net/publications/4101/-In-the-black-Labour

Anthony Seldon, 'The Politics of Optimism', Policy Exchange research note, January 2012, http://www.policyexchange.org.uk/images/publications/pdfs/The_Politics_of_Optimism_-_Jan__12.pdf

Civil Exchange, *The Big Society Audit 2012* (May 2012), http://www.civilexchange.org.uk/wp-content/uploads/2012/09/THE-BIG-SOCIETY-AUDIT-2012finalwebversion.pdf

Legislation

All accessed 9 January 2015

The Housing Act of 1980: http://www.legislation.gov.uk/ukpga/1980/51

1988 Education Reform Act: http://www.legislation.gov.uk/ukpga/1988/40/contents

National School Curriculum (established 1988): http://www.education.gov.uk/schools/teachingandlearning/curriculum

Education (Schools) Act (1997): http://www.educationengland.org.uk/documents/pdfs/1997-education-(schools)-act.pdf

School Standards and Framework Act (1998): http://www.legislation.gov.uk/ukpga/1998/31/contents

Localism Act of 2011: http://www.legislation.gov.uk/ukpga/2011/20/contents/enacted

Health and Social Care Act of 2012: http://www.legislation.gov.uk/ukpga/2012/7/contents/enacted

Public Inquiries:

The Francis Report- the Public Inquiry into the Mid-Staffordshire Foundation Trust, 6 February 2013: http://www.midstaffspublicinquiry.com/report (accessed 9 January 2015)

Index